Buddhism and Waste

Bloomsbury Studies in Material Religion

Bloomsbury Studies in Material Religion is the first book series dedicated exclusively to studies in material religion. Within the field of lived religion, the series is concerned with the material things with which people do religion, and how these things—objects, buildings, landscapes—relate to people, their bodies, clothes, food, actions, thoughts, and emotions. The series engages and advances theories in "sensuous" and "experiential" religion, as well as informing museum practices and influencing wider cultural understandings with relation to religious objects and performances. Books in the series are at the cutting edge of debates as well as developments in fields including religious studies, anthropology, museum studies, art history, and material culture studies.

Christianity and Belonging in Shimla, North India, Jonathan Miles-Watson
Christianity and the Limits of Materiality, edited by Minna Opas and Anna Haapalainen
Figurations and Sensations of the Unseen in Judaism, Christianity and Islam, edited by Birgit Meyer and Terje Stordalen
Food, Festival and Religion, Francesca Ciancimino Howell
Islam through Objects, edited by Anna Bigelow
Material Devotion in a South Indian Poetic World, Leah Elizabeth Comeau
Museums of World Religions, Charles D. Orzech
Qur'anic Matters, Natalia K. Suit
The Religious Heritage Complex, edited by Cyril Isnart and Nathalie Cerezales

Buddhism and Waste

The Excess, Discard, and Afterlife of Buddhist Consumption

Edited by
Trine Brox and Elizabeth Williams-Oerberg

BLOOMSBURY
NEW DELHI • LONDON • OXFORD • NEW YORK • SYDNEY

BLOOMSBURY INDIA
Bloomsbury Publishing India Pvt. Ltd
Second Floor, LSC Building No. 4, DDA Complex, Pocket C–6&7,
Vasant Kunj, New Delhi 110070

BLOOMSBURY, BLOOMSBURY ACADEMIC INDIA and the Diana logo are
trademarks of Bloomsbury Publishing Plc

First published in India 2025
First published in Great Britain 2022

Cover design: Tjasa Krivec
Cover image by Trine Brox

This edition published with permission from Bloomsbury Publishing Plc,
50 Bedford Square, London, WC1B3DP, UK

A catalogue record for this book is available from the British Library.
A catalog record for this book is available from the Library of Congress.
Library of Congress Control Number: 2021947572

ISBN: 978-93-61319-81-5

Series: Bloomsbury Studies in Material Religion
Typeset by Deanta Global Publishing Services, Chennai, India
Printed in India by Manipal Technologies Limited, Manipal

To find out more about our authors and books
visit www.bloomsbury.com and sign up for our newsletters

Contents

Figures

Acknowledgments

Buddhism and Waste is based upon discussions organized by the international, collaborative research project *Buddhism, Business and Believers* at the Center for Contemporary Buddhist Studies (CCBS), University of Copenhagen, during the years between 2015 and 2020. This volume is a direct result of a particularly fruitful CCBS workshop *Buddhist Consumption: Excess and Waste* in Helsingør, Denmark, May 2019. The editors would like to acknowledge financial support from the Danish Council for Independent Research | Humanities. Thanks also to Jane Caple for copyediting the manuscript, to Jørn Borup and Justin McDaniel for their inspiration during the workshop on *Buddhist Consumption*, and to Lalle Pursglove and Lily McMahon at Bloomsbury for taking such good care of our book project.

Note on Sanskrit Diacritics

Diacritics are omitted for Sanskrit terms that are in common English usage (e.g., Mahayana, mandala, sutra, stupa, Vajrayana), unless part of a title (e.g., *Saddharmapundarīka Sūtra*). Other Sanskrit terms (e.g., *dhāraṇī*) and names (e.g., Śākyamuni) are transliterated with full diacritics.

Introduction

A Framework for Studying Buddhism and Waste

Trine Brox

Despite the message of anti-materialism that can be derived from Buddhist philosophy, materiality is an essential constituent of Buddhist places, communities, bodies, and practices. In the words of Fabio Rambelli (2017: 3), material culture "is literally the stuff Buddhism is made of, and it would be misleading to deal with Buddhism in only a dematerialized and disembodied fashion, as if its doctrines and rituals had no material substratum and bodily reach." Buddhism has a concrete, material presence. Material things are important, for instance, in communicating the categories to which people claim or refuse to belong. Robes and haircuts set monastics and tantrists apart from each other and the laity, while some people might communicate their Buddhist identity with prayer beads and amulets. Cairns, prayer flags, stupas, and temples demarcate the sacred spaces in Buddhist landscapes, and public and private Buddhist practice places are packed with items that serve as valuable gifts to deities and ancestors, essential tools for practices, technologies for accumulating merit, recipients of offerings, receptacles for divine powers, and protectors against ills and evils. Such structures and items inspire faith and enable people to feel, relate to, and practice the teachings of the Buddha and accomplished Buddhist masters. But what happens when these things—which define and make Buddhist places, communities, bodies, and practices—are exhausted, dissolved, broken, worn out, excessive, impure, or dead? What are they when people stop engaging with them, when they are left behind, or when they pile up and become too much? What happens when they become waste? How do Buddhists recognize, define, and sort waste from non-waste—and how do new practices of Buddhist consumption result in new forms and new ways of dealing with waste? These are the questions that we ask in *Buddhism and Waste: The Excess, Discard, and Afterlife of Buddhist Consumption.*

Figure 0.1 Withering prayer flags by the lake Namtso in Tibet, September 2007. Photograph by the author.

The chapters of this book pay attention to how material things are integral to religion, the material residues of religious practices, and the ideas that help Buddhists deal with material things. They also privilege material evidence in their inquiries into concepts, practices, socialities, and economies related to Buddhism. We can therefore situate *Buddhism and Waste* within the recent "material turn" in religious studies (Keane 2008; Meyer et al. 2010; Meyer 2012; Morgan 2010). However, that literature has mostly dealt with media and mediation of the sacred, not with how stuff dematerializes and how it is treated when it is exhausted, dissolved, broken, worn out, excessive, impure, or dead. Similarly, although there has been a recent proliferation of studies of Buddhist materiality, Buddhist studies has historically "downplayed or even denigrated material data" (Fleming and Mann 2014: 2). Gregory Schopen (1991, 1998) has pointed this out in several articles and also highlighted the more general disregard in religious studies for precisely the waste dimension that is the focus of this book. Scholars of religions, he argues, "have been particularly uncomfortable, perhaps, when people touched or rubbed or hugged or kissed things, especially when those things were themselves somewhat disconcerting—dead bodies, bits of bone or cloth, dirt or fingernails, dried blood" (Schopen 1998: 256). Yet, as Schopen (ibid.) also remarks, "seemingly dead matter has played a lively role in the history of several major religions." Due to this scholarly neglect, we lack knowledge about an important dimension of religious materiality—waste—even though it is as much an inevitable part of lived religion as production and consumption.

There has been some work to date in Buddhist studies focusing on peoples' detachment from and disposal of things following their use. Examples include studies of memorial services for artifacts in Japan (Gould 2019; Gygi 2018; Kretschmer 2000; Rambelli 2007; Triplett 2017), the deanimation of statues in Vietnam, Korea, and Burma (Kendall 2017; Kendall et al. 2010), the tradition of entombing Buddhist scriptures (Moerman 2010; Salomon 2009; Shen 2019), iconoclasm in East Asia (Rambelli and Reinders 2012), and waste as an environmental issue in Buddhist Asia (Abrahms-Kavunenko 2019; Allison 2014, 2015, 2019; Wang 2019). From this research, we know that the exhaustion and death of artifacts trouble Buddhist practitioners and adherents and that their disposal can become a burden since people recognize endurable values in sacred and animated items. Our volume takes the next step by providing seven analyses of compelling cases that represent contemporary problematizations of Buddhist materiality. Covering a range of Buddhist traditions and geographies, they address various kinds of waste that relate in different ways to Buddhist beliefs and practices—what I refer to loosely in this introduction as "Buddhist waste."[1] By inviting systematic and comparative analyses of Buddhism and waste across Buddhist traditions and geographies, this book provides a new perspective on religious consumption practices and materiality, adding to our understanding of how religious actors generate, interpret, and deal with waste.

Our main contribution is toward the study of religious materiality, but by injecting religion into the study of waste, we also seek to complicate waste as a category and to thereby contribute to waste and discard studies. Waste and discard studies deal with the ideas, discourses, actions, and materialities of discarded materials (Hawkins 2006; Reno 2014; Thompson 2017 [1979]). At present, the field is primarily concerned with macro-level studies of how waste is regulated (modes of governance), accessed (waste citizenship), or distributed (waste networks or flows) (Gille 2010; Reno 2018). While discard studies is an interdisciplinary field, often involving collaborations between geography, archeology, history, anthropology, and economics, it seldom includes religious studies in its interrogations of the systems (social, economic, political, cultural, material) that make and deal with waste.

In this introduction, I discuss the concept of waste and "sacred waste" (Stengs 2014), showing how the waste associated with Buddhism challenges prevailing waste concepts. I look at the inevitable decay of Buddhist artifacts such as a scripture that has been torn and cannot be read or an amulet that has disintegrated and can no longer be worn. Like Irene Stengs' (ibid.) "sacred waste," these items are not the same as the garbage of everyday consumption and should not be treated like other mundane and disposable commodities. Additionally, and this is where this book complicates Stengs' discussion of sacred waste, Buddhists also generate other types of waste, such as the excess from religious practices (for example, food offerings), sanctified leftovers (abandoned family altars), dead actants (buddha statues), poisonous emissions from the production, transportation, and consumption of mass-produced Buddhist commodities, and the everyday garbage that litters Buddhist places. We therefore need a broader range of categories to operate with than that of sacred waste. Buddhist waste is so diverse that we can talk about different classes of waste to which people ascribe different waste conceptions and waste care practices. This introduction offers a framework for studying Buddhism and waste through the categories of excess, discard, and afterlife. This framework exposes the diversity and ambiguity of waste, which can be both burdensome and productive.

What is Waste?

Waste is usually defined in negative terms.[2] As a noun, it is the negative state of a thing, as its many synonyms and near-synonyms tell us. It is that which offends our senses, provoking strong feelings and bodily discomfort when it is "garbage," "rubbish," "sewage," "excrement," or the putrefied "dead." It is the unwanted leftovers and dangerous byproducts of production and consumption when it is "junk," "debris," "pollution," or "litter." As "breakdown," "decomposition," or "worthlessness," waste is the loss caused by consumption, wear, and decay. As "wasteland" or "desert" it is the missed opportunities and unfulfilled potential of that which is untended and unused. As a verb, "to waste" means to get rid of something before it is wholly appreciated or consumed, to use it recklessly or wrongly in some way, or to overspend. Synonymous with "squandering," "wastefulness," and "prodigality," wasting as an action—for example, the provokingly lavish spending of the wealthy—also has negative moral connotations. Since waste is a negative category, it is also a spatial practice. Before they are sorted from non-waste, excrement (Anderson 1995), mass waste (Reno 2014), and e-waste (Lepawsky and Billah 2011) are "matter out of place" that by definition are liminal and dangerous. But once they have been sorted from non-waste and socially and spatially marginalized in the sewers underground, the landfill at the edge of the city, or the Global South far away from the Colonial North (from the perspective of waste imperialism), waste no longer has the disorder of dirt, since it has been placed where it belongs (Douglas 2002 [1966]: 197–8; see also Liboiron 2019).

Waste is also a dynamic category. Both the contents of garbage and the criteria for sorting waste and its opposite (value, purity, sacredness, and so on) can change as "nothing is inherently trash" (Strasser 2000: 5; see also Douglas 2002 [1966]; Reno 2009). Discard studies and waste studies recognize the mobility of things, which shift between various regimes where they enter into different social relations and are interpreted differently (Paine 2014; see also Thompson 2017 [1979]). We can say that waste is "mercurial" in the sense that it "can accumulate, disperse, flow and even return" (Lepawsky and Billah 2011: 123; cf. Hawkins 2006; Gille 2010; Thompson 2017 [1979]). Waste, as formed from a material reality that changes due to usage, degradation, and atrophy, is fleeting. Objects change because they are made of transient materials that break or degrade over time, but these processes can be accelerated by usage and climate. Still, when something moves into the waste category it is not necessarily heading toward the end of a linear life span. A wrecked ship can become "chock-chocky furniture" in Bangladesh (Gregson et al. 2010), rubbish electronics are dismantled and reworked into "new" household hardware sold in China (Lepawsky and Billah 2011), and rat-infested slums are gentrified into high-end living (Thompson 2017 [1979]). If we look toward the religious field, we likewise see how entombed scriptures can become a treasure (Gayley 2007) and the bodily discards of a holy person can become relics (Schopen 1998). Value is subtracted or ascribed to a wrecked ship, rubbish electronics, filthy habitats, withered scriptures, and holy nail clippings according to values, knowledge, and beliefs that determine what is considered waste and what is not. Waste is both a material reality and a social construct.

If the value of waste is generally complicated, there is even more at stake when dealing with religious materiality as it is generated in the setting of rituals, devotion, morality, and the sacred (space, bodies, objects). In religious fields, items can protect people from evil, grant fortune, and give access to the transcendent, which makes religious stuff potent, powerful, and precious. This means that the responsibilities of caretaking and containing these powers are not necessarily discontinued even after consumption, wear, tear, breakdown, and death. Examples include ritual remains in Cuban popular religion (Wirtz 2009), withering icons on Eastern Orthodox home shrines (Riccardi n.d.), wilted flower offerings in Hindu temples (Sinha 2008), Buddhist things and bodies wrecked by iconoclastic destruction (Rambelli and Reinders 2012), and ritually buried scriptures across religions (Myrvold 2010). These examples of religious materiality complicate our understanding of the waste category because when they are used, disintegrated, rotten, destroyed, or discarded, they can still affect the people and environment with which they are entangled.

Anthropologist Irene Stengs (2014) offers the concept of "sacred waste" in conversation with David Chidester (2014) and Crispin Paine (2014) in the *Journal of Material Religion*. She identifies sacred waste as a form of waste that is not worthless, drawing on examples of sanctified leftovers such as the remnants of catastrophes (the dust from Ground Zero in New York, objects washed ashore in North America from the Tsunami in Japan), as well as "damaged sacra" such as worn-out religious texts or icons. These materials have a sacrosanct value enabling "the substance to enforce its ceremonial treatment" (Stengs 2014: 235). In other words, contrary to how people, including scholars, commonly talk about waste as worthless and define it in negative terms, we here have to do with waste that must be handled in ways that respect or contain its enduring value as sacred. Stengs (ibid.) characterizes sacred waste as

> [the] material residues and surpluses that cannot be disposed of as just garbage (or rubble), but neither can be kept or left alone. Its ambiguous nature, charged with a religious, moral, or emotional value on the one hand, but at the same time a kind of leftover for which no proper destination exists, makes sacred waste precarious matter, and hence often a ground for conflict and contestation.

This is waste that "demands special treatment: it must be set apart, for instance by being preserved as a relic or as cultural heritage, or requires to be ritually neutralized" (ibid.). Yet, there are seldom clear protocols to guide how different kinds of sacred waste should be handled (ibid.). This is a key point, since lack of protocol creates uncertainty and burden, and as exemplified in this book, such objects do not always receive the special treatment to which their sacred status entitles them (see also Gould 2019).

In the cases that preoccupy Stengs, waste becomes sanctified because people interact with it as sacred, and this introduces a dilemma of disposability. In this book, we discover that the waste associated with Buddhism is much more diverse. As remarked by Hannah Gould (this volume): "All religious activity generates waste: some sacred, most banal." Yet, scholars have not given much attention to this waste, for instance, the garbage produced during pilgrimage tourism and religious festivals (Williams-Oerberg this volume) or excessive food offerings

(Caple this volume). The chapters in this book deal with post-consumption items that relate to Buddhism in various ways and whose waste nature differs, therefore evoking diverse waste problematics. Some of these items we might call waste in a moral-political sense; they are seen as excessive (Caple; Gould) or are unwanted and have been discarded (Abrahms-Kavunenko; Williams-Oerberg). Other things can be called waste in the sense that they are decayed, broken, or deteriorated, yet are not disposed of as garbage but are reposited (Wilson), recycled, or repurposed (Holmes-Tagchungdarpa), or ritually discarded (Gygi). In the remainder of this introduction, I discuss waste as excess, as discard, and as afterlife, suggesting this as an approach for studying Buddhism and waste. I test this framework with reference to the following seven chapters of this book and the various exhausted, dissolved, broken, worn out, excessive, impure, and dead things they discuss, which are either Buddhist or handled through Buddhist ideas and practices.

A Framework for Studying Buddhism and Waste

Excess, discard, and afterlife are three ways of thinking about Buddhism and waste that reveal particular dimensions of a thing's material properties and social relations, as well as the cultural worlds that they are embedded in. The analytical framework that I propose here is therefore not intended as a model to categorize individual phenomena as belonging to one or another class of waste, as if a thing can only be the excess, discard, or afterlife of Buddhist consumption. These dimensions are not stable. Things (food offerings, ritual tools, icons) can move between them, just as they can move in and out of the waste category. However, this conceptual distinction between excess, discard, and afterlife provides an explorative infrastructure with which to approach the study of Buddhism and waste, highlighting different dimensions of that which is produced, consumed, and residual that can be compared across Buddhist traditions and geographies.

Waste as Excess

Buddhist waste seen through the lens of excess should be understood as a sign of prosperity or material abundance that is subjected to moral judgment. It is related to the verb "to waste," either as the act of getting rid of something before it is completely appreciated and consumed or as the act of reckless and immoderate consumption. Buddhism is fundamentally speaking against excess:

"While Buddhist institutions needed wealth and power to expand and carry out their salvific mission, excessive wealth and power in themselves were essentially against the basic tenets of Buddhism as a religion of renunciation" (Rambelli and Reinders 2012: 5). Anti-materialism has emerged as a dominant trope of Buddhism, and as discussed by Gould (this volume), Buddhist and particularly Zen philosophy and practice has been associated with a minimalist ethic of being and interacting in the material world that has had global appeal. The anti-materialist image of Buddhism is personified by the ascetic monk who displays non-attachment to wealth by wearing only a patched monastic robe.[3] Following the exemplary life of the Buddha Śākyamuni, who gave up his wealth and family to seek enlightenment, monastics are renunciates. Yet, they are dependent upon the generosity of the laity, whose labor and wealth support the Sangha, the community of renunciates. There are numerous stories of how such generosity is rewarded by fabulous wealth, most notably the *Vessantara Jātaka*, the tale of one of the Buddha's past lives, which serves as a model of the perfection of generosity (Sanskrit: *dāna*) for the Buddhist laity.[4] The protagonist, Prince Vessantara, who gives away his riches, his wife and children, and even his own eyes, ends up having his family and sight restored and being showered with jewels (Rozenberg 2004: 509). Other examples include the *Saddharmapundarīka Sūtra* and *Sukhāvatīvyūha Sūtra*, which are rich with "fantasies of plenitude and felicity" describing aesthetically glorious and abundant Buddhist heavens rewarding those who lead moral lives (Ali 2003: 246).

Excess in the form of abundance is an oft-exhibited value in the Buddhist field. Monasteries, temples, and shrines display a plethora of sacred objects, embellished interiors, scriptures with gold ink and semi-precious stones, and elaborate altars crowded with food and cash offerings. This kind of excess not only suggests the precious value of Buddhism's teachings, places, and artifacts but also inspires faith; merely seeing this richness should fill one with devotion. This excess is what Daud Ali (ibid.), in his discussion of Buddhist heavens and celestial gardens, has called an "aesthetics of plenitude" prominent in Mahayana sutras: "This aesthetics saw flowers, jewels, and ornaments as the necessary, felicitous and beautiful accoutrements of a morally sanctioned world" (247). It is not only in Mahayana Buddhism that we find an aesthetics of plenitude. Justin McDaniel (2011: 166) argues that in Thailand, extravagant material wealth is the norm rather than the exception; temples and monasteries are not "aesthetically austere" but, rather, defined by abundance. However, that does not mean that this kind of excess is exempt from moral judgment. As Caple (this volume) discusses, the question is at what point and why such abundance is considered excessive to the point that it becomes wasteful, and who sets the parameters for such an evaluation.

Historically, Buddhist monasteries and monastics have been accused of amassing wealth and being an economic burden on societies' resources by both external and internal critics (see e.g., Caple this volume; Covell 2012; Ornatowski 1996; Rambelli and Reinders 2012). We also find similar lines of argumentation in contemporary Buddhist fields. Buddhist followers variously interpret monastic or individual monks' displays of excess wealth as signs of virtue (since the virtuous receive donations corresponding to their spiritual accomplishments and moral integrity) or as signs of immorality (since the unvirtuous amass wealth instead of distributing it). Guillaume Rozenberg (2004) discusses this distinction in his study of the spectacular birthday celebration of the famous monk Thamanya Hsayadaw in Burma. During the festivities, Thamanya Hsayadaw displayed his superior position by exhibiting the donations he had accumulated (ibid.: 500). Thousands of participants congregated for the birthday ceremony, during which not only the celebrated monk but also the visitors were offered gifts. The visitors received the excess of Thamanya Hsayadaw's accumulated offerings in the form of money and Buddhist objects. This redistribution of excess contributed to the sanctification of Thamanya Hsayadaw but also manifested his saintliness. It relates to what Rozenberg (ibid.) calls an "idiom of detachment" that "publicly demonstrates the excellence of his renunciation" (see also Caple 2020: 32–6). Thus, even with this spectacular display of excess, we return to the trope of renunciation that fundamentally defines monastic Buddhism.[5]

Contemporary excess in Buddhist societies includes the material affluence of Buddhist institutions, the wealth of individual monks, and the mass consumption of material goods, which has accelerated with the rise of consumer capitalism. Buddhists not only participate in consumer society, but also orchestrate the accumulation of material wealth and capital (see Brox and Williams-Oerberg 2020). Elizabeth Williams-Oerberg and Trine Brox (2020: 2) argue that "Buddhism in the twenty-first century is marked by a heightened engagement with capitalism and market economics." Moreover, as Buddhist societies have become wealthier, lay Buddhists have more disposable income to spend on Buddhist practices and institutions, and monasteries and monks generate more excess. The point at which abundance becomes "too much" and is therefore subjected to moral judgment as excess among Buddhists themselves is often unclear and debated (see Caple this volume). The most extreme cases can, however, become local and even international scandals that, for example, expose materialistic monks involved in corruption and embezzlement, or displaying luxury consumer goods in breach of the monastic renunciatory ideal. Yet, it is not only these high profile cases that have given rise to criticism. Buddhist practitioners and monastics are more generally criticized for "their abundant material acquisition, display, and consumption" (Williams-Oerberg and Brox 2020: 13).

The production of excess in contemporary Buddhist societies is supported by an industry that creates "waste snowballs" that run through the entire economy (Gille 2010). For example, in China, the accelerating scale of the religious product economy through serial production and an ample supply of inexpensive Buddhist commodities has resulted in excessive quantities of stuff to consume. Increased consumption has led to larger amounts of waste (see, for instance, Abrahms-Kavunenko this volume). There are reports of accelerated ritual expenses among the Tibetan Buddhist laity resulting from the peer-pressure of displaying financial capability (Jixiancairang 2018) and competitive giving of luxury gifts and large monetary donations to temples and high-ranking lamas among affluent Han Chinese converts to Tibetan Buddhism (Osburg 2020). As discussed in the chapter on excess and waste by Jane Caple (this volume), such "conspicuous generosity" has become an object of critique. Caple examines local concerns about a recent escalation in religious sponsorship and temple building among Tibetans in northeast Tibet during a period of breakneck economic development. This escalation and its accompanying material excesses are seen by some of her Tibetan interlocutors as wasteful in ways similar to other forms of prestige-oriented consumption; they feel that the money could be better used elsewhere (see also Williams-Oerberg this volume). Yet, Caple suggests that it can simultaneously be seen as a moral response to state-sponsored capitalist development and perceptions of a decline in faith. Pointing to the "inherent pull" toward material excess in Buddhist generosity practices, Caple highlights "a tension in Buddhist excess that helps to explain the slippage of generosity practices into a kind of Buddhist waste."

Waste as excess not only relates to overconsumption but also to that which is excessive by not being used. In Gygi's chapter on memorial services for dolls in Japan (this volume), for example, we learn that owners take their dolls to Buddhist temples for ritual disposal as they know that the next generation will not appreciate them. Similarly, in Wilson's chapter, family altars can become unwanted burdens since, as inherited heirlooms, they are not part of the new owner's everyday religiosity in North America and take up a lot of space. Both chapters exemplify how generational shifts can result in changing relations between people and objects, transforming the latter into unwanted material

Figure 0.2 Protection cords, ceremonial scarves, and amulets left along the circumambulation path encircling Ganden Monastery in Tibet, June 2010. Photograph by the author.

excess, dealt with through practices of abandonment. In the chapter by Gould, we learn about the trend of combating excess in both senses of the word—as overconsumption and as the unused—by throwing out stuff. The "modern minimalist movement" that she describes, which is promoted by figures such as the Japanese downsizing expert Marie Kondo, preaches decluttering as a salve for unhappiness in affluent societies. As an "emerging movement in domestic spirituality," which has "an enduring association with Japanese Zen Buddhism," it is usually directed at women who consume from a position of privilege and financial stability and who are the main caretakers in the home (see also Siniawer 2018: 297). Possessed of both material abundance and excess money, Gould shows us, these women are involved in a "competitive minimalism," which draws on images and teachings of the Buddha to signal "lifestyles of non-consumption." In some instances, Buddhism is used as a visual signature, for example, through the placement of a Buddha statue as part of the backdrop of a decluttered, English home. However, in other instances, Buddhism is itself offered by minimalist advocates and other contemporary Buddhist authors as the antidote to the excesses and wastefulness of consumerism in affluent societies like Australia and Great Britain.[6] Many of the superfluous dolls, family altars, and household items that have become waste as excess in these cases share a common fate; as their owners eventually reject and get rid of them they move into the category of waste as discard.

Waste as Discard

Buddhist waste viewed from the perspective of discard typifies the things that are rejected and thrown away because they are considered unwanted, worthless, useless, or dangerous. This waste dimension includes a broad range of things, from sacred objects to consumer goods, which activate diverse disposal methods. These are manifold entities that should not be conflated, but in the contexts discussed here they share a similar post-consumption fate of being discarded. Waste as discard involves many issues that are too complex to be addressed in this brief introduction, but I will point to three striking problematics: (1) the sorting of waste from non-waste; (2) the disposability of things; and (3) the impact of discard in the form of environmental and spiritual pollution.

Discard as an issue of sorting has to do with when and why particular things are classified or treated as sacred or disposable, clean or dirty, living or dead, useful or useless, waste or wanted, eternal or ephemeral, and so on. To understand these sorting practices, we must look at the status of the object before it became waste, how its consumption or usage affects its value, and how its biography determines its waste nature, that is, why it is considered excessive, disposable, or reusable. In this volume, we find that waste care practices for dolls in Japan (Gygi), family altars in North America (Wilson), and statues in the Himalayas (Holmes-Tagchungdarpa) acknowledge the enduring value of these items. People connect with them emotionally, religiously, and morally, which means that they require special handling—similar to the "sacred waste" discussed by Stengs (2014). Concomitantly, they are recognized as waste: the unwanted doll, the neglected altar, and the broken statue are placed into the hands of Buddhist specialists for ritual disposal, safekeeping, or repurposing, respectively. This kind of sorting, based upon status and biography but also the materiality of things, leads us to the second issue regarding disposability.

While litter is managed by professionals to be taken together with household waste to a dumpster, landfill, or incinerator plant, the disposal of sacred or animated items activates a different set of disposal methods. These include immersion (e.g., the woodblocks deposited in a river mentioned by Holmes-Tagchungdarpa this volume), entombment (e.g., relics exhumed and reburied in medieval China; see Shen 2019), cremation (e.g., of unwanted dolls; see Gygi this volume), ingestion (e.g., Tibetan butter sculptures and food offerings devoured by birds and monkeys), and entropy (e.g., traditional prayer scarves placed on sacred rock cairns; see Abrahms-Kavunenko this volume). Rituals may assist these modes of disposal according to a written protocol or vernacular folkways.

In Japanese settings, there is a growing repertoire of disposal rituals that is well described. *Kuyō*, "rites of veneration and separation," are modeled after Buddhist rites and performed for ordinary and sacred things (Gould 2019; see also Gygi 2018; Kretschmer 2000). Most things that are ritually disposed of in Japan are everyday items like needles, clocks, chopsticks, and so forth, but *kuyō* is also performed for Buddhist objects like family altars and prayer beads (Kretschmer 2000: 380). There exist ritual manuals, but Gould (2019) remarks that disposal methods are commonly orthopraxic. Sometimes, the laity conduct ritual disposal; at other times, this responsibility is outsourced to Buddhist specialists (Kretschmer 2000). Mortuary rites are performed because these items have some sort of value, like "sacred waste," and are being unwillingly parted with. The owners do not want to throw their family altars and prayer beads in the bin with the consumer waste but, instead, acknowledge that they still are valuable, even as waste. They feel obliged to care for them beyond their usage (see also Abrahms-Kavunenko; Wilson this volume). Gould (2019: 7–8) calls this "a sense of stewardship" that shows how people are attached to objects and concerned for their welfare after they have been abandoned. In this volume, we learn from Gygi about the memorial services performed for dolls by temples and shrines throughout Japan. By handing over their dolls to Buddhist priests, the owners transfer this stewardship. Ideally the dolls are burned and their owners can witness the ritual mass cremation, which helps them detach themselves from the dolls and relieves them of the burden of disposal. However, nowadays, dolls are usually made of plastics and other substances that emit hazardous fumes if burned. The denouement of the ritual has therefore been moved backstage. Willfully ignored by the owners, the dolls are taken by rubbish men, tipped into a compactor rubbish truck and compressed into doll debris. Gygi argues that owners' ignorance of this breach of ceremonial treatment—the fact that these dolls violently, unceremoniously, and unsentimentally end up mixed in with mundane waste in the compressor truck—enables the former owners "to maintain certain notions about objects, consumption, themselves, and national culture" (Gygi this volume).

Most studies, including Gygi's, discuss disposal as a process of separation and detachment, but there can be bonds between people and things that are not severed through disposal. According to Gould (2019: 4), the rite of *kuyō* is "a kind of affective labour, which works to both venerate and separate the bonds between people and things." Similarly, in a Vietnamese Buddhist context, statues that are considered animated, sacred, and agentive, are desacralized in rituals if they have lost their power, been damaged or have disintegrated, or have to be replaced by bigger statues (Kendall et al. 2010: 71). Regardless of the disposal method, these items were handled respectfully partly because they are efficacious and able to do good for people, but also because they are considered to have punitive powers (ibid.; see also Wilson this volume). It is crucial here to remark that disposability is not necessarily contingent on an item's value in an object hierarchy: precious scriptures are burned, ordinary nail clippings of an accomplished master are upcycled as relics, and mass-produced dolls receive memorial services by Buddhist priests. Instead, disposability is contingent on materiality (can it be destroyed?), biography (wherefrom did it originate?), assumptions about its powers (can it confer blessings, attract fortune, do harm, and will those powers survive if the object is extinguished?), and on its prospects for reuse or recirculation (can it be repaired or re-made?). Non-disposables will be discussed in the next section on waste as afterlife.

The last point regarding waste as discard has to do with pollution. Buddhists operate with different ideas regarding the effects of waste (both religious objects and everyday garbage) and how discard pollutes people and the environment. These ideas are not necessarily only religious but, as exemplified in the chapter by Williams-Oerberg (this volume), may very well be informed by global politics. There is a vast literature on Buddhist environmentalism and "spiritual ecology" containing historical and contemporary writings by Buddhist teachers (e.g., Kaza and Kraft 2000; Payne 2010) and scholarship on Buddhist environmentalist drives. The latter include zero-waste initiatives in Bhutan (Allison 2019), tree ordination in Thailand (Darlington 2012), Green Plans in Japanese Sōtō Zen temples (Williams 2012), recycling schemes by Tzu Chi Organizations in Taiwan (Hsiao et al. 2019), and clean-up campaigns organized by Tibetan lamas in Ladakh (Williams-Oerberg this volume). In doing something for the environment, Williams-Oerberg (ibid.) points out, Buddhist organizations are also picking up a cause that has global resonance. In her chapter on Buddhist organizations' "green" initiatives in Ladakh, she argues that the "greening of Buddhism" has become a means for Buddhist leaders to promote their own ethical standards to expand their particular sectarian organizations. Buddhist environmentalism is a popular cause behind which they can unite. Yet, while they arrange green activities such as tree-planting, the "brown" environmental issues of personal and institutional consumption are ignored. They arrange lavish festivals and rituals that involve mass consumption, thereby feeding into the very problem they try to address through, for example, clean-up drives. Where does the rubbish of the thousands—in some cases hundreds of thousands—of Buddhist followers attending these festivals and rituals end up when there is no proper sewerage system, landfill, or incinerator plant? William-Oerberg's chapter exposes this duality of Himalayan Buddhist expansion (through spectacular religious festivals and environmental campaigns) and Ladakh's massive waste problem (insufficiently attended to through greening campaigns).

Such "brown" matters are also discussed in Abrahms-Kavunenko's chapter on Mongolian waste. Abrahms-Kavunenko explores how mass consumption in the capital of Ulaanbaatar, Mongolia, has resulted in mass-disposed everyday rubbish that lingers as "zombie waste," unable to become organic matter. At the same time, religious offerings have also taken on "a new kind of materiality that lingers problematically," as previously decomposable items like silk scarves have been replaced by polyester and food is now wrapped in plastic. While it is the enormous quantities of everyday waste that make it dangerous, discarded religious items that are unable to decompose pose a threat due to the specific potencies each contains depending on its individual biography. Yet, this kind of pollution of the environment by "undead" everyday garbage and religious offerings is also connected to the people of Mongolia in other ways. Abrahms-Kavunenko's interlocutors suggest that wasting and littering reflect peoples' state of mind. They evaluate others as morally and spiritually degraded by pointing to increased consumerism, air pollution, and casual disposal (see also Caple this volume).

Buddhist communities grapple with different kinds of pollution, as explored in the works of Elizabeth Allison (2014, 2015, 2019). Fears of spiritual pollution or *drib* (*sgrib*) among her rural Bhutanese interlocutors were in tension with waste conceptions promoted by the State. For instance, they refused to burn trash because they worried the smell would offend deities, and they discarded plastic wrappings carelessly in the landscape because "they lack the qualities that cause drib" (Allison 2015: 172; cf., Wang 2019). Allison shows that Bhutanese villagers were more concerned about avoiding spiritual defilement than managing waste. Consequently, unless litter caused ritual pollution, it did not qualify as waste and was therefore of no concern.

These discussions from India, Mongolia, and Bhutan on (at times conflicting) conceptions of pollution as the result of discard are forebodings of the near future. In the wake of a flourishing Buddhism coupled with increased mass consumption, we can expect not only increased pollution but also confrontation regarding sorting issues, the Buddhist environment, and waste management.

Waste as Afterlife

Buddhist waste as afterlife designates a phase in the life of material things, which might be retirement, life after death, or "a period of continued or renewed use, existence, or popularity beyond what is normal, primary, or expected."[7] Michael B. Schiffer (2013: 2) notes how "any entity—person, artefact, organization, or place—that has undergone a change from some sort of 'life' to some sort of 'death' may have an afterlife." I suggest that the recycling, recirculation, repurposing, and repositing of post-consumption things in the Buddhist field can be categorized as afterlife. Recycling can include the processing of an object for reuse, its return to its original condition through deconsecration, or its repair and reassembly. Tibetan ceremonial scarves, for example, can be offered as gifts in a cycle of gift-giving (Harris 2007). When they can no longer be circulated, they may end up as cloths used in temples and monasteries to dust and polish sacred items. Similarly, luxurious textiles such as fabric from painted scrolls are reused in appliques with Buddhist motifs (Reynolds 1992), and newspaper illustrations of religious figures are cut out and recycled on house shrines as idols (Holmes-Tagchungdarpa 2014). Afterlife in the form of recirculation also includes statues that have been dislocated and put into circulation as commodities or gifts, ending up in curio shops, museums, and private collections as commodities, diplomatic gifts, souvenirs, and antiques (Kendall et al. 2010; Martin 2015). Afterlife, therefore, is the life after the consumption and use of a thing. It is the secondary life where that thing enters new relations and is perhaps used for purposes not intended by its original maker. To look at waste from this perspective means that one investigates which and when things are not discarded or destroyed but are, instead, cared for. We should therefore include Stengs' (2014) sacred waste in the category of waste as afterlife.

Stengs focuses on the significance that "sacred waste" has according to its waste nature. Yet, I argue that it is just as crucial to understand the properties of the wasted object *before* it became waste since these can determine its afterlife trajectories. In addition to an item's materiality, it is relevant to look at (1) its biography, that is, its life according to its recognized efficacy, (sacred) status, and relations (accomplishments and associations with sacred places or persons); (2) what is lost, what remains, and what is gained after breakdown or death; and (3) the connections between the afterlife object and the original object.[8] These dimensions can help us understand care practices relating to non-disposable items in terms of their recycling, recirculation, repurposing, and repositing. In Holmes-Tagchungdarpa's chapter (this volume), we learn that statues are non-disposable. As waste, they are ground into dust to become sacred ingredients to sacralize other objects. Other common waste care practices are what we can call "containment" (when non-disposable waste is viewed as dangerous or dirty) or "repositing" (when the waste is seen as valuable). In the latter case, valuable non-disposables such as altars, amulets, prayer wheels, and so forth can be set apart in particularly designated repositories. These include places that are considered pure (such as the cupboard of one's home shrine or a niche in a temple), sacred (circumambulation routes and stupas), or elevated (mountains and trees).

Not all material objects have afterlives, and not all afterlives are considered appropriate. For instance, dolls in Japan are extinguished forever in ritual cremation or disposal (Gygi this volume), while Marie Kondo admonishes her minimalist followers not to pass their excess belongings on but to get rid of them altogether (Gould this volume). Some Buddhist objects are not recycled because they are considered dangerous or polluted such as sacred or ritual objects that have not been adequately maintained through rituals or not been properly

Figure 0.3 Inside a small hut by a circumambulation path that functions as a repository for "sacred waste" such as unwanted painted scrolls, votives, and statues, Dharamsala, India, September 2019. Photograph by the author.

discarded (Abrahms-Kavunenko; Holmes-Tagchungdarpa this volume). In Mongolia, prayer scarves are usually not recycled because they are perceived as carrying the intentions of the person offering them. Instead, they are left on sacred rocks, tied to trees and landmarks, or offered to show respect, but not easily recycled (Abrahms-Kavunenko this volume). The fear that such items have picked up pollution speaks against recycling. This is an interesting ambiguity: old objects are considered powerful as they can have amassed blessings, but at the same time, there is a fear that they have garnered spiritual pollution.

Two chapters in this book are illustrative of waste as afterlife, dealing with the powers and pollution of things that become waste because they decay and break down (Holmes-Tagchungdarpa) or because they are old and unused (Wilson). As demonstrated in the study by Holmes-Tagchungdarpa, such items can "reincarnate" in the sense that they are repurposed or recycled. For instance, Buddhist texts, statues, and stupas, which are considered receptacles of the Buddha's speech, body, and mind, are seen as containers of blessings. When they are exhausted, they can be ground into a powder together with other exhausted objects (such as worn-down monastic robes and prayer beads, and relics such as nail clippings and hair from accomplished masters). In this rejuvenated form, they can be turned into amulets and medicinal pills or become filler to empower other objects. While sacred items can pick up pollution, their powers can also accumulate, making them potentially more efficacious: "the older or more frequently they were used by someone with a lot of *jinlap* [blessings], the better" (Holmes-Tagchungdarpa this volume). What Holmes-Tagchungdarpa shows, in other words, is that far from the efficacy or power of an object dissipating when it becomes waste, it can be transferred and given an afterlife where it serves new purposes.

In contrast, the family altars (butsudan) discussed by Wilson (this volume) have afterlives that in most instances are not productive. What had been important objects of Buddhist worship and ancestor veneration, are discharged from their duties as altars by a new generation of owners. Yet, rather than simply dumping them or throwing them in the trash, the owners recognize, respect, or sometimes fear their religious or sentimental values, and therefore bring them to temples. Wilson (this volume) relates how these reposited family altars pile up in Japanese temples in Canada and the United States: "Squatting in the minister's office, lurking behind the main hall altar area, hiding in libraries and random corners, crammed into closets, basements, and garages—discarded butsudan are ubiquitous at Japanese-American/Canadian temples." They are so many that they constitute a serious storage problem for the temples.

The two chapters by Wilson and Holmes-Tagchungdarpa relate very different afterlives: one reposited in a temple and the other repurposed as a sacred ingredient, one unproductive, the other productive. Yet, both afterlives are predicated upon the powers and values that people associate with these items, and the affective qualities, moral connections, and religious significance that they ascribe to them. These altars and statues evoke a sense of stewardship similar to that which leads people to perform rites of disposal for discarded items such as dolls. Waste seen as afterlife, in other words, shows us that the endpoint of consumption is not inevitably death and discard.

Rethinking Waste

> Waste is what is worthless or unused for human purpose. It is a lessening of something without an apparently useful result; it is loss and abandonment, decline, separation, and death. It is the spent and valueless material left after some act of production or consumption, but can also refer to any used thing: garbage, trash, litter, junk, impurity and dirt. (Lynch 1990: 146)

The framework of excess, discard, and afterlife allows us to explore Buddhism and waste from three angles that offer different insights into the various problematics and stakes of waste and wasting. When waste is studied as excess, it opens up discussion on the ethics and effects of consumption for both individuals and communities (Caple; Gould this volume). When studied as discard, we find that sorting and disposal practices are informed by feelings of obligation and care (Gygi this volume) and ideas about different kinds of pollution (Abrahms-Kavunenko; Williams-Oerberg this volume), among others. As afterlife, we discover that waste can have anti-value that makes it non-disposable (Wilson this volume) and can create new valuables when repurposed (Holmes-Tagchungdarpa this volume).

In that sense, it has been fruitful to explore the many different phenomena that fall within this framework. But can we call all of them "waste" given the term's usual negative connotations as something offensive, unwanted, dangerous, and so forth? If we were to operate with an unequivocally negative definition of waste, like that of Kevin Lynch (1990) cited earlier, then not all things that have moved into the categories of excess, discard, and afterlife of Buddhist consumption would be counted as waste. Using this tripartite framework thus enables us to diversify and problematize the conception of waste as worthless—

as the unavoidably negative end-product of consumption. It adds new insights and greater nuance to our understanding of the ambiguous valence of waste. The waste that we are dealing with in this book is often hard to get rid of. It has enduring value because people feel connected to it, because it is significant, or because it has a new life and purpose. In particular, waste that is in an afterlife state challenges any conception of waste as definitively negative since it demonstrates the potential productiveness, new relations, and renewed value of discarded, worn out, or broken Buddhist stuff.

Unlike the worthless, polluting and "stinky brown waste" that congests streams and accumulates in makeshift piles scattered in the landscape (Williams-Oerberg this volume) or the excess objects cluttering up homes and bringing about unhappiness (Gould this volume), some kinds of waste are not worthless. In several of the cases explored in this book, waste must be handled in a way that both respects or contains the values that are ascribed to it and is practical in view of its material components. It follows that the disposal of Buddhist things has become a growing problem as their quantity and circulation has escalated; Buddhists are increasingly challenged by what to do with the waste generated through consumption. This is especially true for things that have a durable sense of value, even more so when they are sacred (Abrahms-Kavunenko this volume). In that sense, Buddhist waste can resemble sacred waste as characterized by Stengs (2014), that is, as material residues and surpluses that have a sacrosanct value demanding special treatment. Still, this cannot encompass the diversity of the destinies that await materials that rot, decay, or break in the Buddhist field through practice, consumption, or neglect, or things that are problematic or discarded because they are excessive or unwanted.

The category of waste—a generally ignored but important aspect of object biographies—can help us understand the productive, social dimensions of religious materiality. The trajectories that Buddhist things follow are not the same as those of the everyday garbage that is discarded in the dumpster, laid to rest in a landfill, or annihilated at an incineration plant. As related by Holmes-Tagchungdarpa (this volume), when an object is acknowledged as sacred in Vajrayana Buddhism, it never ceases to remain as such. However, it is not only the sacrality but also the animation of or emotional connection to things that complicates disposal. Owners might wish to abandon their inherited altars in North America (Wilson this volume), but they cannot be disposed of like garbage. Instead, the responsibility is transferred to temples, which dispose or reposit them. Buddhism also emerges as a method or ethic to deal with material excess unrelated to Buddhism. That is the case, for instance, when a walking pilgrimage becomes a waste-picking operation in Ladakh (Williams-Oerberg this volume), when a buddha forms the backdrop of a minimalist lifestyle in England (Gould this volume), or when people take their dolls to a temple to be ritually discarded (Gygi this volume). Buddhism can also provide a conduit through which excess wealth or resources can be transformed into other kinds of value through the production of yet more Buddhist things (Caple this volume).

In short, waste is diverse, ambiguous, and burdensome, but it is also productive. Approaching its study through the categories of excess, discard, and afterlife offers a conceptualization of waste that can encompass the variety of post-consumption fates that await stuff that is used, abandoned, worn, and consumed by people in Buddhist places or through Buddhist practices.

About this Book

This book explores the excess, discard, and afterlife of consumption based upon ethnographies of Buddhist waste in Australia, India, Japan, Mongolia, North America, and the Tibetan and Himalayan Buddhist world. This introduction is followed by seven chapters written by scholars from religious studies, anthropology, and language-based area studies. They cover a range of Buddhist traditions, providing new ethnographic data, novel analyses, and thought-provoking insights that speak to ongoing theoretical discussions regarding religious materiality and Buddhist material culture. They also show religion to be a productive topic relevant to waste and discard studies, fleshing out the framework of excess, discard, and afterlife proposed in this introduction.

The overall aim of the volume is to understand the complexity of Buddhist consumption and related conceptions of waste and waste care. Although the chapters deal with unique phenomena, from the mass cremation of unwanted dolls in Japan and tetra-packed milk offerings in Mongolia, to entombed sacred treasures on the Tibetan plateau, they address issues pertinent to scholars, consumers, and practitioners in the Buddhist field and beyond. They include discussion on the moralization of consumption and limits of abundance (Caple, chapter 1), the virtue and art of disposal (Gould, chapter 2), the abandonment of practices and things spurred by generational shifts and wider social changes (Wilson, chapter 3), the difficulty of getting rid of items that we are attached to (Gygi, chapter 4), the potential pollution and prosperity of repurposing practices (Holmes-Tagchungdarpa, chapter 5), the littering of landscapes with things that refuse to disintegrate (Abrahms-Kavunenko, chapter 6), and finally, the appeal of green issues and neglect of the brown (Williams-Oerberg, chapter 7). As well as addressing such topical issues, the chapters facilitate comparison through the diversity of ethnographic contexts that they explore and the material focus of each. Taken together, they thereby challenge our conceptions of waste and contribute to the interdisciplinary study of material religion and contemporary Buddhism.

In the first chapter, Jane Caple explores concerns about Buddhist material excess among Tibetans in northeast Tibet, where there has been a wave of new temple building and escalating levels of expenditure on Buddhist rituals and monastic events. Supporting the Sangha and building temples are ubiquitous forms of Buddhist generosity practice. Why then have some monks and laypeople been critical of such practices in recent years, perceiving them to be excessive and wasteful? Are there limits to how many temples a community should build or to how big they should be? Caple situates these debates in relation to local responses to state developmentalism and market capitalism, exploring the specific contexts in which an impetus toward conspicuous generosity embedded in Buddhist teachings has become problematized. In contrast to external critiques of Tibetan Buddhism as corrupt and wasteful, she argues that these emic concerns about material excess have more to do with a moralization of consumption than of Buddhism or Buddhist practices per se.

While Caple focuses on problematizations of Buddhist material excess, Hannah Gould's chapter explores how popular Buddhist philosophy and praxis stemming from Japan are deployed to deal with the excess of consumer goods in late-capitalist societies around the globe via the discourse of minimalism. Gould examines the works of three Japanese minimalist luminaries that have travelled globally via the "pop Zen" phenomenon, alongside an ethnographic study of minimalist lifestyles in Australia, to investigate how Japanese Buddhism features within lifestyles that value simplicity, contentedness, and skilled detachment. The investigation reveals an emerging movement in domestic spirituality based on an economy of attachment, which promotes heightened emotional skills of disposal and investment in a select number of goods. Minimalism, as a prominent contemporary articulation of Buddhism, is not aniconic or anti-materialist, but full of life-changing magic.

In Chapter 3, Jeff Wilson looks at Buddhist home altars (butsudan) that have long been a mainstay of Japanese-American and Japanese-Canadian homes. These objects are sites of significant religious activity and family meaning. However, as modern social forces break apart extended families and depress Buddhist adherence, these previously cherished small shrines often transform from sacred objects into problematic clutter. Still tinged with holiness, nostalgia, or even the possibility of bad luck, they linger until they can be foisted onto Buddhist temples. As Wilson discusses, this simply passes the problem on, as ministers now have to figure out what to do with them. This chapter considers why butsudan are dropped off at temples, the varying responses of ministers to this sacred rubbish, and what the vast accumulation of discarded home altars at temples in North American and Hawai'i means for traditional Buddhist patterns of practice.

Fabio Gygi's chapter turns our attention to Buddhist rites of disposal in contemporary Japan, more specifically memorial services for dolls (*ningyō kuyō*). How do such rituals facilitate the transformation of cherished objects into waste? Gygi argues, based on six months of ethnographic fieldwork, that these rituals produce ignorance about the fate of the dolls. In order to do this, ritual frames—spatial, temporal, and material—are manipulated to create the impression that the dolls simply disappear. Gygi contends that this is necessary to mitigate the contradiction between feeling sorry for the dolls and the wish to get rid of them. The increase in temples and shrines offering this service in the Heisei era (1989–2019), and the fact that many informants who participated in these rites described them as "*shūkatsu*" (end-of-life preparation), suggest that demographic changes are one of the driving forces behind the popularity of this practice.

In Chapter 5, Amy Holmes-Tagchungdarpa examines the recycling of sacred waste in Tibet and the Himalayas. Objects become sacred through processes of consecration and through their function, location, and association with powerful places and people. When statues, texts, prayer flags, amulets, and other objects age to the point where they are no longer recognizable or functional, or are removed from their original context and rediscovered, they are not simply disposed of. After being awakened, sacred objects remain powerful and venerated as reincarnating agents capable of granting blessings. Instead of disposal, which can attract dangerous forms of ritual pollution, sacred objects are often recycled as *zung* (filling for other sacred objects), become treasures to be cared for in residential shrines or monasteries, or are renovated or refreshed. Although their outer forms might change, Holmes-Tagchungdarpa argues, these sacred objects are thereby reincarnated through recycling, and continue to hold the same efficacy as in their earlier lives.

Chapter 6, by Saskia Abrahms-Kavunenko, delves into the issue of objects that do not disintegrate. In the presocialist period, Mongolian Buddhist offerings were perishable. They were generally made from dairy products and other items that decompose, such as barley grains and prayer scarves made from silk. In the contemporary period, religious items are often mass-produced and are cheap and easy to purchase. Many are now made from materials that cannot decompose. Store-bought imperishable items, such as polyester prayer scarves and food offerings wrapped in plastic, take on a new kind of materiality that lingers problematically. Distinct from ordinary waste, when Buddhist offerings resist entropy, they can become powerful, potentially negatively altering the fortunes of those who mistreat them. Abrahms-Kavunenko utilizes the "undead" as a way of analyzing the differences between ordinary and sacred waste, while foregrounding their material properties.

Elizabeth Williams-Oerberg takes us to the northwest Indian Himalayan region of Ladakh in the seventh and final chapter of the volume, in which she examines the role that Buddhists have played in tackling the problem of waste. In the past few decades, an enormous growth in the tourism industry has put a considerable strain on this fragile, cold desert region, not least in dealing with waste management issues. Tourism has most frequently borne the blame for the waste problem in Ladakh, yet Buddhist consumption and the amount of waste produced at large Buddhist festivals has rarely come into focus. Buddhist-led organizational efforts to address "brown" environmental concerns, such as picking up trash, have become more common, yet it is their "green" initiatives, such as tree-planting and wildlife conservation, that have attracted global attention and awards. What Williams-Oerberg terms Brown Buddhism, which encompasses both Buddhist waste and Buddhist efforts to combat the problem of waste, has not drawn as much global attention as Green Buddhism in Ladakh.

Notes

1 While this volume addresses Buddhist waste in this fairly loose sense of the term, there is an argument for developing a more clearly defined category of Buddhist waste. I will return to this in a future publication.

2 I am inspired by the entry "waste" in the Merriam-Webster Dictionary (https://www.merriam-webster.com/) as well as discussions by Lynch (1990) and Reno (2018).

3 According to Henrik Sørensen (2013: 92), the patched robe signals how cloth that has been discarded should be reused, not out of respect for the material but to convey the message that monks "should not become attached to the luxury of wearing a new, fancy robe." Yet, as Sørensen comments, nowadays one can buy brand new, tailor-made robes made to look like they are produced from recycled and repaired material.

4 I thank Jane Caple for highlighting the important distinction between renunciation and generosity.
5 See Elverskog (2020) for a historical discussion of Buddhism as a "prosperity theology" and Borup (2020) on the emergence of contemporary "Prosperity Buddhism" (see also Jackson 1999) in contrast to this renunciation paradigm.
6 Popular and academic perceptions have, at times, posited Buddhism as a viable counter-narrative to global capitalism, materialism, and mass consumption, for instance Kaza (2005) and Payne (2010). See Brox and Williams-Oerberg (2017) as well as Williams-Oerberg and Brox (2020) for discussions on the misconception of Buddhism as a non-economic religion.
7 https://www.merriam-webster.com/afterlife (accessed November 22, 2020).
8 Here, I am inspired by Schiffer (2013).

References

Abrahms-Kavunenko, Saskia (2019), *Enlightenment and the Gasping City: Mongolian Buddhism at a Time of Environmental Disarray*, Ithaca: Cornell University Press. doi: 10.7591/9781501737664.

Ali, Daud (2003), "Gardens in Early Indian Court Life," *Studies in History*, 19 (2): 221–52.

Allison, Elizabeth (2014), "Waste and Worldviews: Garbage and Pollution Challenges in Bhutan," *Journal for the Study of Religion, Nature and Culture*, 8 (4): 405–28. doi: 10.1558/jsrnc.v8i4.25050.

Allison, Elizabeth (2015), "At the Boundary of Modernity: Religion, Technocracy, and Waste Management in Bhutan," in Megan Adamson Sijapati and Jessica Vantine Birkenholtz (eds), *Religion and Modernity in the Himalaya*, 163–81, New York: Routledge. doi: 10.1017/s0021911818000803.

Allison, Elizabeth (2019), "The Reincarnation of Waste: A Case Study of Spiritual Ecology Activism for Household Solid Waste Management: The Samdrup Jongkhar Initiative of Rural Bhutan," *Religions*, 10 (514): 1–19. doi: org/10.3390/rel10090514.

Anderson, Warwick (1995), "Excremental Colonialism: Public Health and the Poetics of Pollution," *Critical Inquiry*, 21 (3): 640–69. doi: org/10.1086/448767.

Borup, Jørn (2020), "Prosperous Temple Buddhism and NRM Prosperity Buddhism," in Trine Brox and Elizabeth Williams-Oerberg (eds), *Buddhism and Business: Merit, Material Wealth, and Morality in the Global Market Economy*, 59–75, Honolulu: University of Hawaiʻi Press. doi: org/10.2307/j.ctvxhrhh9.8.

Brox, Trine, and Elizabeth Williams-Oerberg (2017), "Buddhism, Business and Economics," in Michael Jerryson (ed), *The Oxford Handbook of Contemporary Buddhism*, 504–17, Oxford: Oxford University Press. doi: 10.1093/oxfordhb/9780199362387.013.42.

Brox, Trine, and Elizabeth Williams-Oerberg (eds) (2020), *Buddhism and Business: Merit, Material Wealth, and Morality in the Global Market Economy*, Honolulu: University of Hawai'i Press. doi: 10.2307/j.ctvxhrhh9.

Caple, Jane (2020), "The Lama's Shoes: Tibetan Perspectives on Monastic Wealth and Virtue," in Trine Brox and Elizabeth Williams-Oerberg (eds), *Buddhism and Business: Merit, Material Wealth, and Morality in the Global Market Economy*, 22–39. Honolulu: University of Hawai'i Press. doi: 10.1515/9780824884161-004.

Chidester, David (2014), "The Accidental, Ambivalent, and Useless Sacred," *Material Religion*, 10 (2): 239–40. doi: 10.2752/175183414x13990269049527.

Covell, Stephen G. (2012), "Money and the Temple: Law, Taxes and the Image of Buddhism," in Inken Prohl and John Nelson (eds), *Handbook of Contemporary Japanese Religions*, 159–76. Leiden: Brill. doi: 10.1163/9789004234369_008.

Darlington, Susan (2012), *The Ordination of a Tree: The Thai Buddhist Environmental Movement*, Albany: State University of New York Press.

Douglas, Mary (2002 [1966]), *Purity and Danger: An Analysis of the Concepts of Pollution and Taboo*, London: Routledge.

Elverskog, Johan (2020), *The Buddha's Footprint: An Environmental History of Asia*, Philadelphia: University of Pennsylvania Press.

Fleming, Benjamin J. and Richard D. Mann (2014), "Introduction: Material Culture and Religious Studies," in Benjamin J. Fleming and Richard D. Mann (eds), *Material Culture and Asian Religions: Text, Image, Object*, 1–17. New York and London: Routledge. doi: 10.4324/9780203753033.

Gayley, Holly (2007), "Soteriology of the Senses in Tibetan Buddhism," *Numen*, 54 (4): 459–99. doi: 10.1163/156852707x244306.

Gille, Zsuzsa (2010), "Actor Networks, Modes of Production, and Waste Regimes: Reassembling the Macro-social," *Environment and Planning A*, 42: 1049–64. doi: 10.1068/a42122.

Gould, Hannah (2019), "Caring for Sacred Waste: Caring for Butsudan (Buddhist Altars) in Contemporary Japan," *Japanese Religions*, 43 (1–2): 197–220.

Gregson, Nicky, Mike Crang, Farid Uddin Ahmed, Nasreen Akhter, and Raihana Ferdous (2010), "Following Things of Rubbish Value: End-of-Life Ships, 'Chock-chocky' Furniture and the Bangladeshi Middle Class Consumer," *Geoforum*, 41: 846–54. doi: 10.1016/j.geoforum.2010.05.007.

Gygi, Fabio (2018), "Things that Believe: Talismans, Amulets, Dolls, and How to Get Rid of Them," *Japanese Journal of Religious Studies*, 45 (2): 423–52. doi: 10.18874/jjrs.45.2.2018.423-452.

Harris, Christina (2007), "Mediators in the Transnational Marketplace: Wholesalers of Tibetan Ceremonial Scarves and the Marketing of Meaning," in Michael Gervers, Uradyn E. Bulag, and Gillian Long (eds), *Traders and Trade Routes of Central and Inner Asia: The 'Silk Road,' Then and Now*, 189–206. Toronto: Toronto Studies in Central and Inner Asia.

Hawkins, Gay (2006), *The Ethics of Waste: How We Relate to Rubbish*, Lanham: Rowman & Littlefield Publishers.

Holmes-Tagchungdarpa, Amy (2014), "Representations of Religion in The Tibet Mirror: The Newspaper as Religious Object and Patterns of Continuity and Rupture in Tibetan Material Culture," in Benjamin J. Fleming and Richard D. Mann (eds), *Material Culture and Asian Religions: Text, Image, Object*, 73–93. New York and London: Routledge. doi: 10.4324/9780203753033.

Hsiao, Hsin Yi, Hsun-Ta Hsu, Debra Boudreaux, and Alice Ting (2019), "Global Grassroots Green Movement Drive by Tzu Chi Foundation's Recycling Volunteers," in Alice M. L. Chong and Iris Chi (eds), *Social Work and Sustainability in Asia: Facing the Challenges of Global Environmental Changes*, Milton: Routledge. doi: 10.4324/9781315514970-5.

Jackson, Peter A. (1999), "Royal Spirits, Chinese Gods, and Magic Monks: Thailand's Boomtime Religions of Prosperity," *South East Asia Research*, 7 (3): 245–320. doi: 10.1177/0967828x9900700302.

Jixiancairang (2018), "Tibetan Pre-Death Ritual (gson chos): A Practice of Merit Accumulation in a Tibetan Community in Reb gong, A mdo," Phd diss., University of Oslo, Oslo.

Kaza, Stephanie (ed.) (2005), *Hooked! Buddhist Writings on Greed, Desire, and the Urge to Consume*, Boston and London: Shambala. doi: 10.1017/s0360966900003856.

Kaza, Stephanie and Kenneth Kraft (2000), *Dharma Rain: Sources of Buddhist Environmentalism*, Boston: Shambhala.

Keane, Webb (2008), "On the Materiality of Religion," *Material Religion*, 4 (2): 230–1.

Kendall, Laurel (2017), "Things Fall Apart: Material Religion and the Problem of Decay," *The Journal of Asian Studies*, 76 (4): 861–86. doi: 10.1017/s0021911817000833.

Kendall, Laurel, Vũ Thị Thanh Tâm, and Nguyễn Thị Thu Hương (2010), "Beautiful and Efficacious Statues: Magic, Commodities, Agency and the Production of Sacred Objects in Popular Religion in Vietnam," *Material Religion*, 6 (1): 60–85. doi: 10.2752/174322010x12663379393378.

Kretschmer, Angelika (2000), "Mortuary Rites for Inanimate Objects: The Case of Hari Kuyō," *Japanese Journal of Religious Studies*, 27 (3/4): 379–404. doi: 10.18874/jjrs.27.3-4.2000.380-404.

Lepawsky, Josh and Mostaem Billah (2011), "Making Chains that (Un)make Things: Waste-Value Relations and the Bangladeshi Rubbish Electronics Industry," *Geografiska Annaler. Series B, Human Geography*, 93 (2): 121–39. doi: 10.1111/j.1468-0467.2011.00365.x.

Liboiron, Max (2019), "Waste is Not 'Matter out of Place,'" *Discard Studies*, 9 September. https://discardstudies.com/2019/09/09/waste-is-not-matter-out-of-place/ (accessed September 7, 2020).

Lynch, Kevin (1990), *Wasting Away*, San Francisco: Sierra Club Books.

Martin, Emma (2015), "Fit for a King? The Significance of a Gift Exchange between the Thirteenth Dalai Lama and King George V," *Journal of the Royal Asiatic Society*, 25 (1): 71–98. doi: 10.1017/s1356186314000157.

McDaniel, Justin Thomas (2011), *The Lovelorn Ghost and the Magical Monk: Practicing Buddhism in Modern Thailand*, New York: Columbia University Press. doi: 10.4000/moussons.2423.

Meyer, Birgit (2012), "Mediation and the Genesis of Presence: Towards a Material Approach to Religion," Utrecht: Universiteit Utrecht Faculteit Geesteswetenschappen. http://www2.hum.uu.nl/onderzoek/lezingenreeks/pdf/Meyer_Birgit_oratie.pdf (accessed September 29, 2013).

Meyer, Birgit, David Morgan, Crispin Paine, and Brent Plate (2010), "The Origin and Mission of Material Religion," *Religion*, 40 (3): 207–11. doi: 10.1016/j.religion.2010.01.010.

Moerman, Max D. (2010), "The Death of the Dharma: Buddhist Sutra Burials in Early Medieval Japan," in Kristina Myrvold (ed), *The Death of Sacred Texts: Ritual Disposal and Renovation of Texts in World Religions*, 147–59. Farnham: Ashgate Publishing. doi: 10.4324/9781315615318.

Morgan, David (ed.) (2010), *Religion and Material Culture: The Matter of Belief*, London: Routledge.

Myrvold, Kristina (ed.) (2010), *The Death of Sacred Texts: Ritual Disposal and Renovation of Texts in World Religions*, Farnham: Ashgate Publishing. doi: 10.1163/15685152-1018b0006.

Ornatowski, Gregory K. (1996), "Continuity and Change in the Economic Ethics of Buddhism: Evidence from the History of Buddhism in India, China and Japan," *Journal of Buddhist Ethics*, 3: 198–240.

Osburg, John (2020), "Consuming Belief: Luxury, Authenticity, and Chinese Patronage of Tibetan Buddhism in Contemporary China," *HAU: Journal of Ethnographic Theory*, 10 (1): 69–84. doi: 10.1086/708547.

Paine, Crispin (2014), "Sacred Waste," *Material Religion*, 10 (2): 241–42.

Payne, Richard (ed) (2010), *How Much is Enough? Buddhism, Consumerism, and the Human Environment*, Somerville: Wisdom Publication.

Rambelli, Fabio (2007), *Buddhist Materiality: A Cultural History of Objects in Japanese Buddhism*, Stanford: Stanford University Press. doi: 10.1086/649531.

Rambelli, Fabio (2017), "Materiality, Labor, and Signification of Sacred Objects in Japanese Buddhism," *Journal of Religion in Japan*, 6 (1): 1–26. doi: 10.1163/22118349-00601001.

Rambelli, Fabio and Eric Reinders (2012), *Buddhism and Iconoclasm in East Asia*, New York and London: Bloomsbury.

Reno, Josh (2009), "Your Trash is Someone's Treasure: The Politics of Value at a Michigan Landfill," *Journal of Material Culture*, 14: 29–46. doi: 10.1177/1359183508100007.

Reno, Josh (2018), "What is Waste?," *Worldwide Waste: Journal of Interdisciplinary Studies*, 1 (1): 1–10.

Reno, Joshua Ozias (2014), "Toward a New Theory of Waste: From 'Matter out of Place' to Signs of Life," *Theory, Culture & Society*, 31 (6): 3–27. doi: 10.1177/0263276413500999.

Reynolds, Valrae (1992), "Ritual Textiles," in Pratapaditya Pal (ed), *Art of the Himalayas: Treasures from Tibet*, 106–8. New York: Hudson Hills Press.

Riccardi, Sarah A. (n.d.), "Sacred Waste," in Max Liboiron, Michele Acuto, and Robin Nagle (eds), *Discard Studies Compendium* [online]. https://discardstudies.com/discard-studies-compendium/#Sacredwaste (accessed August 27, 2018).

Rozenberg, Guillaume (2004), "How Giving Sanctifies: The Birthday of Thamanya Hsayadaw in Burma," *Journal of the Royal Anthropological Institute*, 10 (3): 495–515. doi: 10.1111/j.1467-9655.2004.00199.x.

Salomon, Richard (2009), "Why did the Gandhāran Buddhists Bury their Manuscripts?" in Stephen C. Berkewitz, Juliane Schober, and Claudia Brown (eds), *Buddhist Manuscript Cultures: Knowledge, Ritual, and Art*, 19–34. London: Routledge. doi: 10.1163/001972409x12645171002298.

Schiffer, Michael Brian. 2013. "Afterlives," in Paul Graves-Brown, Rodney Harrison, and Angela Piccini (eds), *The Oxford Handbook of the Archaeology of the Contemporary World*, 247–60. Oxford: Oxford University Press. doi: 10.1093/oxfordhb/9780199602001.013.004.

Schopen, Gregory (1991), "Archaeology and Protestant Presuppositions in the Study of Indian Buddhism," *History of Religions*, 31 (1): 1–23. doi: 10.1086/463253.

Schopen, Gregory (1998), "Relic," in Mark C. Taylor (ed), *Critical Terms for Religious Studies*, 256–68. Chicago: University of Chicago Press.

Shen, Hsueh-man (2019), *Authentic Replicas: Buddhist Art in Medieval China*, Honolulu: University of Hawai'i Press.

Sinha, Vineeta (2008), "'Merchandizing' Hinduism: Commodities, Markets and Possibilities for Enchantment," in Pattana Kitiarsa (ed), *Religious Commodifications in Asia: Marketing Gods*, 169–85. London: Routledge. doi: 10.4324/9780203937877.

Siniawer, Eiko Maruko (2018), *Waste: Consuming Postwar Japan*, Ithaca: Cornell University Press. doi: 10.1093/ahr/rhaa291.

Sørensen, Henrik H. (2013), "Of Eco-Buddhas and Dharma-Roots: Views from the East Asian Buddhist Tradition," in Henrik H. Sørensen and Carmen Meinert (eds), *Nature, Environment and Culture in East Asia*, 83–105. Leiden: Brill. doi: 10.1163/9789004253049_006.

Stengs, Irene (2014), "Sacred Waste," *Material Religion*, 10 (2): 235–38.

Strasser, Susan (2000), *Waste and Want: A Social History of Trash*, New York: Holt: Metropolitan.

Thompson, Michael (2017 [1979]), *Rubbish Theory: The Creation and Destruction of Value*, London: Pluto Press.

Triplett, Katja (2017), "The Making and Unmaking of Religious Objects: Sacred Waste Management in Comparative Perspective," in Saburo Shawn Morishita (ed), *Materiality in Religion and Culture*, 143–54, Wien: LIT Verlag.

Wang, Bo (2019), "Sacred Trash and Personhood: Living in Daily Waste-Management Infrastructures in the Eastern Himalayas," *Cross-Currents: East Asian History and Culture Review*, 30: 101–119. doi: org/10.1353/ach.2019.0009.

Williams-Oerberg, Elizabeth and Trine Brox (2020), "Buddhist Encounters with the Global Market Economy and Consumer Society," in Trine Brox and Elizabeth Williams-Oerberg (eds), *Buddhism and Business: Merit, Material Wealth, and Morality in the Global Market Economy*, 1–21, Honolulu: University of Hawai'i Press. doi: 10.2307/j.ctvxhrhh9.5.

Williams, Duncan Ryuken (2012), "Buddhist Environmentalism in Contemporary Japan," in Inken Prohl and John K. Nelson (eds), *Handbook of Contemporary Japanese Religions*, Leiden: Brill. doi: 10.18874/jjrs.40.2.2013.377-382.

Wirtz, Kristina (2009), "Hazardous Waste: The Semiotics of Ritual Hygiene in Cuban Popular Religion," *Journal of the Royal Anthropological Institute*, 15 (3): 476–501. doi: 10.1111/j.1467-9655.2009.01569.x.

1

Generosity's Limits

Buddhist Excess and Waste in Northeast Tibet

Jane Caple

On a rainy summer's day in 2015, Döndrup,[1] a driver in his thirties, took me to one of the many Tibetan Buddhist monasteries scattered through his natal region in northeast Tibet (Amdo/Qinghai).[2] Since my first visit there in 2009, several new stupas and temples had been built; now more were under construction. This was a monastery renowned locally for its material expansion and relative wealth via its rich sponsors. But the ongoing work there reflected a more general wave of new temple and stupa building in monasteries and villages in the area, as well as escalating levels of expenditure on Buddhist rituals and the sponsorship of monastic events. Although this was partly a result of increased interest in Tibetan Buddhism among affluent urban Chinese (Caple 2015; see also Osburg 2020), there had also been an upsurge in local religious giving paralleling an increase in disposable income among many Tibetans. Wealthier households might spend the equivalent of tens of thousands of dollars on offerings to monasteries, while some communities were pooling hundreds of thousands to collectively fund new temples. As Döndrup and I looked up at a giant buddha statue still encased in scaffolding, its head and shoulders rising above the temples, he commented: "There is enough at the monastery, better to use the money to pay school fees or something like this."

Supporting the Sangha and building and populating religious structures (with statues, art, offerings, etc., as well as with monks) have historically been among the most common forms of Buddhist generosity practice in Tibetan and other societies heavily influenced by Buddhism. The faith and virtue indexed by the spontaneous outpouring of gifts and labor central to the post-Mao revival of monastic Buddhism in northeast Tibet in the 1980s figures as central in narratives of this period as something of a temporal moral utopia (Caple 2019).

Yet, the dynamics and scale of more recent sponsorship practices and projects have been the subject of some criticism and debate, not only among secular intellectuals critical of Buddhism or Buddhist institutions,[3] or people wary of the politics of sponsorship flowing in from Chinese patrons (Caple 2015), but also among local monks and laypeople across social strata participating in these or similar projects and events.

As was implicit in Döndrup's comment, an idea that surfaced in these debates is that Buddhist generosity practices can be excessive to the point of being wasteful in two related but conceptually distinct senses. The first concerns the question of sufficiency and surplus (there was already "enough") and the second, the question of best use of wealth ("better to use the money to pay school fees"). Is there a limit to the number of temples and stupas a Buddhist monastery should have or how big or ornate they should be? Or to how much money a sponsor should offer to monks or how much food should be prepared for a ritual feast? What constitutes "enough"? When and why does a slippage occur that transforms Buddhist generosity practices into zero or negative value—into a kind of Buddhist waste?[4]

The kind of "Buddhist waste" this chapter focuses on is primarily what Joshua Reno (2018) refers to as waste in a "moral-political" sense. It relates to the use and distribution of material resources in ways that are seen as "dangerous or troubling" (ibid.) or "pointless and futile" (Scanlan 2005: 22), rather than to the problem of the inevitability of decay of religious items (Kendall 2017), their end of life and disposal (Abrahms-Kavunenko; Gygi, both this volume), or their afterlives (Holmes-Tagchungdarpa; Wilson, both this volume). It is the kind of waste that is opposed to value in the sense of economic worth and in the sense of ideals relating to what is good, right, or proper (Reno 2017: 17). As Reno points out, it is "correlational" rather than "ontological" (ibid.: 19), being a material entity (object, substance, body) or an expenditure (of energy, resources, time) that exists as waste—as zero or negative value—only in its relation to the human agent(s) who define or relate to it as such.

As the first section of this chapter discusses, despite popular contemporary representations of Buddhism as anti-materialist, Tibetan Buddhism has historically been subject to moral critique for its perceived material excesses and wastefulness. Such etic critiques have filtered into debates among Tibetan urban intellectuals about Buddhism since the early post-reform period (starting in 1978). However, I suggest that there is a difference in recent emic concerns about excessive generosity practices and their wastefulness. The latter have more to do with a moralization of consumption than of Tibetan Buddhism, even if both sets of critiques are centered on similar concerns about communal well-being. Drawing on ethnographic data collected in Geluk (*dge lugs*)[5] monasteries and rural and urban communities on the northeastern edge of the Tibetan plateau between 2008 and 2015, as well as examples from other relevant recent studies,[6] I show how this moralization of consumption provided an impetus for the upsurge in religious giving, while at the same time bringing to the fore a tension in Buddhist excess that helps to explain the slippage of generosity practices into a kind of Buddhist waste.

Tibetan Buddhism as Wasteful

From the mid-twentieth century, popular ideas about Buddhism as anti-materialist have led to its image in the West as a "green religion" naturally "aligned to environmentalism" (Williams-Oerberg, this volume) and a religion that offers, among other things, "a distinctive critique with liberating methods that may be useful in challenging the Western basis of habits of consumption" (Kaza 2010: 39). Johan Elverskog (2020: 55) points out that such representations elide the historical dynamics of the spread of Buddhism in premodern Asia, which depended on a prosperous laity and economic expansion, mandated by the association between wealth and virtue in Buddhist doctrine. Moreover, as Trine Brox points out in her introduction to this volume, material abundance is "an oft-exhibited value" in many Buddhist societies and communities. "Extravagant, material wealth" is displayed in Buddhist spaces such as temples and shrines, as well as being channeled to support communities of monastics, which in Tibet have numbered from the tens to tens of thousands at their peak.

Indeed, given its extent and influence in both society and politics, Tibetan Buddhism has historically been subject to etic moral-political critique for its perceived material excesses and wastefulness. Georges Bataille (1991 [1967]: 93–110), who took "Lamaism" to be the epitome of a peaceful society, was unusual in viewing such wastefulness in a positive light, arguing that it used up surplus energies and resources that elsewhere fueled war. The critique was more generally a negative one. Despite the more recent Shangri-la-ization of Tibet, from the mid-nineteenth century Westerners generally saw Tibetan religion as "superstitious and irrational, an incomprehensible and unconscionable waste of energy and resources" (Jacobson 2004: 58). This is not dissimilar to the Chinese Communist Party's view of Tibetan Buddhism as a "wasteful and oppressive" (Gonkar Gyatso 2003: 147) and "extremely decadent" (Gayley 2011: 462) system, which resulted in poverty and backwardness in premodern Tibet and remains an obstacle to modern progress.

Such ideological critiques had profound historical effects with the incorporation of much of the Tibetan plateau into the People's Republic of China in the early 1950s. The oft-termed "excesses" of the mass campaigns of the Maoist period, which included the so-called Democratic Reforms of the late 1950s as well as the Cultural Revolution, laid waste to Tibetan Buddhist material culture on a mass scale.[7] Religious policy shifted in the post-reform period allowing for Buddhist revitalization, but CCP discourse on "normative Buddhism" continued to represent the generosity practices of the laity as wasteful (Cabezón 2008: 368n35). Similar ideas have also filtered into debates among Tibetan intellectuals about the role of Buddhism in Tibetan culture and development, including the resources funneled into monastic Buddhism and the dynamics of religious giving (Hartley 2002; Peacock 2020; Robin 2008).

In his short story "The Disturbance in D—Camp," first published in the Tibetan literary journal *Drangchar* (*sbrang char*; "Light Rain") in 1988,[8] influential Amdo author Tsering Döndrup (2019: 17–23) provides a cynical perspective on the funding of the early post-Mao reconstruction of Buddhism. The main character is Sökyab, the overzealous leader of a pastoralist encampment, who makes a series of excessive pledges on behalf of the camp to a lama soliciting funds for the reconstruction of an assembly hall. When the lama mentions how much other camps have pledged, Sökyab offers more. On announcing to the camp members how much they each must contribute, Sökyab reminds them that the project "is for the benefit of all sentient beings, and it's for your own benefit too" and then threatens to kick out any households that do not pay. During the first round of fundraising, two families are unable to scrape together the required donation and are expelled; the head of one is so furious that he falls off his yak and dies. During the second round, only seven families contribute, and the majority are sent away. Apparently oblivious to the material conditions of the herders, the lama—the corrupt Alak Drong who features in several of Tsering Döndrup's stories—bemoans the stinginess of the people of this degenerate era ("No piety at all!"). Despite being threatened with the wrath of the Dharma protectors as well as expulsion, none of the remaining families give anything when asked for a third donation. The only tent left in the camp is Sökyab's, who goes mad.

I mention this particular story in some detail since, as I will go on to discuss, it resonates with certain aspects of more recent debates about generosity practices, the dynamics driving their escalation, and their perceived wastefulness. At the same time, it is in stark contrast to the narratives I collected among people who participated in the first flush of Geluk monastic revival in northeast Tibet in the 1980s. Those narratives emphasize the agency and faith of individuals and communities in rebuilding and repopulating their monasteries and reviving public religious practice (Caple 2019: 25–32). It was partly in relation to this time, remembered as one of faith and purity, that people understood and compared the oft-cited moral degeneracy of the present. Increasing economic-mindedness, marked not least by competitive consumption, was perceived to be paralleling a weakening of faith and communal cohesion.[9] Contemporary generosity practices were understood in relation to this sense of the times and to a moralization of consumption that seems to have provided impetus to both the upsurge in religious giving and interpretations of it (or at least its escalating dynamics) as wasteful.

Moralizing Consumption

Although spanning only four decades, the post-reform period has been one of tremendous change. Following decollectivization in the 1980s, Tibetans experienced a gradual shift away from reliance on primarily agricultural or pastoralist livelihoods, and for a minority, state employment, through integration into China's burgeoning market economy. This accelerated with the state's drive to open up its "western regions" from 2000 and again after unrest broke out across Tibetan areas in 2008. Economic marketization led to increased reliance on cash, a general increase in disposable income as well as debt, growing inequalities within and between communities, and a newly emerging economic elite. In the relatively low-lying agricultural area where I did much of my fieldwork, Tibetans sought a cash income through various means, including working on construction sites, driving trucks or informal taxis, setting up small businesses (sometimes collective, sometimes private), or by engaging in the production and trade of Buddhist art and statues. However, the most common source of household cash income was, as for rural Tibetans elsewhere, the harvesting and trade of "caterpillar fungus" (*Ophiocordyceps sinensis*), a medicinal fungus that can be found only on the Tibetan plateau and had come to command dizzying prices on the Chinese market by the early 2010s (its value has fluctuated since).[10]

During an interview in 2015 with Könchok—a senior monk at a reputed scholastic monastery—I mentioned that every year there were many visible changes in the region's villages. These had partly occurred as a result of state-led redevelopment under the Party-state's "Building a New Socialist Countryside" program, which included subsidies for villagers to construct "'comfortable' and modern housing" (Duojie Zhaxi 2019). People had also been investing their own capital or borrowing funds to build new houses or remodel existing ones, for example, by adding a second story, building a new elaborately carved household shrine, fitting a "modern" kitchen or, in one house I visited, installing a solar-powered shower. Several men I knew had also bought cars, and even urban apartments. Könchok's immediate response to my general comment about the "many changes" was unequivocal. "This is bad," he said. When I asked him to elaborate, he explained that making houses and buying cars was now what people thought about; their minds (*sems*) were changing, and they were becoming increasingly competitive. This was a recurring trope, not only in my many conversations with Könchok over the years, but also among other people who saw an increasing economic-mindedness among Tibetans as both a cause and effect of their preoccupation with consumer culture and its competitive dynamics.

As Emily Woodhouse (2012: 91) emphasizes in her discussion on house building in eastern Tibet (Kham), increasing consumption among Tibetans does not necessarily mean that they are now "more concerned with displays of wealth" than they were in the past. Rather, it reflects increased access to consumer goods via new markets and rising levels of income. But "sudden access to cash," in particular through the caterpillar fungus trade, "has certainly allowed an unprecedented and ostentatious display of wealth, and fueled greater competition" (ibid.). House building or remodeling in particular has been one of the most common ways to demonstrate wealth and modernity in my field areas and beyond (see Sulek 2012; Woodhouse 2012). Certain more "traditional" forms of conspicuous consumption have been heavily criticized by Tibetan Buddhist leaders in exile, including the 14th Dalai Lama and the 17th Karmapa, and in Tibet (e.g., Khenpo Jikmé Puntsok, Tsultrim Lodrö). Particular targets have been excessive meat consumption, which was historically related to the display of wealth and strength in Tibet (Barstow 2018), and the wearing of endangered animal pelts as trims on Tibetan coats. As Holly Gayley (2013: 262) highlights, the tension between such practices and the Mahayana ethic of compassion for all sentient beings is only part of the problem;[11] viewed through an international lens, they are also considered wasteful and morally "vulgar" habits, bad for Tibetans' global image as kind, compassionate, and naturally "green," and reinforcing the image of Tibetans in China as backward (see also Yeh 2013).

Beyond these specific critiques, more general moralizing of conspicuous consumption, whether house building or pelt wearing, has centered on its competitive dynamics and the impact on communal well-being. This is not to say that ideas about character connected to Buddhist ethics or global environmental discourse were absent from local moral discourse. Könchok's comments on the negative change in people's minds flowed into a panegyric on an American scholar he had worked with several years back. Commenting that this scholar was "the best (*gcig po*)," Könchok elaborated on his virtues, which centered on his erudition ("he is like my teacher"; "he has written many books!") and his generosity and frugality. This scholar earned a salary but was careful with it, Könchok said. When he saw sick people without money, he sent money, and for the four years he had visited Amdo, he had worn the same clothes and shoes. Könchok recalled that once, when the scholar had a hole in his sock, "he had a needle and thread in his bag and sewed it up. Me, I would throw the socks away and buy new ones!" When the scholar ate, Könchok recalled, he ate only a little, and when he drank, he drank only a small amount: "He cares about the world and does not waste anything and makes sure the tap is closed because so much water is wasted in the world. There are no people like this in the world!" In this case, global environmental discourse filtered into his assessment of character and moral rectitude, becoming entangled with the virtues of simplicity, moderation, and generosity that he had espoused in earlier interviews, largely in relation to fellow monastics.

Although beyond the scope of this chapter to examine in detail, it is also important to note that responses to contemporary consumption practices and conceptions of waste are also entangled with the "lingering sensual effects" of past experiences (Povrzanović Frykman 2016). The most powerful example came from Penden, a teacher, as he recalled how his parents often talked about the suffering and hunger they had experienced during the period from 1958 to 1976. "Food," he said, "was the most important thing for them of course." The rapid implementation of collectivization in northeast Tibet in 1958 meant that China's Great Leap Forward famine hit the region severely (Wemheuer 2014). Since there was little food available, people resorted to eating what they could find, including grass, leather, and, in the words of an elder woman, "all sorts of animals we'd never normally consider as food" (Nyangchakja 2015: 262; see also Naktsang Nulo 2014: 234–64). One time, Penden's mother told him, the army had killed someone and then thrown the body into the river. People were so hungry that they ran after the human corpse, grabbed it and started to cut pieces off with their knives. His grandmother and some fellow villagers got the head and used it to make a big dinner. "[They had] no desire to eat these things, but their hunger .... So [I was] told don't waste food." Although his younger brother had pleaded with their mother to stop talking about this suffering, Penden said that for him it was "interesting"; moreover, "we have to remember." When his mother saw a tiny piece of food on the floor, he said, she would pick it up and touch it to her head (a way of interacting with the sacred or efficacious among Tibetans), saying "this is treasure, it is important for people, don't waste [it], don't put food on the floor."

However, the generally shared concern emphasized by Könchok, Penden, and others who questioned the value of prestige-oriented consumption (in which many themselves engaged) related to its economic and social implications for communal well-being. Conspicuous consumption such as house building not only highlighted but also increased disparities (see also Duojie Zhaxi 2019), exerting pressure on people to spend beyond their means, which could cause economic hardship, result in indebtedness, and encourage gambling addiction. Competitiveness was also seen as damaging to cohesion within and between communities, as well as causing conflict over contested rights to resources or suspicions of corruption. Woodhouse (2012: 91) makes a similar observation in her discussion on house building in eastern Tibet, which, she says, "attracted no verbal reflection on environmental consequences . . . concerns were mainly focused on social problems created by competition, and housing taking priority over more vital necessities such as food and clothing."

Similar dynamics are also reflected in Emily Yeh's (2013) discussion on the complex "set of interpretations, debates, and motivations" that led some Tibetans to participate in the mass burning of animal pelts across Tibetan areas in 2006 following a speech by the Dalai Lama. While loyalty to the Dalai Lama was the primary motivation, Yeh (ibid. 332–3) found that for many participants the burnings also "encapsulated a critique of deepening inequality" amid concerns about the competitive pressures of pelt consumption. These pressures had led to jealousy and rivalry, as well as indebtedness among those who spent all their money and borrowed more to buy pelts and jewelry to wear at weddings and festivals. Moreover, the money that was being spent on pelts could otherwise be used on, for example, agricultural inputs, children's education, or health care. Some people had felt that destroying the pelts was itself a waste. Why not sell them or put them in a museum? But by burning them and thus obliterating their value in every sense (cash, use, symbolic), participants were attempting "to articulate a vision of a moral economy" that was, in effect, a refusal of the conversion to *homo economicus* implied by state-led marketization (ibid.: 338).

The upsurge in religious giving in northeast Tibet occurred in the broader context of these socioeconomic changes and moralization of consumption.

The wastefulness and the economic-mindedness driving the latter was often associated with a weakening of faith. From one perspective then, generosity practices, like the spectacular burning of animal pelts, could be a way for people to articulate a moral economy and moral community grounded in a regime of value alternative to that of state developmentalism and capitalism. As John Scanlan (2005: 22) points out: "Whilst waste clearly stands for a remainder; a potential exhausted through use, 'to waste' is equally to squander in the distinct sense of not making the *best* use of something (time, resources, opportunities and so on)." Taken in this sense, waste "symbolizes an idea of improper use, and therefore operates within a more or less moral economy of the right, the good, the proper, their opposites and all values in between" (ibid.). It is a "defect of effort in the face of the presence (or likely appearance) of something else that would bring one back into equilibrium with the world and so avoid a falling away into the pointless and futile." As a way to balance aspirations for prosperity and modernity with Tibetan and Buddhist values, spending surplus income on sponsoring monastic events or building temples could be that "something else."

Articulating a Moral Economy

In the mid-2000s, a pastoralist community funded the construction of a large prayer wheel, housed in its own wooden hall, with money they had received in the settlement of a long-running, violent land dispute with another community. They had also used some of the collective capital accumulated from leasing out communal land for the caterpillar fungus harvest (the rest was ploughed into a collective business venture). As told to me by a community elder a decade later, they had wanted to do something special with the money to give thanks to the Buddha for the wealth they had received, to honor the ancestors upon whose land they had profited, and to benefit the many people from their community who had died during the Maoist period when religious practice was banned. Prayer wheels, as receptacles of sacred text, are believed to generate fortune, happiness, and merit when they are turned (see Brox forthcoming). One of the community-appointed organizers of the project said that, after discussion, they had decided to build the wheel on the outer circumambulation circuit of a big regional monastery rather than a local monastery, since more people would interact with it, generating more merit. A young man in his late twenties recalled the celebration that was held when the wheel was completed. They had invited a lama and the village had come together, "singing songs and feeling successful."

They had not spent money for nothing, he said; they had "spent money for something for this life and the next life."

Charlene Makley (2018: 153–95), writes about the construction of a new Buddhist temple in northeast Tibet in 2005–6 as a form of "Buddhist counter-development." Her case is that of a temple built in a precarious community struggling to secure its continuity and fortune in the context of both state-led development and competing territorial claims from a neighboring, more affluent and (locally) powerful village. From what I know of the two communities and their projects, it is doubtful that the construction of the prayer wheel could be read as Buddhist counter-development in quite the same way. Both projects had their own specific local logics and meanings. But what these and other contemporary Buddhist generosity practices have in common is their engagement in a moral economy of the good and the meaningful that, even if implicitly, responds to prevailing Party-state conceptions of modernity and religious waste, capitalist ideals of productivity and value, and emic perceptions of societal moral decline.

As told to me, the project to build a giant prayer wheel was an exemplary use of a community's collective wealth. As a way of investing in communal fortune, it was a project of both moral and economic value. These are interdependent from a Buddhist perspective, as expressed succinctly in an early nineteenth-century teaching on cause and effect given by the great Tibetan yogin, Shabkar Tsokdruk Rangdrol (1781–1851): "poverty comes from avarice . . . abundance comes from generosity" (Shabkar 2001: 294–6).[12] It was also a project that would bring benefit to both self and others. As other scholars have observed, this is a line in the sand for a moral economy among contemporary Tibetans engaging in business (Robin 2017; Saxer 2013; Trine Brox pers. comm.). It is a way to resolve the tension between the kind of economic-mindedness required to make profits and Tibetan and Buddhist values, and by extension a way to resist assimilation (see also Gayley 2013: 258).

Finally, the project was part of a momentum toward an upsurge and escalation in religious giving, which ran in parallel to rising income levels and was partly based on the circulation of ideas about, and examples of, *how* best to use excess wealth as a moral Tibetan individual or community. When discussing what to do with their capital, I was told, the community who made the prayer wheel had taken inspiration from a giant prayer wheel at a highly reputed monastery elsewhere in northeast Tibet. They had not had the experience to build a wheel quite as large as that one. According to one community member, theirs was also "not beautiful" due to some problems with its construction. But they hoped that by building their prayer wheel in such a prominent location they would inspire others to do the same. Theirs did subsequently become the first of several ever-larger prayer wheels housed in increasingly grand halls built on that same circumambulation path. This momentum seems to have accelerated in the wake of state repression of Tibetan protests in 2008, as a response to the deaths of fellow Tibetans, fears about a return to the past "excesses" of the Maoist period, and an increased sense of urgency in bolstering a distinct, often faith-based Tibetan identity. Although it was mostly inferred—it is difficult and dangerous for people to talk openly about such issues—a few people I spoke with explicitly stated that these dynamics had, at least partly, spurred their own or others' religious giving.

During an interview in the county town in 2014, Lobsang, a retired official, told me that families in a nearby, relatively wealthy village were "begging the [local] monastery" for the chance to "cook" (*bskol*; i.e., sponsor) the annual Prayer Festival, Mönlam, a one-day event that, he estimated, would cost a family somewhere between 150,000 and 200,000 yuan (ca. US$23,000–31,000).[13] Positioning this in direct opposition to other (secular) forms of consumption he said: "Someone with faith would first consider cooking for the monastery, given the money. But faithless people would consider building a house or buying cars." In practice, people would attempt to do both. But the idea that prospective sponsors were vying to spend tens or even hundreds of thousands of yuan on such events was not mere hyperbole on Lobsang's part; between the time I left the field in autumn 2009 and returned in summer 2012, one regional monastic center with several hundred monks had started compiling waiting lists for sponsorship of two of its calendrical events. Senior monks at some other monasteries also reported that more people were coming forward to make pledges, "cook" for the monks, or contribute to monastery funds; as already noted, there was also a proliferation of religious construction. Moreover, the amounts of sponsorship were increasing as the "standard" in, for example, cash gifts to monks and the scale of religious construction projects rose.

There is an inherent pull toward escalation in Buddhist generosity practices, based on the idea that the more generous the gift, the more merit one will accrue. On the one hand, generosity cannot be "measured" since it pertains to the state of mind and motivation of the donor, which is central to its karmic effect. On the other hand, the association of generosity that is oriented upward (e.g., feeding monks, building temples) with the practice of faith and reverence (Caple 2020: 23 7) gives impetus toward material abundance and excess. Doing faith and reverence involves taking every care and effort, including, for example over the quality of offerings, albeit ostensibly within one's means. When building a temple, one would aspire to source the finest materials, and employ the most skilled carpenters, artists, and craftspeople of various specialisms to lay the gold roofs, carve intricate beams and pillars, paint murals, embroider or paint *tangkha*, craft the statues, and so on. Moreover, gifts from the faithful tend to be enumerated, whether in the (auto)biographies of Tibetan Buddhist masters or contemporary donor lists. While this might be partly a question of transparency on the part of monastic authorities (Caple 2020: 34–5; Wood 2013), it also serves to publicly document generosity and faith in a quantitative form. The amount people donated was consistently mentioned when people talked about religious giving and figured in their understandings of the merit that would be accumulated, although generosity was also evaluated in relation to a donor's wealth and social position (Caple 2017: 153; Jixiancairang 2018: 249).

Yet, it is in this tendency to excess and escalation that religious giving, as a grassroots moral-economic practice in northeast Tibet, has been wrought with tension and contradiction. This can be illustrated with reference to another collectively funded project, which involved the rebuilding of a monastery's protector deity temple by its main patron village and its monks in 2014–15.[14] There was some disagreement about whether the old temple should be replaced, but the main focus of debate seems to have been about how the project should be funded. In the end, it was decided that households would not be required to pay a minimum fixed amount (the system of funding critiqued in "The Disturbance in D—Camp"). Instead, both villagers and monks should "donate according to their will" and "based on their faith and economic capacity" (Caple 2017: 149–51), partly in recognition of the growing wealth disparities. Their pledges were made in public, at a meeting of villagers and monks in front of the monastery's assembly hall.

As it was described to me, the "voluntary" rather than obligatory mode of donation was important to the project as a moral and thus meritorious and meaningful communal endeavor, as was the enormous amount of money pledged by monks and villagers—over 5 million yuan in total (ca. US$750,000). But some of my interlocutors, both within and without the community, were ambivalent if not critical about this and similar projects. They saw in them the same competitive dynamics, pressures, consequences, and wastefulness as in secular forms of consumption (house building, pelt wearing, buying cars). Thus, Könchok's response to this project and other local generosity practices was the same as his response to the "many changes" in villages; it was "not good (*mi hra gi*)." If one person was to donate 1,000 yuan, the next would give 2,000. If one village was to build a temple, the neighboring village would build a bigger one.

This was "very difficult for the local people." People might think it is "good and virtuous," he said on one occasion, "but mostly it is competition." It is here that we find the slippage that transforms contemporary generosity practices into a kind of Buddhist waste.

Conspicuous Generosity

The idea that escalations in sponsorship and temple building were, like house building and other forms of conspicuous consumption, primarily competitive and prestige-oriented was a common thread in critiques of or ambivalence about contemporary Buddhist giving. Moreover, they generated the same concrete concerns: the pressures being placed on community members, particularly those who were relatively poor, to give and give generously and beyond their means; the implications of one-upmanship for social harmony and communal cohesion; and the other uses to which the resources might have been put. Thus, the same set of complex "interpretations, debates, and motivations" (Yeh 2013) that were at least partly driving the upsurge in religious giving as a response to economic marketization and political precarity were also feeding into the reception and interpretation of generosity practices and perceptions of their wastefulness.

This is encapsulated in Jixiancairang's (2018: 249–59) analysis of the escalating costs of pre-death rituals (*gson chos*) in his natal village in northeast Tibet. These rituals, which are held by children for their parents "to accumulate merit as a preparation for a peaceful death and a desirable rebirth" (ibid.: 265), consist primarily of recitation of texts by religious specialists and communal feasts. The latter are "considered as food donations (*sbyin pa*) by the villagers" (268) and hence a form of generosity practice. Although there had been an increase in the cash gifts given to the religious specialists, it was mostly the increasing extravagance of the feasts—which account for over 80 percent of the expenditure (235)—that had driven up the costs of these three-day events "from approximately 30,000 CNY in 2010 to 65,000 CNY in 2016" (236). Those families performing the rituals explained that "the more one spends, the more merits one accumulates" (249), and some villagers approved of the increasing expenditure, seeing it as "evidence that the family has performed a very good pre-death ritual" (250). But most saw it as competitive and prestige-oriented and were critical of the waste involved, even if, in practice, they might do the same.

These feasts were seen as wasteful in two senses. First, there was the large quantity of food that ended up being thrown away because there was too much to be consumed (254–5); this food literally became garbage. Second, the increasing costs of the ritual meant that (like animal pelts or house building) it was "a big financial challenge for the majority and for the poor in particular" (252). In 2016, the average non-farm income of the more than 90 percent of villagers who were neither public sector employees nor ran their own businesses was 18,000 yuan. There was therefore a perceived wastefulness in this particular use of the villagers' limited financial resources, which many of Jixiancairang's interviewees felt "could more constructively be used for purposes such as education, health care, and basic nutrition" (254). As one of his informants (aged 49), put it: "On one hand, people spend much money on food at the ritual, on the other hand, much of this food is wasted. It is utterly meaningless" (254–5). Yet, despite these critiques and the introduction by collective assent of rules to curb expenditure and consumption, in practice most families flouted the rules, and costs continued to rise (256–8). Jixiancairang attributes this to concerns about prestige (257), not only among the rich, but also among the poor, for whom "ostentatious ritual consumption protects against shame, social exclusion, and the social stigma of poverty" (253).

Even putting to one side the question of whether the escalation in giving was motivated by faith or competitiveness (or both), not everyone agreed that sponsoring increasingly spectacular monastic events, rituals, or temples was necessarily the best use of wealth, even among those with money to spend. Some of my interlocutors were frustrated at what they considered to be the misguided priorities of their fellow Tibetans. Among monastics, the most common critique was that resources would be better spent on supporting monastic education (Caple 2019: 81; see also Dreyfus 2003: 255–6), while lay critics tended to advocate for generosity that would aid the poor, fund education and health care, and build capacity among Tibetans to survive, perhaps even thrive in a socioeconomic environment in which they were marginalized. Such views reflect reformist ideas about monastic Buddhism and the modernist emphasis on social engagement espoused by the 14th Dalai Lama, among other Buddhist leaders.

But even among these critics, perceptions of waste were often related to the question of scale and the tendency toward escalation rather than to absolute value. "Ask him," one of my research assistants nudged me several times during an interview with a senior monk who had led several temple building projects, "ask him why they are building *so much* [emphasis mine]." Although the moralization of consumption was being extended to Buddhist generosity practices, that did not mean that these practices were seen as inherently wasteful. For example, Penden commented that a new temple that had been constructed in his natal village was "very big." The temple serves as the practice space for the village's non-monastic tantrists or *ngakpa* (*sngags pa*). They had needed a new one, Penden told me, but a small one would have sufficed since there were fewer *ngakpa* these days. Despite being one of the "modernists" who expressed frustration at others' priorities (he tended to advocate for spending on education), Penden did not see the project as wasteful per se. Rather, at some undefinable point it had spilled over into this category.

The temple had been sponsored by the villagers. According to Penden this meant that "things were very hard for a few years." As discussed elsewhere, the hardship that people might experience financing such projects can be perceived as an individual or collective virtue; carrying such an economic "burden" can be experienced as positive (Caple 2017: 153). But, like the food wasted at pre-death rituals, for Penden there was a futility or meaninglessness to this expenditure that related to its scale. Echoing the common trope in evaluations of escalating giving, he believed that the size of the project was driven by competitiveness; when he had asked villagers why they had made such a large temple, he claimed, their response was that a neighboring village had made a new temple. But his critique did not stop there. He also made the satirical observation that "before, there were many *ngakpa* but no money to build a big temple, now they have money to build a big temple but there are no *ngakpa*!" In a similar vein, when I was telling Könchok about my visit to a historically significant monastery in the north of Qinghai and mentioned the large assembly hall under construction, he commented that there were now only thirteen monks. "A very big building and waste of money for no reason," he remarked.

These and similar comments point to an additional layer of perceived meaningless, hence, waste in such projects, which extends beyond their limited use value, and the other purposes to which at least some of the resources ploughed into them might have been put. Elizabeth Williams-Oerberg (this volume) discusses ambivalence about the latter kind of Buddhist waste in Ladakh, giving the example of a palace constructed for a six-day Buddhist festival, which was afterward left empty, wasting away. In northeastern Tibet, this kind of excess-as-waste loops back into the sense of the times as morally troubled and precarious. To illustrate this with a final example, I will return to the visit to the monastery with the giant buddha statue with which I opened this chapter.

In a refrain that will by now be familiar, as we were walking around the monastery that day in summer 2015, Döndrup remarked that all of the building work at the monastery was probably to compete with a nearby monastery, which had also been expanding; perceptions of competitiveness were not limited to the practices of the laity. But he had also reacted to the apparent lack of life in this Buddhist space. On pulling up to the monastery, I had pointed to a new prayer wheel hall under construction, which sat on a corner of the monastery's empty circumambulation circuit, which was also being renovated. He exclaimed: "Look—all this. [*pause*]. But no-one comes here to do *kora* [circumambulate]. Our [village] temple is very small, but there are always people doing *kora*." Later, Döndrup acknowledged that this was his first visit to that monastery. Had we returned on another day, when the work was complete, perhaps we would have seen villagers and monks circumambulating, reciting *maṇi*, and turning their new giant prayer wheel. He also admitted to being prejudiced, stating: "Anyway, I don't like [this monastery's patron village], so don't listen to what I say!"

But, like Penden and Könchok's comments, Döndrup's response to the "excess" we encountered that day also spoke to broader concerns that Buddhist materiality was coming to stand in for, rather than act as a support for, Buddhist practice (Caple 2019: 81). There was nothing wasteful about a prayer wheel that was turned, generating blessings and merit, but what value did it have if people no longer had the faith or time to interact with it? There was great merit and hope in the post-reform resurgence of the "Buddhist landscape" (Elverskog 2020) through reconstruction of richly ornamented temples and assembly halls. But what kind of future would there be if there were no virtuous Buddhist monks or tantrists to assemble in them? Rather than being the "something else" that could provide equilibrium, balancing aspirations for prosperity and a modern lifestyle with Tibetan and Buddhist values, Buddhist generosity practices were themselves at risk of "falling away into the pointless and futile" (Scanlan 2005: 22).

Conclusion

The modern minimalist authors and communities in Japan and Australia that Hannah Gould (this volume) discusses are critical of perceived material excess in modern consumer society in terms of its effects on the self. The problem with "excess objects," she argues, is not that they are lying unused, excess to requirements, but rather that "they are seen to expend people's mental energies and thus, ultimately, to rob people of their potential happiness." This is what makes them waste, in the sense of something discarded or rejected, and wasteful, in the sense of an unproductive or meaningless expenditure of resources. In contrast, the conceptions of waste and wastefulness that I have discussed in this chapter tend to center on the social rather than psychological implications of a competitive impulse toward material excess. The minds and motivations of individuals, and thus the karmic effects of their practices, remain ultimately unknowable to others, albeit frequently guessed at. But the social dynamics and consequences of consumption are legible to its critics. This is how generosity practices, just like house building or pelt wearing, can become excessive to the point of being wasteful, expending resources that could have been used elsewhere in ways that are seen to be harmful or meaningless.

Yet, these same practices have also been a way for Tibetans to articulate an regime of value alternative to CCP discourse on religion and to state capitalism. Despite debates about their prestige-oriented motivations, the individuals and communities engaging in conspicuous generosity through their sponsorship of monastic events or building of temples were not just showing off their prosperity. They were also publicly expressing certain values and beliefs, reasserting their faith and virtue in the wake of both economic change and political uncertainty, and (oftentimes at least) using their resources in ways they believed would bring benefits to both themselves and others. Given the decreasing political space for social activism, including welfare initiatives and environmental protection, it must be noted that there are, in practice, limited options for Tibetans who aspire to do some good with excess cash.[15] When talking about what they perceived to be competitive giving, even relatively vociferous moral critics like Könchok and Penden tended to acknowledge that their fellow Tibetans believed that what they were doing was good.

There is therefore an important difference between these critiques of contemporary religious giving and the sardonic take on monastic reconstruction penned by Tsering Döndrup in the 1980s, even if their readings of the impulse to excess and its negative consequences might be similar. In "The Disturbance in D—Camp," herders are coerced into giving beyond their means by an overzealous leader who is keen to please and impress a corrupt lama. That leader expels families who lack the means to contribute. The story can be read as primarily a critique of power and corrupt establishment. In a hypothetical remake set in 2015 and narrated by, for example, Könchok or Penden, we would likely see the herders themselves vying to out-pledge each other as well as other encampments. Any impoverishment, community disintegration, or ostracization of members would come from within, rather than being imposed top-down. It would primarily be a critique of contemporary consumer society and corrupted minds (perhaps also, by implication, state-led development), with moral agency ascribed as much to the public as to the religious and political establishments. In some respects, this twenty-first-century remake poses an even greater threat of reducing Buddhism-in-practice to a state of negative or zero value. Given a Buddhist twist, either story might take a further step to convey the message that the impulse toward excess, whether on the part of the monastic establishment or the laity, is a corruption or misunderstanding of Buddhist doctrine. It does not matter how much one gives; motivation is what counts. Yet, it is hard to argue against the idea that an impetus toward conspicuous generosity is embedded in Buddhist teachings and is what historically fueled Buddhist expansion (Elverskog 2020). The slippage of Buddhist generosity practices into a kind of Buddhist waste thus reflects a tension within Buddhism itself. But quite *how* this tension plays out—and its consequences and stakes—is historically dependent.

Notes

1 All personal names of my interlocutors have been changed.

2 This project has received funding from the European Union's Horizon 2020 research and innovation program under the Marie Sklodowska-Curie grant agreement No. 747673. I gratefully acknowledge the financial support of the Leverhulme Trust for fieldwork conducted between 2012 and 2015; and the UK's Economic and Social Research Council (ESRC) and Arts and Humanities Research Council (AHRC), and the Higher Education Funding Council for England (HEFCE) for fieldwork conducted between 2008 and 2009 under a White Rose East Asia Centre (WREAC) Doctoral Scholarship. I owe an enormous debt of gratitude to the monks and lay people who shared their knowledge, stories, and opinions with me, but who must remain anonymous.

3 By "secular intellectuals," I am referring to those Tibetan intellectuals "who see religion as an inherently regressive and repressive force and seek its marginalization from the public domain" (Gayley and Willock 2016: 16), as well as less radical figures who have not rejected Buddhism but have been highly critical of corruption within institutionalized Buddhism and the socioeconomic impacts of religious financing. For a discussion of the "secular" as a concept in Tibetan cultural worlds, see Gayley and Willock 2016; on Tibetan intellectual critiques of Buddhism, see Hartley 2002; Peacock 2020; Robin 2008.

4 Ideas about excess and waste also extend to the monkhood. On the idea that there are "too many monks," see Caple 2019: 149–153. I leave this out of the present discussion, which focuses on generosity practices.

5 Tibetan terms that are not translated are transcribed according to the "THL Simplified Phonetic Transcription of Standard Tibetan" (Germano and Tournadre 2003). Although not always reflecting the phonetics of oral Amdo Tibetan, it is the only relatively standard transcription system for Tibetan. I have privileged its legibility for a wider readership over the desirability of being faithful to local sounds. At the first occurrence of a term, I add the transliteration in brackets, following the so-called "Wylie" system. Where readers of Tibetan might benefit from knowing the original Tibetan of key terms that are translated, I have added the transliteration of the original term in brackets, following the so-called "Wylie" system.

6 Much (although not all) of my research was conducted in Repgong or neighboring areas, which today fall under the administration of Qinghai province and are situated at its eastern edge, abutting Gansu province. The ethnographic studies that I draw on for other specific examples (Jixiancairang 2018; Makley 2018) are also based on fieldwork in Repgong.

7 For descriptions of the desecration, smashing, burning, and looting of objects, texts, and structures, see Arjia Rinpoche 2010 and Naktsang Nulo 2014. For images, see Tsering Woeser 2006.

8 My thanks to Christopher Peacock for supplying this detail (pers. comm. February 7, 2021).

9 See Abrahms-Kavunenko (this volume) on a similar dynamic in Mongolia, where the early postsocialist period (starting in 1990) is discussed "as a kind of golden period" pitted against "lax morality and financially driven intentions in the present."

10 In some villages, land reclamation for urban expansion meant that households no longer had any land and were entirely reliant on other income sources, but in most cases land was still being farmed on either a household or collective basis.

11 This is a tension with a long history. Elverskog (2020: 59) claims that nowhere in the Buddhist teachings is "wealth and status one-upmanship" among the laity critiqued and that, historically, "conspicuous consumption defined the moral rectitude of the [lay] Buddhist elite." However, Geoffrey Barstow's (2018) study of Tibetan religious discourse on meat consumption from the tenth to mid-twentieth centuries shows that there was historically at least some tension and debate concerning *certain* culturally and socially valorized ways of publicly displaying wealth and strength in Tibet (see also Shabkar 2001: 192-3, 505, 507).

12 When Shabkar puts this teaching into verse it is clear that the abundance he is referring to is not a mental or spiritual "fullness" (Gould, this volume). It is material: "Be generous: you will be wealthy / Make many offerings: You will have horses and chariots" (Shabkar 2001: 296). Local ideas about fortune are, of course,

more complex and relate to various forces and relations between human and nonhuman beings (see e.g., Makley 2018; Coma-Santasusana 2020).

13 For a more detailed account of expenditures at a similar event, see Caple 2020: 23–6.

14 This project is discussed in greater detail in Caple 2017.

15 My thanks to @tenzin_time (*Twitter* comment, November 2019) for prompting me to reflect on this point. It is one that I will explore further in the future.

References

Arjia Rinpoche (2010), *Surviving the Dragon: A Tibetan Lama's Account of 40 Years Under Chinese Rule*, New York: Rodale.

Barstow, Geoffrey (2018), *Food of Sinful Demons: Meat, Vegetarianism, and the Limits of Buddhism in Tibet*, New York: Columbia University Press.

Bataille, Georges (1991 [1967]), *The Accursed Share: Volume 1*, New York: Zone Books.

Brox, Trine (Forthcoming), "What is the Value of a Tibetan Prayer Wheel?" *Social Compass.*

Cabezón, José (2008), "State Control of Tibetan Buddhist Monasticism in the People's Republic of China," in Mayfair Mei-hui Yang (ed), *Chinese Religiosities: Afflictions of Modernity and State Formation*, 261–91, Berkeley and Los Angeles: University of California Press.

Caple, Jane (2015), "Faith, Generosity, Knowledge and the Buddhist Gift: Moral Discourses on Chinese Patronage of Tibetan Buddhist Monasteries," *Religion Compass* 9 (11): 462–82.

Caple, Jane (2017), "The Ethics of Collective Sponsorship: Virtuous Action and Obligation in Contemporary Tibet," *Religion and Society* 8: 145–57.

Caple, Jane (2019), *Morality and Monastic Revival in Post-Mao Tibet*, Honolulu: University of Hawai'i Press.

Caple, Jane (2020), "The Lama's Shoes: Tibetan Perspectives on Monastic Wealth and Virtue," in Trine Brox and Elizabeth Oerberg-Williams (eds), *Buddhism and Business: Merit, Material Wealth, and Morality in the Global Market Economy*, 22–39, Honolulu: University of Hawai'i Press.

Coma-Santasusana, Maria (2020), "Releasing Lives on the Grasslands of Amdo: Entanglements of Human and Animal Vitality," *Revue d'Etudes Tibétaines*, 55 (Juillet): 54–78.

Dreyfus, George (2003), *The Sound of Two Hands Clapping: The Education of a Tibetan Buddhist Monk*, Berkeley: University of California Press.

Duojie Zhaxi (2019), "Housing Subsidy projects in Amdo: Modernity, Governmentality, and Income Disparity in Tibetan Areas of China," *Critical Asian Studies*, 51 (1): 31–50. doi: 10.1080/14672715.2018.1543548.

Elverskog, Johan (2020), *The Buddha's Footprint: An Environmental History of Asia*, Philadelphia: University of Pennsylvania Press.

Gayley, Holly (2011), "The Ethics of Cultural Survival," in Gray Tuttle (ed), *Mapping the Modern in Tibet*, 435–502, Andiast, Switzerland: IITBS.

Gayley, Holly (2013), "Reimagining Buddhist Ethics on the Tibetan Plateau," *Journal of Buddhist Ethics* 20: 247–80.

Gayley, Holly, and Nicole Willock (2016), "Introduction: Theorizing the Secular in Tibetan Cultural Worlds," *Himalaya* 36 (1), Article 8. http://digitalcommons.macalester.edu/himalaya/vol36/iss1/

Germano, David, and Nicolas Tournadre (2003), "THL Simplified Phonetic Transcription of Standard Tibetan," *The Tibetan & Himalayan Library*. https://www.thlib.org/reference/transliteration/#!essay=/thl/phonetics/

Gonkar Gyatso (2003), "No Man's Land: Real and Imaginary Tibet: The Experience of an Exiled Tibetan Artist," *The Tibet Journal*, 28 (1/2): 147–160. http://www.jstor.com/stable/43305422

Hartley, Lauren R. (2002), "'Inventing Modernity' in Amdo: Views on the Role of Traditional Tibetan Culture in a Developing Society," in Toni Huber (ed), *Amdo Tibetans in Transition: Society and Culture in the Post-Mao Era*, 1–26, Leiden: Brill.

Jacobson, Calla (2004), "Spirituality, Harmony, and Peace: Situating Contemporary Images of Tibet," *Himalaya*, 24 (1), Article 16. http://digitalcommons.macalester.edu/himalaya/vol24/iss1/16

Jiaxiancairang (2018), "Tibetan Pre-Death Ritual (gson chos): A Practice of Merit Accumulation in a Tibetan Community in Reb gong, Amdo," PhD diss., University of Oslo.

Kaza, Stephania (2010), "How Much is Enough? Buddhist Perspectives on Consumerism," in Richard K. Payne (ed), *How Much is Enough? Buddhism, Consumerism, and the Human Environment*, 39–62, Somerville, MA: Wisdom Publications.

Kendall, Laurel (2017), "Things Fall Apart: Material Religion and the Problem of Decay," *The Journal of Asian Studies*, 76 (4): 861–86. doi:10.1017/S0021911817000833.

Makley, Charlene (2018), *The Battle for Fortune: State-Led Development, Personhood, and Power Among Tibetans in China*, Ithaca and London: Cornell University Press.

Naktsang Nulo (2014), *My Tibetan Childhood: When Ice Shattered Stone*, trans. Angus Cargill and Sonam Lhamo, Durham: Duke University Press.

Nyangchakja (2015), "Witness to Change: A Tibetan Woman Recalls Her Life," *Asian Highlands Perspectives*, 37: 250–278.

Osburg, John (2020), "Consuming Belief: Luxury, Authenticity, and Chinese Patronage of Tibetan Buddhism in Contemporary China," *HAU: Journal of Ethnographic Theory*, 10 (1): 69–84. doi:10.1086/708547.

Peacock, Christopher (2020), "Intersecting Nations, Diverging Discourses: The Fraught Encounter of Chinese and Tibetan Literatures in the Modern Era," PhD diss., Columbia University.

Povrzanović Frykman, Maja (2016), "Sensitive Objects of Humanitarian Aid: Corporeal Memories and Affective Continuities," in Jonas Frykman and Maja Povrzanović

Frykman (eds), *Sensitive Objects: Affect and Material Culture*, Lund: Nordic Academic.

Reno, Joshua (2017), "Wastes and Values," in Daniel Sosna and Lenka Brunclíková (eds), *Archaeologies of Waste: Encounters with the Unwanted*, 17–22, Oxford: Oxbow Books.

Reno, Joshua (2018), "What is Waste?" *Worldwide Waste: Journal of Interdisciplinary Studies* 1 (1): 1–10. doi:10.5334/wwwj.9.

Robin, Françoise (2008), "'Oracles and Demons' in Tibetan Literature Today: Representations of Religion in Tibetan-Medium Fiction," in Lauren R. Hartley and Patricia Schiaffini-Vedani (eds), *Modern Tibetan Literature and Social Change*, 148–172, Durham, NC: Duke University Press.

Robin, Françoise (2017), "Gangshun and the Rise of Capitalism with Tibetan Characteristics," *High Peaks Pure Earth*. https://highpeakspureearth.com/2017/poem-this-is-how-we-quietly-work-by-gangshun-with-accompanying-essay-by-francoise-robin/ (accessed May 6, 2020).

Saxer, Martin (2013), *Manufacturing Tibetan Medicine: The Creation of an Industry and the Moral Economy of Tibetanness*, Oxford: Berghahn.

Scanlan, John (2005), *On Garbage*, London: Reaktion Books.

Shabkar Tsokdruk Rangdrol (2001), *The Life of Shabkar: The Autobiography of a Tibetan Yogin*, trans. Matthieu Ricard and Padmakara Translation Group, Ithaca: Snow Lion Publications.

Sulek, Emilia R. (2012), "Everybody Likes Houses. Even Birds Are Coming!" in Hermann Kreutzmann (ed), *Pastoral Practices in High Asia*, 235–55, London: Springer. doi: 10.1007/978-94-007-3846-1_13.

Tsering Woeser (2006), *Forbidden Memory: Tibet during the Cultural Revolution*, trans. Susan T. Chen, Lincoln, NE: University of Nebraska Press, Potomac Books. doi:10.2307/j.ctvzxxbdk.

Tsering Döndrup (2019), *The Handsome Monk and Other Stories*, trans. Christopher Peacock, New York: University of Columbia Press.

Wemheuer, Felix (2014), *Famine Politics in Maoist China and the Soviet Union*, New Haven, CT: Yale University Press.

Wood, Benjamin (2013), "The Scrupulous Use of Gifts for the Saṅgha: Self-Ennoblement through the Ledger in Tibetan Autobiography," *Revue d'Etudes Tibétaines*, 26: 35–55.

Woodhouse, Emily (2012), "The Role of Tibetan Buddhism in Environmental Conservation under Changing Socio-Economic Conditions in China," PhD diss., Imperial College London.

Yeh, Emily (2013), "Blazing Pelts and Burning Passions: Nationalism, Cultural Politics, and Spectacular Decommodification in Tibet," *The Journal of Asian Studies*, 72 (2): 319–44. doi:10.1017/S0021911812002227.

2

Modern Minimalism and the Magical Buddhist Art of Disposal

Hannah Gould

There is a Zen *kōan*, popular within Western Buddhist circles, that provides one of the most intriguing insights into ideas about materiality in Japanese Buddhism. During the Tang Dynasty, a traveling Zen Master named Tanka found lodging at Yerinji Temple. It was a dark and stormy night, and he was so cold that he decided to use the temple's large wooden Buddha statue to make a fire. Upon discovering this, the temple's Abbot expressed great displeasure. As D. T. Suzuki (2011) retells it:

> "How dare you burn up my wooden Buddha?"
>
> Said Tanka, who looked as if searching for something with his stick in the ashes, "I am gathering the holy śarīras [Buddhist relics][1] in the burnt ashes."
>
> "How," said the keeper, "could you get śarīras by burning a wooden Buddha?"
>
> "If there are no śarīras to be found in it, may I have the remaining two Buddhas for my fire?" retorted Tanka.
>
> The shrine-keeper later lost his eye-brows for remonstrating against the apparent impiety of Tanka, while the Buddha's wrath never was visited upon the latter.

The Abbot's pained reaction, suggesting that the statue is sacred or at least deserving of respect, is mocked by Tanka as a limited view of Buddhist material cosmology. If the statue is merely an effigy, and not the real substance of Buddha, then why should it not be used as firewood?

On one level, this *kōan* presents the kind of aniconic or anti-materialist attitudes—exemplified in the aphorism, "If you meet a Buddha on the road, kill him!"—that have come to characterize Zen Buddhism in the contemporary world (Rambelli and Reinders 2012; Winfield and Heine 2017: xvi). It is this disenchanted form of Buddhism that has been described as its most palatable iteration for white Protestant communities, not only attracting converts, but also garnering a prodigiously positive impression within global popular culture (Tweed 2008). Suzuki initially appears to affirm this position, siding with the "higher spiritual attainment" of Tanka. However, he also warns novice practitioners against freely burning statues from the conviction of their superior insight; Buddhist icons still deserve respect. It is the caution of the Abbot and his reverence for powerful things that I think most resonates with the material ethics expressed in the Buddhist discourses of the modern minimalist movement.

I found myself returning to this *kōan* recently, when I stumbled across a striking image of modern minimalism in *The Guardian* newspaper. The article, entitled "'I gave away our stuff': The minimalists doing more with less" (Thornhill 2019), was published in early 2019, at the height of the craze for domestic decluttering helmed by Marie Kondo that swept across much of the English-speaking, Netflix-watching world. The article detailed the experiences of a young woman, Georgina, who had decided to downsize her family home and give away three-quarters of her possessions to live a "simpler life" with her family in Cornwall, saving money and finding sanity along the way. It was not the content of the article that intrigued me; personal testimonies of middle-class white women espousing the powers of minimalism as a means to escape the tyranny of modern life had veritably blossomed into a new journalistic subgenre that year. Instead, I was struck by the cover image. In it, Georgina, dressed in a pair of light-blue jeans with blonde wavy hair to her waist, sat cross-legged on the floor. The room's interior reflected the particular aesthetic that writer Kyle Chayka (2016), in an article for the *New York Times*, has called "the oppressive gospel of minimalism . . . white walls interrupted only by succulents." Only one other décor element appeared at home in this environment: a large golden statue of the Buddha. At no point during the article is the statue mentioned. Georgina is not identified as a Buddhist, and Buddhism is not presented as motivating her transformation. Instead, the ostentatious golden Buddha appears to fade into the background as a natural and thus unremarkable part of the material ecosystem of contemporary minimalism. Like white walls, succulents, and self-help books, Buddha becomes a conspicuous signal of lifestyles of non-consumption.

In this chapter, I show how popular Buddhist philosophy and praxis stemming from Japan is deployed to deal with the excess of consumer goods in late-capitalist societies around the globe via the discourse of minimalism. The "new" or "modern minimalist movement" is a lifestyle trend that gained global popularity in the mid-2010s, post global financial crisis, via a wave of popular media (see Meissner 2019). Broadly, the movement is characterized by its active curation of material absence as a moral or psychological good under the principle of "less is more." On one level, it consists of practical advice about how to manage the flow of consumer goods in and out of one's home, from navigating holiday gift-giving etiquette to recycling milk bottles. On another, it represents a system of ethical living and self-improvement premised on deeper ontological assertions about the nature and relation of people and things. Modern minimalism draws on diverse sources, including Scandinavian design, Buddhist teachings, the visual vernacular of Instagram, and Japanese architecture. More pointedly, as what I believe to be a significant vehicle for Japanese Buddhism's contemporary global transmission, it is an example of "oriental globalization" or Easternization (Nederveen Pieterse 2006: 411) that speaks to Asia's continued influence within new spiritual movements.

Even when cast as minimalist, Buddhism constitutes an ethics of being in and interacting with the material world. Production, consumption, and disposal are a central part of how Buddhism is lived. In recent years, scholarship has been particularly attuned to these dimensions of the religion (e.g., Gould 2019a; Winfield and Heine 2017). However, production and consumption have overwhelmingly captured attention to the neglect of decay, disposal, and recycling as sites of meaning-making (Wirtz 2009: 276–7). People often make quite complex judgments about how to dispose of goods, informed by broader religious and cultural ideas of value. Indeed, Joshua Reno (2016: 5) argues that "waste is not only made by us . . . waste makes all of us." All religious activity generates waste: some sacred, most banal. In many cases, Buddhism also specifies methods for dealing with unwanted, spent, or surplus goods. For example, as I have previously described (Gould 2019b) and Fabio Gygi articulates in this volume, the practice of *kuyō* (供養), or rites of veneration and separation, are applied to sacred tools and inalienable personal goods at temples across Japan in order to ease people's feelings of continued stewardship toward things.

In comparison to formal temple rites, Buddhism's expression in modern minimalism proves a more nebulous research subject, manifesting in snatches of popular culture and within people's private homes. This chapter represents a first scholarly attempt to map how the minimalist movement takes and remakes from (Japanese) Buddhism, drawing on data from discourse analysis of minimalist literature and popular media, as well as interviews. I focus on three books that have received commercial success in both Japanese and English, taking them as representative of Japanese Buddhism's varied articulations within the minimalism movement: Marie Kondo's *The Life-changing Magic of Tidying: The Japanese Art* (Kondo 2015), Sasaki Fumio's *Goodbye, Things*

(Sasaki 2015), and Shoukei Matsumoto's *A Monk's Guide to a Clean House and Mind* (Matsumoto 2011).[2] These works are discussed in relation to data from interviews with self-identified minimalists living in Australia and participant-observation at minimalist meet-up groups. Some research participants self-identify as Buddhist, but the majority do not. Many fall into the category of "Buddhish nones" (Oakes 2015) or "night-stand Buddhists" (Tweed 1999), who read Buddhist texts, attend meditation classes, or soak up cultural ideas about Buddhism without themselves subscribing to the religious identity or beliefs.

As previous studies of global Buddhism have established, not all religious ideas or practices travel well or find purchase. Jeff Wilson (2014: 3), in his study of the practice of mindfulness in America, argues that "members of the new culture take from Buddhism what they believe will relieve their culture-specific distresses and concerns, in the process spawning new Buddhisms (sometimes, crypto-Buddhisms) that better fit their needs." At the same time, cultural encounter gives rise to novel hybrids or creoles that draw on, but are distinct from, the particular (social, political, religious) context of each (see Rocha 2006). This chapter will articulate exactly what brand of Buddhism has found expression in modern minimalism and what this reveals about contested categories of "waste" and "excess."

Modern minimalism declares the vast majority of consumer goods to be excess and prescribes Buddhist philosophies and practices, particularly those centered on attachment or detachment and disposal, as a kind of life-changing "magic." Unlike earlier waves of minimalism that drew attention to the environmental consequences of overconsumption, modern minimalists center their ethics around the intimate relationship between people and their domestic possessions. Advocates suggest that what is wasted through excess consumption and possession is the psychological and physical energy that people spend in caring for stuff—energy that might be better invested in more meaningful projects of self-creation. Excess objects are classified as waste not because of their unexpended production value or use value, but because they are seen to expend people's mental energies and thus, ultimately, to rob people of their potential happiness. My investigation thus reveals an emerging movement in domestic spirituality based on an economy of attachment, which promotes heightened emotional skills of disposal and investment in a select number of goods. I conclude by suggesting that, alongside mindfulness, attachment and detachment have become central Buddhist skills within popular culture. Minimalism, by borrowing models of attachments and detachment from Buddhism, is not aniconic or anti-materialist, but full of life-changing magic.

Making Minimalism Buddhist

The term minimalism derives from an artistic movement of the late 1960s and early 1970s, in which artists shunned the deep personal investment that characterized earlier schools, like Abstract Expressionism, and, instead, sought to present the reality of the art itself, its medium and form. As a lifestyle practice, minimalism has roots in the West in the "voluntary simplicity" or "simple living" countercultural movements that proliferated during the same period (Shi 2001: 3). In Japan, minimalism is influenced by a distinct but cross-pollinating tradition of decluttering and home organization, reaching back to an emerging "waste consciousness" of frugality after World War II (Siniawer 2018: 270). Voluntary simplicity, like minimalism, is an omnibus label, broadly defined as "an oppositional living strategy that rejects the high-consumption, materialistic lifestyles of consumer cultures and affirms what is often just called 'the simple life' or 'downshifting'" (Alexander and Ussher 2012: 2). It responds to an age of unprecedented material wealth (albeit with serious inequality of distribution) within late-capitalist societies and the perceived harms that arise therein—what Meissner refers to as "the world of too much" (2019). Today, the average US household possesses the highest average number of domestic goods at any time in history and personal storage facilities represent a multi-billion-dollar industry, with approximately 21 square feet of rentable space available per household (ibid.). Minimalists are motivated by an array of causes, from lessening one's environmental impact to gaining financial independence and reclaiming mental well-being. As an umbrella term, it thus potentially includes penny-pinching budgets, lavish lifestyles in high-end interiors, and anti-capitalist movements. Minimalism is to be distinguished from poverty by its premise of material wealth, but the comingling of these threads in a single discursive space reveals deeper inequalities at work in minimalism today; it is a relative condition of necessity for some and a luxury for others.

Strains of modern minimalism are more or less tied to organized religion. Joshua Becker, author of *The More of Less* (Becker 2018), teaches a kind of Christian prosperity gospel via minimalism. Becker proclaims Jesus (alongside Buddha) to be a minimalist and interprets the parable of Jesus advising a rich young man to sell his goods and donate the proceeds as a lesson in self-improvement, as much as it is a lesson in charity.[3] This brand of minimalism fits into a broader media ecosystem of simple living populated by Mennonite YouTube channels and evangelical "mommy bloggers," continuing a historical legacy of Quakerism in US simple living movements (Shi 2001). Other religious influences are less explicitly affirmed, contested, or even denied by their promoters. Like other Japanese popular culture phenomena that have gripped the global imagination, significant media attention has been devoted to identifying the religious motivations of Japanese minimalist authors. After Marie Kondo's Netflix series launched in 2019, her gospel of "spark joy," her practice of conversing with goods, and even her neat dress were held up as evidence of the influence of Shintoism in her work. Much was made of Kondo's part-time job as a shrine attendant or *miko* (巫女), despite this being a relatively common casual job for students. Kondo herself commented, in a 2015 Reddit Q&A session, that: "It [Shintoism] influences me, but not as strongly as you might think." Joylon Baraka Thomas (2019) makes important critiques of such "culturalist readings" of Kondo, which reduce her to a mouthpiece of her socioreligious context through liberal application of the term "animist." As I go on to describe, Japanese minimalist authors appear to make very deliberate decisions about how to position themselves in relation to religious and cultural phenomena in different contexts. At the same time, their work is often appropriated. At the height of the Kondo craze, several temples and online sangha claimed minimalist credentials to attract new followers and demonstrate their relevance to the zeitgeist. Minimalism is also the subject of extensive posts on sites like *Buddhist Boot Camp*[4] and *Tricycle*, often as part of a broader schema of mindful living.

Minimalism is most strongly and consistently identified with the Zen Buddhism of Japan. This association has a long history, with "Thoreau and the 'hippies' of the 1960s" looking to Eastern spirituality for minimalist inspiration (Shi 2001: 4). The figure of the world-renouncing ascetic monk looms large in this cultural exchange, although not always as a positive image. Reflecting on the inspiration behind his minimalist lifestyle, Rohit, an IT specialist in his mid-thirties living in Melbourne, recalls reading that monks are "only allowed to own like three or five items—a robe, a bowl, a needle . . . or something. That really made me think about what I actually need in life." However, Rohit later called this level of restriction "a bit extreme." Many minimalists, in fact, define their lifestyle *against* the perceived austerity of the ascetic. Minimalist interior designers Fortin and Quilici (2018: vii), for example, cast "traditional minimalism" as

> an austere philosophy of stripping down to the bare essentials and questioning what is required for one's basic survival. It conjures imagery of ascetic, Thoreau-like solitude owning a single fork and knife while foraging berries from surrounding woods.

This lifestyle is deemed incompatible with commitments to family, friends, and work, which equally feature in the contemporary good life. Fortin and Quilici (ibid.) define new minimalism as a "mindful, intentional way of living, prioritizing relationships and experiences above material things." This "middle path" between asceticism and "over-the-top" consumerism (ibid.: viii), which equally draws on Buddhist discourses, overwhelmingly characterizes the minimalism I encountered in Australia and in online transnational spaces.

Zen Buddhism seeps into minimalism as a "cool commodity" and part of a "commodified, global folk Buddhism" (McMahan 2008: 262). Jørn Borup (2015: 72) suggests that Zen derives its power from its status as a "floating signifier," or infinitely malleable reference that can be readily applied to disparate phenomena, from voting to eating to sex (see also Wilson 2014: 6). Zen is thus a kind of meta-narrative or brand of authenticity, semantically equivalent to truth. Its intertwinement with minimalism is not just a result of Western appropriation; it also occurs in Japan. There, Zen is liberally co-opted by minimalist authors to support a range of different value propositions, from environmentally driven, anti-consumerist, and zero-waste lifestyles, to the disposal-focused, aesthetically driven practices of contemporary lifestyle movements (Siniawer 2018: 275). Of all strands of Buddhism, Zen appears uniquely detachable from a specific context, while retaining its emotive connotations and cool appeal. It is notable, for example, that Shōkei Matsumoto's (2011) *A Monk's Guide* is marketed as "ancient Zen household techniques," despite the author being ordained in the Jōdo Shinshū (True Pure Land) tradition. Zen provides both "ancient wisdom" and a distinct visual aesthetic of empty rooms, clean surfaces, and natural textures. This overlaps with the persistent, worldwide "fascination with the abstract, idealized category of 'The Japanese House,' and by extension Japan" as a site of elegance, cleanliness, and simplicity (Daniels 2009: 1) .[5] As Inge Daniels' (2009) work shows, this abstract image is entirely romantic, and contradicted by the everyday bric-a-brac, overflowing storage, and complex disposal systems that people in Japan live with.

The association between Zen and minimalism is more than cultural collocation or attractive branding; it is part of the project of Buddhism modernism. The Zen that entered the Western intellectual tradition in the late nineteenth century was cast as a meditation-orientated, psychological practice (Borup 2015: 70). This so-called Protestant Zen was produced by stripping away the cultural "stuff" of Buddhism—its idols, incense, robes, and so on (all that is smelly and fetishistic)—to create a pure philosophy that could be synthesized with a scientific worldview. It is this formation of an aniconic or anti-materialist

Buddhism that is positioned as an ancient salve for a degenerate materialism infecting the modern West (Rambelli 2007). Meanwhile, Daniel Miller (2001) identifies how moral castigations of contemporary consumer culture often, and he argues too enthusiastically, place blame on US cultural imperialism, such that consumerism becomes synonymous with "McDonaldization." This sets up a dichotomy between a maximalist US and minimalist Japan that belies the lived realities on the ground. The form of Buddhism invoked in the modern minimalist movement also falls between these two extremes, as authors work to promote their lifestyle practice within, not against, consumer culture.

Marketing Minimalism

Wilson (2014: 136) declares mindfulness to be both "the ultimate Buddhist product" and a challenge to capitalist routes of circulation, as it is not immediately apparent how it can be bought and sold. Minimalism is perhaps an even more direct challenge in this regard, seemingly taking direct aim at the logic of accumulation. However, in both cases, the market has found a solution in the production and marketing of books, podcasts, self-help courses, and functional tools to support practice. These are the vehicles via which minimalism has traveled, although their profusion and commercialization are not without controversy. Some minimalist luminaries offer their insights online for free. Others, such as the popular American duo *The Minimalists,* invite followers to borrow their books from a library or to first purchase them and then give them away.

In Japan, decluttering guides form part of a larger subgenre of "conduct literature" (Bardsley and Miller 2011) on topics ranging from seasonal home decoration to funeral etiquette. These works represent a powerful normative force in regulating etiquette, particularly among their target audience of women (ibid.: 15–16), who bear the overwhelming burden of managing domestic space and waste disposal (Siniawer 2018: 9–10). Japan is home to a distinct literature on decluttering with long historical lineages and distinct philosophies. One subgenre asks readers to consider what would happen to their possessions if they were to die tomorrow, prompting a kind of "death cleaning" (a trend also prominent in Swedish minimalist texts). Another uses dharmic teachings to reframe people's emotional connection to things. For example, the minimalist system created by Yamashita Hideko, called *danshari* (断捨離), draws heavily on yogic and Buddhist teachings. The term encompasses all parts of the consumption/disposal cycle; the first character 断 *dan* means "refuse," the second character 捨 *sha* means "dispose" and finally 離 *ri* means "separate," referring to a psychological separation of oneself from materiality. Yamashita's prodigious works are bestsellers and she runs a wildly popular seminar series, but her books have not been translated into English (although they do appear in German).

Three authors have crossed the linguistic and cultural divide, with best-selling books and other media launching them into relative degrees of fame. They stake out distinct positions in relation to the "cool Zen" phenomenon. Shoukei Matsumoto's *A Monk's Guide to a Clean House and Mind* was published in English in 2011. The book typifies the visual style of the genre, with short paragraphs, hand-drawn line illustrations, and ample negative space. It amalgamates a series of short essays on properly caring for one's home possessions, body, and mind, with exact specifications for cleaning routines and anecdotes about the significance of particular objects to Zen. Matsumoto (2011) focuses on cleaning, suggesting that it is "carried out not because there is dirt, but because it's an ascetic practice to cultivate the mind" (3). Matsumoto is a younger priest and a cosmopolitan figure, having graduated from Tokyo University's School of Religious Studies and attained an MBA at the Indian School of Business. He is active in the kind of projects that John Nelson (2013) has termed "experimental Buddhism," which are aimed at reviving religious participation and making Buddhism relevant to modern concerns. In particular, he is one of the original co-founders of higan .net, an "online temple," and of the *o-tera-no-mirai* project, which connects individuals to local temples outside of formal ancestral parishioner relations. In both *A Monk's Guide* and international talks, Matsumoto appears to embrace the discourse of "cool Zen" and more broadly the international cultural capital of "cool Japan" and "cool Zen," affirming minimalism as an inherent virtue of the Japanese; "Japanese people take cleaning very seriously. . . . Buddhist monks have a motto: 'Live to clean and clean to live'" (Matsumoto 2011: 3).

In contrast, Marie Kondo's body of work reveals a more cautious approach to Zen's global cultural capital. Kondo's minimalist empire originates from a single volume published in Japanese in 2011 and translated into English in 2015, which guides the readers through a once-in-a-lifetime process of significantly downsizing their possessions. Her empire has subsequently blossomed into weekly podcasts, a decluttering training program, a homeware range, a global network of certified consultants, and several spin-off books, including an illustrated manga version and a guide to workplace minimalism. Kondo's Netflix series *Tidying Up with Marie Kondo* was released on January 1, 2019, capitalizing on the tradition of New Year's resolutions and sparking a pop culture phenomenon, to the extent that "to kondo" has entered popular lexicon. Each episode of the series shows Kondo intervening in the life of a struggling, maximalist family. The family's stunned, almost reverential response to Kondo's demeanor as she taps books to "wake them up" and "greets the house" by kneeling on the floor in silence and bowing, underscores her positioning as a source of "ancient wisdom from the East." As I have noted, Kondo herself is more circumspect about the spiritual origins of her practice, but both direct marketing and popular media coverage of her products and services lean heavily toward these spiritual tropes.

Finally, Sasaki Fumio's work, *Goodbye, Things* (Sasaki 2015), reveals both a romantic idealization of the "minimalist heart" of Japanese culture and a self-conscious reflexivity toward the cool Zen discourse. Sasaki's work is striking for a number of reasons, not least in terms of gender; the Japanese decluttering literature is overwhelmingly dominated by female authors and directed toward women. Sasaki presents himself as a former "loser" who has shaken off normative masculine expectations of marriage, children, and a corporate job in order to pursue happiness via minimalism. His strain of minimalism is also notably more hard core than those of Kondo and Matsumoto in the extent of material simplification prescribed. I identify romantic visions of premodern bliss in Sasaki's work, as he suggests that before industrialization "Japanese culture used to be a minimalist culture" (Sasaki 2015: 42) and admires an age of sturdy stone tools and earthenware built for "purely functional reasons" (ibid.: 68). Sasaki also outright acknowledges the influence of Buddhism on his thinking, but notes that he is most directly inspired by the Buddhist aesthetics of Apple products and Steve Jobs, whom he declares "the perfect minimalist" (ibid.: 201):

> The products that Jobs created always avoided excess. . . . I think this is all due to the fact that Jobs had been a minimalist, and he was known to be a believer in Japanese Zen, which teaches minimalism.

Despite being initially hesitant about meditation, Zen, and yoga because of their "New Age, sketchy feel" (ibid.: 206), Sasaki first engaged with meditation after taking a class with a local priest. He bolsters his support of the practice by noting that companies like Google and Facebook are "pretty heavily into Zen and meditation" (ibid.: 206). Sasaki's attitude is an interesting example of the "looping effect" or "feedback loop" (McMahan 2008: 57) that arises through transnational exchange of ideas, as the cool Zen narrative returns to audiences in Japan (Borup 2015: 73). Both Job's minimalism and his Buddhism are often touted by minimalist teachers. His recent biographers are more circumspect, suggesting that "while nobody who knew him well during his later years would have called Steve a 'devout' Buddhist, the spiritual discipline informed his life in both subtle and profound ways" (Schlender and Tetzeli 2015).[6] Regardless of the facts, the figure of Steve Jobs is a prime example of the ambiguous but inextricable mélange of Buddhism and minimalism in popular culture. This intersection gives rise to distinct practices and philosophies that exceed their source materials, as I explicate in the next section.

Key Values of Modern Minimalism

As noted previously, minimalist texts function both as practical housekeeping advice and as a material ethics. These two layers cannot be separated and even modest descriptions about seemingly meager things reveal deeper value propositions. Although there is certainly no unified doctrine of modern minimalism, the movement coalesces around certain key ideas that are taken up and debated in the community. In particular, three concepts speak to how Buddhism and minimalism interfuse: diagnosis, treatment, and goal.

The Diagnosis: Wanton Attachment

Modern minimalism begins from the assumption that contemporary society is excessive, in both the sheer quantity of material goods and the psychospiritual burden they impose. Material things, particularly mass-produced goods in disordered disarray, prove inauthentic or without meaning as the commodity fetish, for all its allure, wears off soon after purchase. Sasaki (2015: 59), for example, discusses how new purchases momentarily satiate boredom, but "the glory of acquisition starts to dim with use." This conflicted feeling is summarized as "being overwhelmed and yet alienated" (Chayka 2019). For members of the minimalist community I worked with in Melbourne, it was most frequently discussed in reference to the keen, almost visceral discomfort they felt when visiting the homes of their parents, who they often labeled "hoarders." As Kristin, a copyeditor in her thirties, noted: "I've tried helping mum clean it up, but she just insists, 'I like my clutter' (sigh). Really, it pains me to visit her there, with all that clutter and . . . that stress."

This diagnosis of excessive materiality appears to counter the positive reframing of consumption by scholars of the material culture turn, including Miller (1987), whose ethnographies of shopping and home life present the practice of consumption as an appropriative act, generative of personalized meanings and authenticity. Indeed, this diagnosis more closely aligns with earlier Frankfurt school critiques of the alienating effects of mass consumption.[7] However, in minimalism, material goods are framed not just as inauthentic or alienating, but as veritably parasitic, feeding on the mental energies and agency of the individual. As Sasaki (2015: 23) phrases it: "I've found that the less stuff I own, the less my stuff owns me." Stuff saps our attention, until we become "like a slow computer" (ibid.: 49), unable to process the data of the world around us. Similarly, Kristin cautioned that excess stuff "weighs you down." This vein of minimalism cleaves strongly toward what Wilson (2014: 91) refers to as "the great bugaboo of Buddhism," namely, attachment, a byword that ricochets through minimalist texts. Rohit told me that "The more stuff I have then the more attachments I have, and you end up getting attached to things rather than fulfilling the greater purpose of your life." Similarly, others in the community described minimalism as a "process of getting better at detaching from stuff."

Crucially, not all goods appear equally liable to generating such parasitic affections, nor are all such attachments considered negative. For some self-proclaimed "hardcore minimalists," stuff is always secondary to mental goods. Sasaki (2015: 28) elevates experiences, time spent with others, and personal growth as the "real pleasures in life." This is a central plank of the popular anti-materialist discourse that Miller (2001) identifies, which pathologizes "attachment or devotion to objects that is at the expense of an attachment or devotion to people" (227). For most minimalists, however, the condemnation of thing-attachment is not so complete. Things retain an important space in Kondo's heart and upbringing. She reflects that "Because I was poor at developing bonds of trust with people, I had an unusually strong attachment to things" (Kondo 2015: 208). Many minimalists in the Melbourne community maintained beloved objects or collections, such as Rohit's Mustang or Kristin's pottery. Further, certain goods, notably books (and perhaps Buddha statues), appear a protected class curtailed from the taint of materialism. Of all Kondo's decluttering commandments, her instruction to limit oneself to thirty books received the most ire and represented the greatest cleave from her readership. A series of critical opinion pieces with titles like "Going Against the Decluttering Craze: The Book Hoarders Who Defy Marie Kondo" (Long 2019) espouse the inherent morality of books. The selective valorization of goods can be contested. For example, Kondo's attempt to launch a homeware store, featuring products like a US$132 tote bag, a US$64 soil rake, and a US$124 leather tray, was widely mocked as hypocritical and price-gorging.

In this manner, the minimalist's world appears humming with power, and this power demands a practiced response. Attachment is not inherently negative, but it is at least a scarce resource, worn down through contemporary excess. This resource is consumed not only by the psychic weight of possession, but also by the time taken for the cleaning and display of goods in the home. Kondo (2015: 236) argues that "human beings can only truly cherish a limited number of things at one time." For her, "truly cherishing" includes running your hands over clothes and "thanking" socks at the end of the day. Matsumoto (2011: 1) similarly prescribes a routine of intensive daily cleaning, so that people and things might "support each other's existence." Scholar of North American decluttering movements Katie Kilroy-Marac (2016: 20) makes the argument that within these communities, possession of things is insufficient to demonstrate social distinction; "one must also demonstrate an active engagement in practices related to the curation and management of one's object world." Objects become meaningful when they are invested with personal time and energy, such as through cleaning. However, no amount of curation or organizational prowess can save one from rampant stuff without first practicing mass disposal.

The Treatment: Disposal

If an excess of material attachment is the disease, then its course of treatment comes in the form of divesting or detaching from goods. Given the immediate excess of things, the modern minimalist movement is focused on downsizing, ideally once and en masse, rather than on curtailing new consumption. Within minimalism, disposal is invested with extraordinary power to transform not only domestic space, but also one's happiness and life trajectory. As Kondo (2015: 4) states, "a dramatic reorganization of the home causes correspondingly dramatic changes in your lifestyle and perspective." For many members of the Melbourne community, their turn to minimalism was precipitated by momentous life events, such as moving cities, divorce, or the death of a loved one. Minimalist authors encourage readers to make minimalization itself into a significant event. Kondo promotes her method with a "one-time-and-you're-done" guarantee, promising readers that they will never have to declutter again: "It brings about a change so profound that it touches your emotions and will irresistibly affect your way of thinking and your lifestyle habits" (ibid.: 18). Disposal does not, however, come easily to most, and divestment from stuff emerges as a practical and emotional skill that needs to be (re)learned. Sasaki (2015: 82) argues that most people are "simply inexperienced" at disposal and have acquired "learned helplessness" from previous failed attempts. Building up this muscle requires investment and time; as with learning a language, "you can't become a master at *danshari*, or de-cluttering and parting, overnight."

Minimalist authors vary in the criteria they set for the retention or disposal of goods. Some, like Sasaki, are functionalists, judging goods on the basis of whether or not they are part of "the absolute minimum you need" (Sasaki 2015: 24). In contrast, Kondo focuses on the interaffectivity of people and things, teaching people to hone their skills of strategic investment in goods that "spark joy." This affect is embodied, as each object must be held, caressed, and even smelt before a decision can be made. Both standards ultimately prove subjective and malleable. Although Sasaki (2015) initially endorses Kondo's "killer phrase" and its philosophy, he eventually urges his readers to transcend it, to "be brave and let go of things that spark joy" (106). Indeed, he appears to operate, at least personally, on a principle of "discard now and ask questions later," having himself repurchased and then disposed of items several times as the need arose.

As disposal can be challenging, minimalist luminaries shepherd their readers through the rollercoaster of emotions it generates. Sentimental items, such as photographs and keepsakes, prove particularly difficult in this regard. This category is what Daniels (2009) has called "troublesome things," objects that are unwanted but cannot be easily parted with due to feelings of obligation or attachment. Similarly, the disposal of unutilized or underutilized objects can generate feelings of "wasted value," which are a major concern for minimalist authors. Kondo (2015: 65) actively encourages people not to offer goods second-hand to one's circle, as it hinders the flow of those items out of the home and also "transfers the guilt" of disposal to another. She declares, instead, that "to throw away what you no longer need is neither wasteful nor shameful" (ibid.: 71). Sasaki (2015: 134) similarly wrestles with guilt stemming from the waste created by discarding serviceable items, but reasons that "the real waste, though, is the psychological damage that you accrue from hanging on to things you don't use or need" (see also Matsumoto 2011: 4). In this manner, minimalist authors construct a value system in which people's personal energies and lifestyles, rather than objects themselves, are subject to wasting, as they become consumed by an excess of unsatisfactory attachments. Getting rid of objects—even serviceable, valuable, or attractive items—is thus a necessary sacrifice to maintain the welfare of the mind.

In this way, modern minimalism diverges sharply from earlier, equally Buddhist-inspired, domestic-organization movements from Japan. Before "spark joy," there was *mottainai* (もったいない). This similarly enigmatic phrase can be glossed as "Oh, what a waste!" It describes an affective condition of guilt or sadness when disposing of something before its potential utility has been exhausted. In this philosophy, ideas of waste and value are less human-centered, being considered within an object's own life trajectory rather than through its relationship to the consumer. Eiko Maruko Siniawer (2018) describes how, at the turn of the twenty-first century, *mottainai* was promoted as a lost Japanese virtue from the era of postwar frugality and a means to tackle the contemporary pathology of affluence. Like spark joy, the philosophy of *mottainai* traveled globally, entering into United Nations environmental discourses via the efforts of political activist and Nobel Prize winner, Wangari Maathai, among others. Heightened awareness of *mottainai* might inspire practices of mending or repurposing goods, and, by extension, a consideration of the ecological impacts of new consumption. In comparison, the modern minimalism movement is significantly less concerned with the material trajectory or environmental ethics of waste (ibid.: 271). This is not to say that environmentalism is irrelevant to contemporary minimalist authors and practitioners, many of whom also pursue more ethical consumption practices and continue to struggle with feelings of guilt. However, it is rarely ranked as the primary motivator for adopting a minimalist lifestyle and is placed below ideas like freedom, simplicity, and ease.

One way to address lingering guilt is through the practice of gratitude. Kondo (2015: 71) suggests that people actively acknowledge the contribution objects have made to their life and then "let them go with gratitude." Clothes that have been purchased but never worn, for example, are thanked as an important lesson to be more discerning in personal fashion choices in the future. In Kondo's Netflix series, participants were instructed to say "thank you" aloud to objects before putting them in bin bags (a task many only half-seriously performed). The practice of gratitude as a means to disentangle oneself morally and psychologically from unwanted or spent objects has resonances in the ritual practice of *kuyō* (供養) in Japan. Waste disposal companies in contemporary Japan may employ Buddhist priests to conduct rites on unwanted items, from teddy bears to eyeglasses, before removing these objects from the home, out of site and out of mind. As Fabio Gygi (this volume) describes, ritual practitioners often take great care to obscure the eventual fate of objects or to disrupt their material continuity through transformation, in order to soothe emotions related to their transition from the state of beloved possessions to simple rubbish.

Although the emotional skill of disposal is to be cultivated (or at the very least, outsourced), in excess it can be equally harmful. Just as mindfulness practitioners are warned against getting too attached to the identity and ego that can accompany expertise in mindfulness (Wilson 2014: 91), minimalists are warned to not become obsessed with disposal. Kondo (2015: 45–7) describes a low point early on in her minimalist journey when she became "virtually a 'disposal unit'" to the point of stealing her sibling's goods to dispose of them. These habits lead to stress, sadness, and eventually more shopping to fill the void, and fuel the desire to dispose. Sasaki (2015) also warns people against comparing the paucity of their possessions to that of others, as each person's minimalism and definition of what is necessary to live a good life is different. Competitive minimalism is a substantial feature of online forums, however, where participants frequently post images of their household décor, and debate whether or not it can be rightfully labeled "minimal." Sasaki (2015: 150) cautions that "minimalism is not a rite of penance, nor is it a competitive sport. It is simply a means to an end." The exact nature of this end state, however, is one of the more ambiguous facets of the movement.

The Goal: Abundance

All moral judgments of material excess imply a definition of sufficiency (see also Caple this volume). However, so much of the modern minimalist literature focuses on disposal that the nature and virtue of this ideal state—whether or not it is ever obtained—is difficult to pin down. Sasaki (2015: Chapter 4), for example, emphasizes the self-actualization found through minimalism, listing over twenty personal gains from the practice, including more time, enjoyment of life, more freedom (traveling to new countries, changing jobs), more self-confidence (writing a book, dating a girl, talking in public), better concentration, better inter-personal relationships, more money, and better security. Kondo (2015: 210) similarly enumerates a long list, from discovering one's vocational calling, to gaining confidence in social relationships, and learning to live in the moment. In this manner, minimalism can appear a panacea, in which the shortcomings of modern life are alleviated by learning to deal with stuff. Perhaps the most unified description of its power is that minimalism creates a sense of material satiation, whereby a minimalist environment is not experienced as punishing or ascetic, but, rather, creates a feeling of abundance or fullness. Such a feeling was central to what members of the Melbourne minimalist community commonly referred to as "a simple life," "intentional living," or "having just enough to be happy."

In published works, the language of absence/abundance often plays on seemingly contradictory collocations. One minimalist blogger, Mihoyo Fuyji, who grew up in a Japanese temple family and runs the site "Zero=Abundance,"[8] positions the value of *kū* (空) meaning "emptiness," "void," or "sky" as the core tenet of both Buddhism and minimalism. Matsumoto (2011: 124) similarly explains that "there is an old Zen saying that goes 'where there is nothing, there is everything.'" Ideas of abundance fuse mental freedom and cultivated intentionality or mindfulness. Matsumoto (2011: 123) draws an analogy between the minimalism process and the pilgrimage of itinerant preacher Ippen Shōnin, noting that "by not being anchored down by worldly possessions, his mind was able to achieve true freedom." For Matsumoto, this freedom includes appreciation of the seasons and appreciation for objects and their true nature through acts of cleaning and organizing the home. For many minimalists, this freedom extends more broadly. Kristin explained that what she values is "a life that matters, that is conscious . . . a satisfaction in being the type of person I want to be," while Rohit strove to achieve "intentionality in my higher purpose." Such ideas of inner abundance contend with the visual character of minimalism promulgated on social media, which Kristin dismisses as "Pinterest Minimalism" that is overly focused on display. Indeed, very few minimalists even mentioned material objects when discussing the goal of their practice, and few appeared concerned with cultivating a particular visual aesthetic, such as that of white walls and succulents.

Given minimalism's strong link between domestic order and mental contentment, it was interesting to see how the minimalist community reacted to the COVID-19 pandemic of 2020, in which social distancing measures in place in Victoria, and around the world, closed public venues and forced people to spend many more hours at home. In online forums, some minimalists expressed regret about the objects they had previously chosen to dispose of, particularly workout gear, puzzles, a television, and supplies for hobbies. In contrast, for those currently in the throes of decluttering, isolation appeared to provide extra motivation and time to dispose of goods. For the hardened minimalists I talked to, the sudden context of social isolation appeared largely to confirm the feeling of self-sufficiency and contentment they derived from their domestic space. Emma, a youth counselor, was living alone in a small apartment when the restrictions were imposed (she rented the apartment pre-furnished after moving to Melbourne with a single suitcase). She remarked how unaffected her daily life was by the restrictions and how stable this made her feel:

> For people who have bought expensive cars and suits, all of that has just been proven irrelevant at this point in time, because people are forced to get back to

> the basics. Like, I have a friend who is a shopaholic, and she can't go out to the shops obviously, and it's a real problem for her. But for me, well, with no excess stuff I can just live, walk, eat simply. . . . I don't feel like I lack anything, I feel full.

This sense of fullness or wealth—even in the face of extreme uncertainty or upheaval to the everyday—is one of the most enduring selling points of minimalism, equally espoused by the community and by prominent authors. And stability has been in high demand in recent years. Chayaka (2019) concludes his work by suggesting that minimalism is "an inevitable societal and cultural shift responding to the experience of living through the 2000s." For younger generations who have lived through a series of financial crises and expanding income inequalities, the (material) wealth of the baby boomers appears unattainable, while precarity reigns. By framing material absence as an experience of wealth, minimalism provides a means to cope with precarity. Or, in its most insidious reading, the edict "less is more" can be interpreted as coercive, convincing people to be happier with less, and thus demand less structural change. Of course, the two statements are not mutually exclusive.

Conclusion

On its surface, minimalism's enduring association with Japanese Zen Buddhism appears a natural reflection of a shared commitment to anti-materialism, natural fibers, and white walls. However, as this chapter has outlined, a more complex ethics concerning material culture, in terms of both its parasitic power and potential as a source of freedom or joy, characterize the modern minimalist movement and how its advocates engage with Buddhist philosophy and practice. This is, perhaps, not surprising. Wilson (2014: 6) asserts that "things that move are things that more easily fit into prevailing worldviews." The hybrid form that is Japanese minimalist Zen is not one that radically challenges a capitalist logic of accumulation, as some previous simple living movements have done. Like the mindfulness gurus that preside over app empires, minimalist authors sell many millions of books, embark on speaking tours, and build global homeware empires. Modern minimalism largely shies away from any outright condemnation of new consumption, and very rarely touches upon the extraordinary environmental consequences of continued accumulation and waste disposal, or our moral obligation to the planet and/or future generations. Rather, its leaders counsel people to develop emotional skills of detachment so as to relieve the perceived mental burdens of stuff and ultimately, to create mental abundance through material absence. This model of attachment and detachment, more so than even mindfulness or Zen aesthetics, is the central Buddhist attribute taken up within minimalism. In this new lifestyle movement, the golden Buddha statue thus appears to encode a deeper set of value propositions on attachment and abundance.

Notes

1 *Śarīras* are usually small pearl-like objects found in the cremated ashes of Buddhist spiritual leaders.
2 The label "minimalist" is not always self-ascribed. Marie Kondo, for example, is keen to disassociate herself from it, stating on her website that: "Minimalism champions living with less, but Marie's tidying method encourages living with items you truly cherish" (see www.konmari.com). As I will describe, this sentiment, in fact, closely reflects modern minimalist thinking, whether or not she takes up that mantle.
3 Gospel of Matthew 19:16-30; Gospel of Mark 10:17-31; Gospel of Luke 18:18-30.
4 *Buddhist Boot Camp* is a popular website with a podcast, blogs, and a series of books, run by Timber Hawkeye, offering "secular and non-sectarian" Buddhist teachings. See https://www.buddhistbootcamp.com
5 Japan is not the only source of cultural wisdom and aesthetics that the modern minimalist movement draws on. Scandinavian culture and design are another key source of inspiration. For example, Fortin and Quilici (2018: viiii) extol the virtues of the *lagom*, a Swedish word they translate as "just the right amount," as the guiding principle for their "middle way" new minimalism.
6 Jobs is said to have meditated regularly, read Shunryu Suzuki's famous text, *Zen Mind, Beginner's Mind,* consulted with a Japanese monastic, and made Asian spirituality a frequent topic of conservation in business meetings. See Schlender and Tetzeli (2015).
7 On the scholarly debates about consumption, see Miller (2001); Graeber (2011).
8 See website: www.interactiongreen.com

References

Alexander, Samuel and Simon Ussher (2012), "The Voluntary Simplicity Movement: A Multi-national Survey Analysis in Theoretical Context," *Journal of Consumer Culture*, 12 (1): 66–86. doi: 10.1177/1469540512444019.

Bardsley, Jan and Laura Miller (2011), "Manners and Mischief: Introduction," in Jan Bardsley and Laura Miller (eds), *Manners and Mischief: Gender, Power, and Etiquette in Japan*, 1–28, Berkeley: University of California Press.

Becker, Joshua (2018), *The More of Less*, Colorado: WaterBrook Press.

Borup, Jørn (2015), "Easternization of the East? Zen and Spirituality as Distinct Cultural Narratives in Japan," *Journal of Global Buddhism*, 16: 70–93.

Chayka, Kyle (2016), "The Oppressive Gospel of 'Minimalism,'" *The New York Times*, July 26. https://www.nytimes.com/2016/07/31/magazine/the-oppressive-gospel-of-minimalism.html

Chayka, Kyle (2019), *The Longing for Less: Living with Minimalism*, London: Bloomsbury Publishing.

Daniels, Inge (2009), *The Japanese House: Material Culture in the Modern Home*, London: Berg.

Fortin, Cary Telander and Kyle Louise Quilici (2018), *New Minimalism: Decluttering and Design for Sustainable, Intentional Living*, Seattle: Sasquatch Books.

Gould, Hannah (2019a), "Domestic(ating) Buddha: Making a Place for Japanese Buddhist Altars (butsudan) in Western Homes," *Journal of Material Religion*, 15 (4): 488–510. doi: 10.1080/17432200.2019.1632107.

Gould, Hannah (2019b), "Caring for Sacred Waste: The Disposal of *butsudan* (Buddhist Altars) in Contemporary Japan," *Japanese Religions*, 43 (1 & 2): 197–220.

Graeber, David (2011), "Consumption," *Current Anthropology*, 52 (4): 489–511. doi: 10.1086/660166.

Kilroy-Marac, Katie (2016), "An Order of Distinction (or, How to Tell a Collection from a Hoard)," *Journal of Material Culture*, 23 (1): 20–38. doi: 10.1177/1359183517729428.

Kondo, Marie (2015 [2011]), *The Life-Changing Magic of Tidying: The Japanese Art*, Trans. C. Hirano. London: Vermillion.

Long, Amanda (2019). "Going Against the Decluttering Craze: The Book Hoarders Who Defy Marie Kondo," *The Independent*, April 13. https://www.independent.co.uk/life-style/marie-kondo-bibliophiles-books-decluttering-tidying-a8864926.html

Matsumoto, Shoukei. (2011), *A Monk's Guide to a Clean House and Mind*, Trans. I. Samhammer, London: Penguin Books.

McMahan, David L. (2008), *The Making of Buddhist Modernism*, Oxford: Oxford University Press.

Meissner, Miriam (2019), "Against Accumulation: Lifestyle Minimalism, De-growth and the Present Post-ecological Condition," *Journal of Culture Economy*, 12 (3): 185–200. doi: 10.1080/17530350.2019.1570962

Miller, Daniel (1987), *Material Culture and Mass Consumption*, London: Wiley.

Miller, Daniel (2001), "The Poverty of Morality," *Journal of Consumer Culture*, 1 (2): 225–43. doi: 10.1177/146954050100100210.

Nederveen Pieterse, Jan (2006), "Oriental Globalization," *Theory, Culture & Society*, 23 (2–3): 411–413. doi: 10.1177/026327640602300274.

Nelson, John (2013), *Experimental Buddhism: Innovation and Activism in Contemporary Japan*, Honolulu: University of Hawai'i Press.

Oakes, Kaya (2015), *The Nones Are Alright: A New Generation of Believers, Seekers, and Those in Between*, London: Orbis Books.

Rambelli, Fabio (2007), *Buddhist Materiality: A Cultural History of Objects in Japanese Buddhism*, Stanford: Stanford University Press.

Rambelli, Fabio and Eric Reinders (2012), *Buddhism and Iconoclasm in East Asia: A History*, London: Bloomsbury.

Reno, Joshua (2016), "Waste and Waste Management," *Annual Review of Anthropology*, 44: 557–72. doi: 10.1146/annurev-anthro-102214-014146.

Rocha, Cristina (2006), *Zen in Brazil: The Quest for Cosmopolitan Modernity*, Honolulu: University of Hawai'i Press.

Sasaki, Fumio (2015), *Goodbye, Things: On Minimalist Living*, Trans. E. Sugita, London: Penguin Books.

Schlender, Brent and Rick Tetzeli (2015), *Becoming Steve Jobs: The Evolution of a Reckless Upstart Into a Visionary Leader*, New York: Crown Business.

Shi, David E. (2001), *The Simple Life: Plain Living and High Thinking in American Culture*, Athens: The University of Georgia Press.

Siniawer, Eiko Maruko. (2018), *Waste: Consuming Postwar Japan*, Ithaca: Cornell University Press.

Suzuki, D. T. (2011), *Essays in Zen Buddhism*, 1st series, London: Souvenir Press.

Thornhill, Jo (2019), "'I Gave Away Our Stuff': The Minimalists Doing More With Less," *The Guardian*, September 29. https://www.theguardian.com/money/2019/sep/29/i-sold-our-house-and-gave-away-our-stuff-the-minimalists-doing-more-with-less

Thomas, Joylon Baraka (2019), "Domesticity & Spirituality: Kondo Is Not an Animist," *LA Review of Books*, February 8. https://marginalia.lareviewofbooks.org/domesticity-spirituality-kondo-not-animist/

Tweed, Thomas A. (1999), "Night-Stand Buddhists and Other Creatures: Sympathizers, Adherents, and the Study of Religion," in C. Queen and D. R. Williams (eds), *American Buddhism: Methods and Findings in Recent Scholarship*, 71–90, Richmond: Curzon.

Tweed, Thomas A. (2008), "Why Are Buddhists So Nice? Media Representations of Buddhism and Islam in the United States Since 1945," *Material Religion*, 4: 91–93. doi: 10.2752/175183408X288168.

Wilson, Jeff (2014), *Mindful America: The Mutual Transformation of Buddhist Meditation and American Culture*, Oxford: Oxford University Press.

Winfield, Pamela and Steven Heine (2017), "Introduction: Zen Matters," in P. Winfield and S. Heine (eds), *Zen and Material Culture*, xii–xv, Oxford: Oxford University Press.

Wirtz, Kristina (2009), "Hazardous Waste: The Semiotics of Ritual Hygiene in Cuban Popular Religion," *Journal of the Royal Anthropological Institute*, 15 (3): 476–501. https://www.jstor.org/stable/40541695

3

The Afterlives of Butsudan

Ambivalence and the Disposal of Home Altars in the United States and Canada

Jeff Wilson

Closets Full of Altars

While Alice Unno was growing up in the small city of Lodi, California, in the 1930s, the social life of her family revolved around the Buddhist temple, but the family's true religious heart was found at home:

> It was really important to my parents that we had an *obutsudan* (Buddhist altar) at home. My parents always told us that if ever there were a fire, the altar was the first thing we had to take out of the house—that and the drawer underneath it, which contained the sūtras and important papers like birth certificates. I was always scared dusting the altar because it was so special and sacred. My mother always said you shouldn't just use an ordinary rag. There was a special cloth to clean it with. We bowed to it in the morning and evening before we went to sleep. (Unno 2008: 176)

Buddhist home altars remain common items in Japanese-American and Canadian homes over eighty years later. But while some retain their place as cherished objects, a great many butsudan no longer enjoy such privilege.

Squatting in the minister's office, lurking behind the main hall altar area, hiding in libraries and random corners, crammed into closets, basements, and garages—discarded butsudan are ubiquitous at Japanese-American/Canadian temples (see Figure 3.1). Numbers vary, but in some cases, there are so many that they present a serious storage issue for temples. Even when space is not an issue, larger concerns are provoked by their presence. How did they get here? To whom did they belong? Why were they abandoned? What should the temple do with

Figure 3.1 Old butsudan, memorial plaques (*ihai*), and even cremains huddle in a space behind the main altar area at the Toronto Buddhist Church. Photograph by the author.

them? What obligations do the temples have? What does their abandonment and subsequent disposal reveal about American/Canadian Buddhism and society?

This study draws on three sources of data to begin grappling with these questions: First, visits to dozens of temples throughout Hawai'i, the mainland United States, and Canada in order to observe the presence and storage of butsudan; second, conversations with members of Japanese-American/Canadian Buddhist communities, including structured interviews with twenty-six temple ministers and seven laypeople, numerous unstructured conversations with other ministers and lay members, and occasional attendance at butsudan seminars hosted by temples; third, collection and analysis of temple newsletters, websites, books, Dharma school materials, and other publications that discuss butsudan. Site observations took place at temples of various Buddhist denominations, but all interviewees were members of Jōdo Shinshū (often called Shin in English) Buddhist temples. Jōdo Shinshū is the largest Buddhist tradition in Japan and was the first to be brought to Hawai'i and North America.[1]

Although characterized as central to Buddhist identity and activity in Japanese-American/Canadian communities (at least for previous generations), butsudan have received very little attention in studies of Buddhism in Canada and the United States. No full treatment has ever been attempted, let alone a study of their disposal. The comparative profusion of studies on meditation and other practices in North American Buddhism is striking. This immediately suggests a larger neglect of attention to Buddhism and domestic spaces, material culture, and lived practice, as well as a preference for analysis of white Buddhist communities and forms of practice that concern white Buddhist Studies researchers (who are often members of those communities).

This near-total lack of work on butsudan outside of Japan presents a serious challenge. Patterns of butsudan ownership have not been accurately recorded over the approximately 130 years that they have been present here; shifting usages are at best anecdotally noted; and no standards of analysis or common scholarly discussions exist. Indeed, economic and material objects, processes, and perspectives in general are among the most neglected aspects of American and Canadian Buddhism by the academy.

What are Butsudan?

As a word, butsudan may be translated as "buddha (*butsu*) altar (*dan*)." They are often given the honorific "O" (great/respected). English speakers refer to them as home altars or home shrines. As an object, butsudan are domestic Buddhist altars that have been commonly found in Japanese households. Their presence became near-universal over the course of the Edo period, due to both government enforcement of butsudan use as a strategy for countering the threat of Christianity, and their promotion by Buddhist sects and butsudan artisans (Rambelli 2010: 73–4). During this time the butsudan evolved into a tall box-like cabinet with closing doors and interior shelves. Variations of size and ornamentation were dependent on cost, denominational affiliation, or the preferences and skills of the craftsperson. More than just a box, the butsudan also typically included scrolls or statues of buddhas and other spiritual figures, candles and candleholders, vases, bowls or shelves for offerings, memorial plaques (*ihai*) for deceased family members and *ihai* holders, family memorial registers (*kakochō*) and *kakochō* stands, an incense burner or bowl to receive incense, and other paraphernalia (see Figure 3.2).

Naturally enough, patterns of butsudan use and piety differed regionally, according to denominational affiliation, and by individual family or personal interest. Thus any given household could diverge from the general pattern described here. But overall, as shrines for the buddhas and ancestors, butsudan

Figure 3.2 Items left over from discarded butsudan fill the shelves of a storage room at the Lihue Hongwanji Mission in Kaua'i, Hawai'i. Photograph by the author.

held an honored place in homes. They were often kept in a separate room (*butsuma*) or in a prominent place in a common room. Here they received daily attention, ranging from a quick prayer in the morning or evening to twice-daily home services with offerings, extended sutra chanting, and participation by the whole family. Buddhist monks were invited into the home to perform memorial services at the butsudan on anniversary dates of deceased family members and during the mid-summer Ōbon festival season.

Butsudan were sites of multiple meaning. On one level, they were Buddhist objects, with a central object of worship derived from an orthodox Buddhist denomination (such as a specific buddha, Buddhist deity, Buddhist denominational founder, or mandala). Prayers to the buddhas ensured prosperity for the household and, especially, protection in the next life, as the buddhas helped spirits to reach the Pure Land, heavenly realms, or other positive rebirths.

On another level, butsudan use maintained and extended older East Asian forms of ancestor veneration. Deceased family members were enshrined in or next to the butsudan via *ihai* and similar items, becoming objects of worship. These family spirits offered protection and assistance, while their veneration enforced family ties and hierarchies, and assisted the integration of the family within generalized neo-Confucian patterns of social arrangement. Ancestor veneration variously provided the opportunity to take comfort in the face of loss, show gratitude to deceased benefactors, display and reinforce proper relationships within households, and ensure the continuance of the family line over generations.

On yet another level, the butsudan was an agent of forces beyond the household, as it knit families into programs of surveillance by the government, webs of family obligation (*danka seido*) to particular Buddhist lineages and temples, and customer-merchant-craftsman relationships with manufacturers and repairers of butsudan. Butsudan certainly also served various non-religious functions, such as display of wealth and status.

Journey to the West: Butsudan beyond Japan

It is unknown when the first butsudan was set up outside of Asia, but it is likely that it arrived in Hawai'i by the end of the nineteenth century.[2] The first migrant laborers were the Gannenmono, who arrived in the Kingdom of Hawai'i in 1868. Formal Buddhist practice did not emerge until after significant immigration began in 1885. By 1889 Buddhist temples were forming, and at some point after that butsudan began to appear in plantation homes. As Hawai'ian historian David K. Abe (2017: 142) notes, "the *butsudan* was not a part of the *Issei*'s [first generation Japanese immigrant] daily religious activities in the early years of the *Issei* period, for the reason that the newly arrived Japanese migrant laborers had not yet lost any family members in their new homeland or back in Japan." These early immigrants were also unable to afford butsudan at first, but as they gradually saved and improved their conditions, as their parents in Japan aged, and as they married and began to produce the second generation—cementing their existence as new Hawai'ians, not just migrants—butsudan began to crop up. Japanese-Hawai'ian oral lore holds that a butsudan was often the first item sent for from Japan once a family reached a certain level of basic financial security. Patterns in North America were similar, with a slight lag as it took longer for Japanese communities to be established along the West Coast.

In his study of rural Japanese-Hawai'ian coffee farmers, Abe (2017: 141) makes an observation that generally holds true for North America as well:

> Buddhism was not practiced only in the temples: it was also practiced in each household. No matter how financially constrained a family might be, they made sure to construct a *butsudan* . . . for their home. The ownership of a *butsudan* was so tied to their Japanese identity that not having a *butsudan* was considered

> impossible. This symbol of their religion was placed in the entrance to their homes and played an important part in their everyday lives. Through the act of praying and laying out offerings each day, they were able to establish a strong connection to their cultural heritage and to maintain their ethnic identity over a long period.

Here we see a fourth level of meaning that the butsudan took on after migrating to areas outside Japan. Beyond Buddhist, ancestor/family, and community functions, the post-Japan butsudan assumed a central role in displaying and reinforcing Japanese identity in Hawai'i and North America.

Constructing a butsudan from local materials was perhaps a common first step, followed eventually by the more expensive option of buying a "real" butsudan from Japan, despite (or perhaps because of) the cost involved. Such butsudan signaled strong Buddhist commitment and the attainment of relative prosperity, as well as providing a solid visual and material link to the homeland. This was especially important given that butsudan served as devices for rites and images that maintained family ties that were under strain, due to either death or dislocation. The first generation's deceased parents and ancestors honored daily at the butsudan were not present, even as ashes. They were far away in Japan, inaccessible in a literal sense but available imaginatively through the portal of the Japan-derived butsudan.

The advent of World War II and the incarceration of Japanese-Americans and Canadians was a watershed moment for butsudan, as it was for all aspects of Buddhist life. In the fearful atmosphere of government surveillance and oppression many families destroyed anything that might make them a target of suspicion, including Japanese language materials, items and artifacts from Japan, and, in some cases, butsudan (Williams 2019: 113). Others were lost when the Japanese of North America were forced into concentration camps, leaving behind most of their possessions, many of which were irretrievable after the war. In the camps, Buddhists built new butsudan out of scrap lumber. Some of these wartime butsudan still survive and are often objects of particular reverence within the community. Like the Japanese-Americans/Canadians themselves, such butsudan are survivors of a massive trauma inflicted by their own governments (Fujimura 1985: 80, 94).

Coming out of the camps, some families were able to retrieve their butsudan from storage, and a few carried camp-made butsudan with them. Others had to start all over again, saving money and eventually sending for a new butsudan from Japan. Butsudan ownership reached new heights in the postwar period, as Buddhists cultivated tight-knit, comprehensive communities that provided everything from basketball leagues, dances, beauty contests, and scouting to Dharma schools for children.

This initial burst of American and Canadian Buddhist activity began to wane in the 1970s, as the first generation disappeared and the second generation aged. The third generation—who had not experienced the camps, rarely spoke Japanese, and felt fully American/Canadian—were noticeably less committed to traditional Buddhist patterns. This would eventually contribute to the abandonment of butsudan use by large portions of the community.

Today, butsudan can still be found in many Japanese-American/Canadian homes. They can also often be found in the homes of non-Japanese people who have joined Japanese-derived Buddhist denominations, such as the Buddhist Churches of America. Though still very much a minority in most groups (Sōka Gakkai International–USA being an important exception), such converts constitute a growing proportion of the membership of historically Japanese-American and Canadian Buddhist organizations.

Current butsudan are acquired via many methods. The most common is inheritance from older family members, especially after death or when an elder is moved to a nursing home. Most new butsudan are still imports from Japan. These are often bought through middlemen, such as the Buddhist Churches of America's bookstore (based in Berkeley), certain temples, and occasional Japanese merchants, but some people do order them direct. Not all butsudan originate overseas. Occasionally, someone will commission a butsudan from a local carpenter. More often, they will buy one from a craftsperson in the Japanese-American/Canadian Buddhist community who constructs and sells butsudan as a sideline or retirement project; it is never their sole occupation. People rarely build their own; those who do are almost always professional or amateur carpenters or craftspeople, since even a relatively simple design requires considerable expertise.

Finally, some people acquire used butsudan. This is especially true of newer, non-Japanese Buddhists. It is possible to buy new and used butsudan from eBay, Amazon, and similar online stores, but second-hand butsudan are typically received from temples, all of which have a supply on hand.

Why Are Butsudan Abandoned?

Los Angeles Hompa Hongwanji Buddhist Temple is the largest Japanese-American temple in LA in terms of both its size and membership. About once a month it receives a call from the public: someone has a butsudan that they do not want, would the temple please take it?[3] Other temples throughout North America and Hawai'i receive similar requests, varying in frequency from monthly to once every few years in rough proportion to the size of the surrounding Japanese-American/Canadian population.[4] For the most part, butsudan arrive in the wake of a death. A grandparent or parent has died, and their butsudan has been orphaned. In the past (and still often in the present), such butsudan would be inherited by the (typically adult) children of the family, especially the family of the oldest son. The butsudan would then become the focus of ritual for the new generation, who thus move into the role of family head. For some families, the butsudan is a cherished religious or nostalgic object, whose care passes smoothly to the next generation. For others, it is a problem that must be dealt with, as noted by one minister:

> Almost in every case it's the third generation. The Sansei [third generation], the Baby Boomer generation. They're no longer Buddhist, and their Nisei parents passed away, and the butsudan was in the home. They knew they shouldn't just throw it in the trash, but they didn't know what to do about it. The logical place is to take it to the temple [chuckles]. At least then it's off their conscience.[5]

By far the most common reason why butsudan are turned over to temples is that the inheritors are not willing to use them. Though raised as Buddhists or in a household that included some measure of Buddhist practice, the younger generation are disinterested in maintaining domestic Buddhist traditions. Often, this indicates that they are not Buddhist. They may be Christian, whether through the influence of friends or family members—many Japanese-Americans/Canadians grow up in a mixed religious household.[6] Or they may simply be indifferent toward religion, as an American minister noted:

> In some cases, the person is something else, some version of Christianity, and in other cases the person is not religious at all, and they associate it with the other assorted Japanese knick-knacks around their parents' house. But they recognize that this thing should go to the temple and the other things can go to the local antique store.[7]

Alternatively, they may retain an interest in Buddhism but feel disinclined to continue owning and maintaining a butsudan. The association of butsudan with Japan, premodern ancestral ideas, and chanting—precisely what made then compelling to many first- and second- generation immigrants—can make them unappealing to many third- and fourth-generation Americans and Canadians. These younger Buddhists may be drawn, instead, to meditation and other aspects of supposedly modern Buddhist practice. Or they may already have their own more space-efficient and "modern" butsudan and thus have no need for additional inherited ones.

Even among Buddhist families with Buddhist children, the new heads of the family may feel that they do not know how to use a butsudan. Many older family members never provide explicit training or instruction to their children and grandchildren, assuming, instead, that proper behaviors will be picked up through observation. But these younger generations have often grown up with comparatively less exposure to Japanese customs and in an era when there is less need for temples and communities to operate as (among other things) protective ethnic enclaves. On inheriting a butsudan, they often discover that they don't know what it was that Ojiichan or Obaachan (Grandpa or Grandma) really did in front of the butsudan each morning. This is especially true in religiously blended households, where older members may keep their practices discreet in order not to cause friction with Christian relatives. Uncertain how to use the butsudan, the new generation may retain it for a while, but eventually it often ends up disposed at the nearest temple.

Lack of space also leads to butsudan abandonment. The owner of the butsudan may not have died, but, instead, become too old to care for themselves unassisted, and their move to a nursing home or the home of a son or daughter has necessitated a downsizing of possessions. If there is no one in the family willing to take the butsudan, it ends up at a temple. In some cases, the temple may provide a smaller butsudan that can be accommodated in the new dwelling, while agreeing to take the larger one. Even families that are not experiencing an immediate change in circumstances may get rid of butsudan due to the space they occupy, as a layperson explained to Hawaiʻi Public Radio:

> That was part of the reason Corday Feagins' family returned their butsudan to the Honpa Hongwanji. "Nobody had a place for it," said Feagins. "It was pretty big." The family shrine, close to six feet tall, was actually built into the wall at her grandfather's house in Salt Lake. Much of the loss, she said, is simply generational. "A lot of families don't extend the information to their children. My grandparents never talked to me about it and my children have never grown up with it," she said. "They have no idea what a butsudan is." (Solomon 2015)

As Corday Feagins' case shows, space issues dovetail with loss of interest in or knowledge about butsudan, meaning that there is little argument that such a space-intensive object should be kept.[8]

Fear can also be an important factor in the decision to turn over newly inherited butsudan. Some people see butsudan as creepy and worry that they may be haunted. This may be expressed as actual fear of ghosts or more generalized concern about *bachi* (bad luck), which is connected to Japanese spirit beliefs. Butsudan are already partially enmeshed within the weave of *bachi* beliefs, as failure to present special *mochi* (rice cakes) to the buddhas and spirits of the butsudan on the second day of the year was believed to invite *bachi* into one's life for the new year (Abe 2017: 247). The specificity of this belief has waned, but the connection of butsudan to *bachi* lingers. Since ancestral spirits are enshrined in the *ihai*, it is easy to understand where fearful attitudes may come from. One minister lamented his inability to get Japanese-Canadian families to take old butsudan: "Japanese people, immigrants from Japan, they don't want to take over someone else's butsudan. It's Japanese superstition: 'Oh, there might be a ghost or spirit in the butsudan, we don't want to take it from someone else.'"[9] Furthermore, the butsudan itself is a dark, mysterious cabinet where older Japanese members perform incomprehensible (to many younger people) rites and sometimes directly speak to the dead. Many observers have noted that in Japan belief in spirits and psychic powers has risen at the same time as adherence to orthodox Buddhist tradition has waned; "superstitious" and folk practices often do seem to persist when formal religious practice and belief have become attenuated (Ambros 2010). This is reflected in a famous scene from the popular J-horror film *Juon* (2002), where a murderous ghost emerges suddenly from a butsudan and pulls a terrified teenage girl into its dark recesses to her doom.

In short, butsudan can become useless clutter to indifferent children, evidence of blasphemous idol worship to Christian inheritors, or even objects of fear to the superstitiously inclined. This surely leads to some being thrown out by their new owners, while others try to sell them to local antique shops, online (thus their presence on eBay; Amazon butsudan are typically new), or even to temples, which always decline to purchase them. One interviewee noted a large butsudan in a local antique shop that had been converted into an entertainment system, with a television in the place where a buddha used to sit.[10]

Yet the evidence is clear that significant numbers of butsudan do not receive such ignoble treatment. Despite their new owners' wish to be rid of them, the butsudan are carefully deposited at Buddhist temples, unlike many other objects that are simply discarded. The bursting closets and cluttered basements of temples demonstrate that these unwanted objects retain a type of power over their former owners, such that they are treated with greater respect than mere rubbish. They are not important or valuable enough to command continuing presence in the home, yet they are able to marshal sufficient respect that they get a second chance at life in the care of the temple. They are neither treasure nor trash, it seems. As such, butsudan represent a type of sacred waste, identified by Irene Stengs (2014: 236) as that which must be removed, yet at the same time must not be treated as ordinary waste. Regular garbage goes to the dump, but butsudan that have outlived their purpose (most often) go to the temple.

How Do Temples React?

Temple ministers and office staff do not look forward to receiving the inevitable calls from people who wish to drop off butsudan, but neither do they react strongly to the situation. Only one minister I spoke with refused to accept butsudan, and then only because their temple is already so overloaded with extra butsudan that they have become a serious burden. This refusal thus indicates a previously liberal policy of acceptance, which will presumably return if the temple manages to deal with its backlog. All other temples accepted unwanted butsudan, whether willingly or grudgingly.

When families drop off butsudan, the ministers' top priority is usually making the family feel comfortable. Rather than chastising them for failing to maintain the family tradition, many ministers indicated that they make extra efforts to communicate that it is okay that they are abandoning their deceased loved ones' butsudan, often thanking them for showing respect to the object and the deceased family member. Ministers are accepting of the situation and make no real efforts to change it. Only one minister indicated that they had ever made even minimal attempts to convince families to keep butsudan (and these had been successful only a single time). Privately, many ministers experience a mix of happiness and sadness when old butsudan come in:

> I appreciate that people have the respect to put it someplace that it belongs. But it does make me sad that people don't want to keep it. Within my own family, I don't think anyone has an obutsudan except for me, and I inherited my grandparents' because no one wanted it. It makes me sad that no one would want it. But like I said, I appreciate that they bring it to some place instead of just throwing it out.[11]

A minority of ministers suggest that families make a modest donation (perhaps US$100 or less) when dropping off a butsudan. This is due to the burden that butsudan storage creates, as well as the general tendency toward falling temple memberships and therefore declining finances. Occasionally, if it is determined that the butsudan comes from a sect other than the temple's affiliation, the minister will suggest that it be taken to a more appropriate temple. But often the temple will simply accept these butsudan and either treat them the same as regular butsudan, or deliver them to the correct sect if they happen to be among the minority of temples located near a temple in the proper lineage.

New Homes for Old Butsudan

After butsudan are handed over, they cease to be a problem for the family and become a problem for the temple instead. How are they to handle these objects, which hover between sacred and worthless? The most immediate reaction is typically to defer any action. Butsudan are put into storage, whether in the minister's office, a corner or shelf in a semi-public space such as the library, or a less accessible spot such as the equipment and preparation area behind the altar (see Figure 3.3). There they can be safely left for a time, not bothering anyone. In only one case have I found a minister who does anything other than just putting them somewhere: this minister performs a ceremony soon after receiving an old butsudan.[12] He noted a high number of people who expressed fears of *bachi*, and thus he reassures them by saying that he will conduct a service of gratitude to the butsudan (which seems to act as an exorcism in the eyes of the owners). After the ceremony, he puts the butsudan in storage.

Temples sometimes make efforts to relocate butsudan with new owners. One makes periodic announcements at Sunday services that used butsudan are available.[13] Some use annual community events, such as bazaars, as a vehicle to give away butsudan. They might be displayed as silent auction items or simply listed as available to good homes. Temples may place advertisements of current butsudan stock in their newsletters or social media, or display them at the temple, often with a sign urging adoption. While finding examples of these practices is not difficult, it should not be overexaggerated. Adoption efforts are sporadic and may occur only every few years or more. Placement of butsudan is rarely a high priority for ministers or temples.

That said, ministers are often passively on the lookout for possible new owners. New temple members who show an interest in setting up a butsudan may be taken to see the temple's stock. Local practices differ widely on what happens next. Some temples simply give away butsudan, along with all the *butsugu* (ritual objects) associated with proper butsudan use. Others ask for a donation, with a minority going so far as to show potential owners catalogs of new butsudan as a

Figure 3.3 Retired butsudan rest in boxes at the Vista Buddhist Temple in southern California. Photograph by the author.

way of establishing just how valuable these objects potentially are. Even temples that do not ask for donations directly are usually happy to receive them. While ministers universally use the language of donation, the exchange of cash for a butsudan could be seen as a purchase. But regardless of how the exchange is interpreted, it should not be imagined that significant amounts of money are usually changing hands. No temple makes any appreciable amount of its annual budget from the trade in used butsudan.

Furthermore, the number of old butsudan successfully placed in new homes is a small fraction of the volume that are continually brought to the temples. Demand is low. Moreover, since many Japanese-American/Canadian members fear the possibility of haunting, the primary "market" for old butsudan comprises new members, especially those from non-Japanese backgrounds. Unaware of beliefs about *bachi*, their ignorance apparently makes them immune to bad luck or spirit attack.[14]

Some butsudan find new careers after they cease to be home altars. Ministers may give them to funeral homes for use when they have Japanese-American/Canadian clients.[15] In one case, a large butsudan was gifted to a local multidenominational Buddhist centre for use as an altar in their main worship/meditation space.[16] Another minister permitted a member to take away an old butsudan for use as a storage cabinet—it went from housing buddhas to housing books and tools.[17] Perhaps the most interesting story came from a temple located in a city with a significant film and television industry. This minister receives calls every few years from production assistants seeking a Buddhist altar for some scene they are filming, and the minister sells them a butsudan in a decent condition, from the temple's closet.[18] These butsudan end their affiliation with the temples by graduating to become movie stars; I can only speculate about what happens to them next.

The Ultimate Fate of Unwanted Butsudan

If all efforts to give away old butsudan fail, they face eventual destruction. This may happen when a temple collects too many and has to make room, or if a temple closes down due to diminished membership. Even at healthy temples with adequate space, all butsudan are living on borrowed time. Sooner or later, new ministers will be assigned who are less inclined to hang on to dust-covered unwanted butsudan. They were not the ones who received the butsudan in the first place and thus have no particular feeling of obligation or guilt toward the family—a family they will not know.

In Japan, the most widely acceptable method for disposing of sacred objects is burning. This precedent is also recognized widely (but far from universally) in Hawai'i and North America. When too many butsudan have gathered at a temple, the minister will often decide the time has come to respectfully destroy them. Most of the fieldwork for this chapter was conducted at temples in the Jōdo Shinshū tradition, which has no official ceremony for burning or destroying butsudan. Ministers therefore adapt other common service formats, mirroring, for instance, typical human memorial rites. As one minister put it succinctly:

> We'll have a ceremony where we burn the obutsudan and then at the same time we'll be chanting Juseige or something to express our gratitude for what it's done for the family. It would probably be either at a temple or at a person's house.[19]

This minister's ceremony falls into the most common pattern. An officiant often begins by ringing a bell, then ritually invites buddhas to come and sanctify the service (Sanbujo), chants a short sutra extract (Juseige or Sanbutsuge), and finishes by dedicating merit. As the above-mentioned interviewee indicates (and many other interviews corroborate), the intention of the ceremony is to express thankfulness for the labor provided by the butsudan over the years. No minister suggested that the ritual has any exorcistic function or that it deals with spirits in any way, nor was it thought of as an "eye-closing" rite to desanctify the butsudan or its associated items.[20] It is possible to overstate this point but, generally speaking, Jōdo Shinshū is less hospitable to the diffuse Japanese world of spirits, curses, and related practices than other forms of Buddhism. Most temples don't have dedicated fire pits, so the actual burning may take place in the parking lot or at a member's private residence. One minister takes them with him on camping trips and uses them as firewood.[21]

Another pattern of disposal is through coordinated regional efforts. In certain areas where a critical mass of Japanese Buddhist temples exists, one may take on the responsibility of holding an annual burning ceremony. For instance, in the San Francisco Bay Area this is handled by a particular Jōdo Shinshū temple. A minister explained the process:

> What we would do is set up a table in the *hondō* [main worship hall] and people would bring the things in and set them up in the *hondō*, and then we would chant Juseige in the *hondō* with all of these things. Ideally the way it would work is people would actually come with their own stuff, and we would invite them at the beginning of the ceremony to bring their stuff up, put it on the table themselves, offer incense, *gassho* [bow] before the *onaijin* [altar area], return to their seats, all together chant Juseige, then bring the things out to the back garden area where we have a dedicated campfire barbecue sort of grate thing that one of our members purchased just for this. And then we start with some papers just to get everything going, and then everything gets added to the fire and burned.[22]

Such idealized communal services often fail to fully reflect the reality of these outsourced services. Other ministers I spoke to in the area paid little attention to the burden placed on this temple; they were mostly relieved that there was somewhere they could reliably drop off their old butsudan so that they became someone else's problem. The current minister grumbled about driving home from local ministers' meetings with a pickup truck full of other temples' discarded butsudan, and yearned for a more meaningful situation:

> Ideally people are bringing their own stuff and actually participating. In recent years it sort of degenerated to people just dropping off stuff and not participating

> in the ceremony, so I'm thinking for next year I actually want to sort of crack down on that a little bit. It's like, "If you're going to do this, that's great, but it's only meaningful if you actually participate in the ceremony." I don't want this to just be the other place to take your recycling. This isn't like taking your e-waste to the recycling center.[23]

In the Los Angeles area, butsudan disposal is handled by a local Japanese-American Zen temple. The other Japanese Buddhist temples know that they can take butsudan to this temple, so they often do so, and do not bother to hold their own burning ceremonies. Attitudes range from approval of these ceremonies because burning is the appropriate disposal method to simple relief that someone else takes care of the problem.

Burning, however, presents its own challenges. California has a serious wildfire problem, which has been exacerbated by climate change and settlement patterns. In many areas private fire pits are banned, and temples have had to stop holding burning ceremonies.[24] In Los Angeles, the Zen temple uses sneaky tactics to get their work done. Since fire is illegal within the city, it hauls its annual cache of butsudan to the coast and, under the pretense of holding a beach bonfire (which is permitted), surreptitiously burns them.[25]

Another problem is presented by the butsudan themselves. Many are covered in black lacquer, and some have plastic elements incorporated into them. These materials can produce acrid black smoke which some ministers worry is bad for the environment or the health of those present at the burning. These misgivings have inhibited some from burning butsudan as they used to earlier.[26]

In the face of these issues around burning, some ministers are using another disposal method: they are throwing the butsudan out. This is not something that they usually tell members or those who drop off butsudan:

> I don't feel that sacredness about it, I would sneak it into a dumpster. . . . I would tend to sneak it into a dumpster, disguised as something, if I had to get rid of it [laughs].[27]

All the ministers who admitted to throwing out butsudan also said they took measures to do so covertly, as they feared that they would offend their members (though temple office staff are sometimes aware of the practice). This sometimes led to comical situations. Worried that homeless people would go through the trash and leave butsudan sitting kerbside in front of the temple, ministers were hiding them inside other items headed for the garbage bin; this is not an easy prospect, as even smaller butsudan are fairly sizable. Some regretted their actions:

> So this lady brought in her butsudan, and it was kind of ratty. It wasn't that ratty, but the guy who fixes our obutsudans, he said "We can't fix it," so he takes it out to the garbage bin. He just puts it in there. And then the next day the lady calls and she says she changed her mind [laughs]. Everyone just starts screaming! [laughs] We ran out there to get the obutsudan, and thank goodness the garbage guys didn't come yet and it was still at the top of the garbage. So we just pulled it out, cleaned it up, and then put it in the office. She got it back. It was just so funny, everyone just let out this scream [laughs]. Our secretary just screamed. It wasn't funny at the time, but now . . .[28]

Those who throw away butsudan don't hold services for them. These ministers expressed a range of attitudes, from treating butsudan as mere inert objects to admitting chagrin at the practice and feeling it was a shame (but doing it anyway). Some tried to offset their misgivings by at least putting the butsudan in the recycling bin, rather than simply tossing them in the garbage.

How Do Temples Contribute to the Loss of Butsudan Practices?

Nearly all the ministers I interviewed expressed some form of sadness at the decrease in butsudan usage that has caused their temples to overflow with old home altars. Yet, these same ministers were rarely making even basic efforts to try and reverse the trend. Only a small handful were actively engaged in teaching their members about the proper use and care of butsudan or about their significance in Buddhism. As one minister put it, "I probably do a very poor job of that. Probably over the time that I've been here teaching [more than ten years], I've taught about it two or three times. . . . So I would probably have to take a failing grade, an F, on that one."[29] The (mostly unconscious) expectation that older family members would teach younger ones to honor and use the butsudan persisted, despite the counter-evidence—the piles of abandoned butsudan, which were regularly added to. Another minister said, "I never thought about it. . . . To me as the resident minister of [two temples] I never taught or explained to members or non-members what the meaning of butsudan is or how we use it."[30]

In short, temples were not commonly taking the initiative in buttressing member understanding and enthusiasm around butsudan. Even when the issue was raised in my interviews, no one expressed an intention to change their habits:

guilt was readily expressed, but it appeared insufficient to effect adjustments in practice. This is ironic given that there is evidence that Buddhist ministers were effective in establishing butsudan practice among the first generations. Abe (2017: 142) quotes a Hawai'ian Nisei:

> When my father died, we didn't know anything about the Japanese altar, so I remembered the priest came to our house with this little tiny altar—not like the big ones we have these days. It was small and cheap and he set it up and taught us how to ring the bell and put the *senko* [incense] and with the *juzu* [beads] and all that . . . . [It was] lucky the priest taught us how because my mother had little experience with doing these kind of Buddhist things.

Abe (ibid.: 143) continues that it was on such occasions that ministers "educated the community about essential Japanese Buddhist spiritual beliefs." He cites another Nisei informant who, like several others, stated: "'Learning from the priest was probably a better way to learn about Buddhism than from my parents, who didn't know anything about Buddhism but just believed, with no questions. . . . . So, for me it was a good experience.'"

In earlier eras it was also common for a temple minister to call periodically on parishioners at their homes. These served as both social and religious visits, since the minister would usually begin by proceeding directly to the butsudan to show respect to the Buddha before sitting to eat snacks and drink tea with his host. Often such visits included a short home service before the butsudan led by the minister. Furthermore, it was common for ministers to be invited to conduct services at the butsudan on the memorial dates of household ancestors, as well as during the mid-summer Ōbon period. Both practices have gradually waned in the United States and Canada, to the point that many ministers now make few or no home visits.

Ministers might more aggressively suggest to their members that such visits be maintained. This could have multiple effects, including more income for the temples and ministers, which both receive an envelope of donations when a minister performs a service; tighter bonds between members and the temple and, presumably, tighter bonds with Buddhism itself; and higher retention of butsudan over the generations, since younger people would observe the use of the butsudan in the home, not just its presence, and have greater opportunities to learn about Buddhism from the visiting minister. But ministers show little interest in pushing home rituals that have fallen out of routine for their members.

Another lost opportunity is the moment when someone calls to inquire about dropping off a butsudan, or when the butsudan is actually left at the temple.

Ministers could make an effort to convince the new owners that butsudan are valuable and useful, and perhaps offer to teach them how to properly use and care for them. Instead, they almost invariably take the butsudan without any attempt at counseling or intervention.

Once an old butsudan is received, efforts to rehouse it are often sporadic and lackluster. Ministers and temples are fairly passive about their stores of butsudan, mostly reacting to requests rather than actively trying to cultivate interest among the laity in taking them. A minister may write an article about leftover butsudan once every several years, or put a few out for possible adoption at festivals, but they rarely make more dedicated efforts, such as organizing adult education workshops or sermons about butsudan.

All of this seems to be connected with a general attitude of non-evangelism. For over four generations Jōdo Shinshū and related Japanese Buddhist organizations in Hawaiʻi and North America have been strongly oriented toward serving a built-in audience of Japanese-American/Canadian Buddhists. This guaranteed membership has been a boon and a handicap. In earlier eras it meant that Buddhist organizations had little need to proselytize their traditions. Given that Japanese Buddhist groups were often under suspicion, sometimes outright persecution, from the white community, this non-evangelizing stance was helpful in minimizing friction with outsiders. But the complacency bred by such (temporary) solid membership foundations, combined with larger social forces (discussed later), has sometimes left these temples without the knowledge, practices, and outlooks necessary to thrive in changed circumstances. The heaps of abandoned butsudan are only the most visible sign of a more general long-term decline that these communities are experiencing.

Shifting Social Patterns and the Loss of Butsudan Traditions

Although ministers are doing little to keep butsudan traditions alive, there are also larger social patterns at work that make any effort to keep butsudan in homes a steep hill to climb. Even in Japan, modern times present complex challenges for butsudan. As Hannah Gould (2019: 202–3) explains, urbanization, changing family structures, and secularization have weakened the household lineage system "via which the butsudan, family grave, and obligation to care for the ancestors are inherited." The decreasing numbers of children born to inherit butsudan increasingly lack interest and knowledge, with the consequence that "*butsudan* are increasingly becoming surplus domestic goods" (ibid.).

All of these factors are also at play within Japanese-American/Canadian communities, and there are ways in which the North American/Hawaiʻian situation exacerbates or further contributes to these trends. Butsudan traditions have mostly been passed down through the family. This process operated smoothly enough in earlier periods when families were relatively intact. But in the postwar period dramatic shifts occurred in family patterns in the United States and Canada. Where previously multiple generations often lived in the same home or nearby, the trend toward nuclear families increased significantly. Thus young family members typically grew up with less exposure to their grandparents, who were often the ones to maintain butsudan traditions and demonstrate them to their children and grandchildren. Beyond the simple breakup of multigeneration homes, increased mobility within Canadian and, especially, American life meant that young parents often established their households in completely different parts of the country, away from their parents and natal communities. Thus the family butsudan, which typically resided with the oldest generation, became an unfamiliar object rather than the focus of nostalgia as in earlier eras. Rising divorce rates further complicated things, so that children and grandchildren sometimes had even less engagement with Buddhist parents and grandparents.

The relative breakdown of the Japanese-American/Canadian community is a further specific part of the equation. After decades of intense discrimination, Asian-Americans/Canadians in general and Japanese-Americans/Canadians in particular made significant gains in mainstream social acceptance in the postwar years. This was the result of a combination of rising concern over civil rights, admiration for military contributions by Japanese-Americans, Japan's role as a close American ally in the Pacific, greater travel and communication between North America and Japan, continual efforts by Japanese-Americans/Canadians to demonstrate their loyalty and adherence to mainstream values (including by conversion to Christianity in many cases), and other factors.

On the whole, this had felicitous effects for Japanese-Americans/Canadians, whose lives became measurably easier. But for Buddhism it was a (barely discerned) challenge. Lowered persecution meant fewer pressures keeping Japanese-Americans/Canadians within their ethnic communities, while greater accessibility to mainstream professions, social clubs, and other institutions meant expanded opportunities beyond those communities. Outmarriage became a trickle and then a flood, with Japanese-Americans/Canadians the most likely of all Asian-American groups to marry outside their ethnicity (Qian et al. 2001). This had a particular effect on Buddhists, as spouses were unlikely to be Buddhist, and Christians tended to be more insistent on raising children in their religion. Those who did not abandon Buddhism altogether nonetheless often made significant concessions, such as hiding their butsudan or Buddha images in their bedrooms or closets in order not to upset non-Buddhist family or friends.[31] This privatized butsudan use, removing it from the shared family sphere and preventing it from being handed down to the next generation.

Even when spouses did not insist on Christianity, many mixed families dealt with potential conflict by raising children with no particular religion. At the same time, North American and Hawai'ian society were slowly creeping toward greater secularization. Religious adherence and church attendance have plunged for mainline religious institutions across the board, whether Christian, Jewish, or Buddhist (Clark and MacDonald 2017). Religious institutions have lost much of their power and a significant amount of their role in the lives of many Americans (and an even greater percentage of Canadians), while secular entertainment and social opportunities have blossomed, presenting intense challenges to Sunday morning religious activities. It bears noting that the least religious region of North America/Hawai'i—the West—is also the place where most Japanese temples are found (Roof and Silk 2005).

All of this adds up to serious disruption to the internal community and larger social patterns that kept Buddhist institutions and families flourishing. Even as Buddhism has gained ever more attention from the mainstream as an attractive spiritual choice, its oldest American and Canadian communities have withered under the pressure of cultural and demographic change. Blows to Buddhism affect butsudan use, as does the relative disintegration of families. Abandoned butsudan are collateral damage of the reordering of American and Canadian life.

Conclusion

What does attention to butsudan and their declining fortunes reveal about American/Canadian Buddhism? There are at least four takeaways. The first is that abandoned butsudan reveal the importance of a seriously overlooked aspect of Buddhism in North America/Hawai'i: its domestic presence, as well as the waning power of older domestic Buddhist traditions. Butsudan are part of a largely extra-temple set of practices and customs that have escaped the notice of previous historians and anthropologists, who have focused on temples and meditation centres. How ordinary Buddhists practice (and do not practice) their religion in everyday life demands greater attention.

Second, noting the surfeit of butsudan at temples reveals the presence and historical importance of material culture in North American/Hawai'ian Buddhism. This is an aspect of Buddhist practice and life largely neglected by earlier studies. By looking at temple-stored butsudan and understanding how they got there, many other aspects of American/Canadian Buddhism come into focus. Butsudan suffer now precisely because they were such an assumed part of earlier American/Canadian Buddhist life that they needed little marketing and reinforcement from institutions. Additionally, looking at how temples handle old butsudan reveals the presence of a larger variety of abandoned objects. Temples also receive books, *nenju/juzu* (rosaries), *monto shikisho* (member's stoles), *ihai*, *omamori* (protective talismans), and other material traces of Buddhism. These too have to be dealt with in some fashion, but I was initially unaware of their volume. Only butsudan were large and distinctive enough to catch my eye in the back rooms of the temples I visited.

Third, while temples receive a variety of objects, there is nonetheless something unique about butsudan. Butsudan enshrine deceased members of the family, as well as buddhas who act as quasi-ancestors. They become more than inanimate objects: they are invested with presence, and the vocabulary around them reflects this. Turned-in butsudan are spoken of as "orphaned," and members are urged to "adopt" them (see Figure 3.4). Successful adoptees are described as being placed into "loving homes" ('Butsudan Adoption Program' 2015). Other abandoned items are not treated with such affective language, and temples do not run advertisements urging members to take home excess *nenju*, *monto shikisho*, and so on. Ministers were significantly more likely to throw other objects away, but often stopped short of disposing of butsudan without at least some effort to place them with new families. They were also more likely to hold burning ceremonies for butsudan, despite the greater effort it takes to destroy large and sometimes chemically dangerous home altars.

Butsudan thus reveal the intriguing grey zone between the holy and the mundane. As Caroline Hirasawa and Benedetta Lomi (2018: 219) put it: "The afterlives of sacred objects are especially useful in understanding how the lines between the sacred and the ordinary can be blurred or redrawn." In many cases, butsudan lack adequate value for families to keep them. Yet, these cherished objects of their ancestors retain sufficient sacredness or meaning that families seek as their final resting place the middle ground of the temple, which is neither too close (as is the home), nor too far (as is the dump). Or for some, they are sufficiently scary for a temple to be brought in to handle the

Figure 3.4 Orphaned butsudan cry out to be adopted at the Mōʻiliʻili Hongwanji Mission in Honolulu, Hawaiʻi. Photograph by the author.

dangerous forces they contain, even though the families otherwise have little use for Buddhism.

What we have here is a journey towards waste occasioned by a transformation in value. When a butsudan is purchased or homemade, a level of value is placed upon the object itself, the uses to which it may be put, and the system in which it and its uses are embedded. The ritual work that owners reproduce (regularly or irregularly) animates this value, so that it moves from being latent, potential, and/or symbolic to becoming temporarily active.

If the butsudan lives long enough, it may outlast the life spans of those who normatively value it and are willing to activate its possible value through use. As the systems of value in which the butsudan was previously enmeshed deteriorate and die off, the butsudan as an object risks dying as well—often quite literally—as physical destruction is ultimately the fate of many butsudan. Yet, even when the standard value of a butsudan has deteriorated, it often retains vestiges of its earlier values, such that it is not easily disposed of. Buddhism as a formal system of meanings may have passed away, but so-called superstition endures; those who used the butsudan may no longer be around to value it, but because they used to use it, it retains historic value as a relic of those lost loved ones. In other words, it ceases to have value as a Buddhist object but potentially acquires some degree of nostalgic value due to its association with former owners, or a degree of anti-value as the abode of spirits, that has to be dealt with carefully.

This mirrors the possible death and social dislocation process for humans in Japan, who may fall from memory after death and become *muen botoke* (spirits without connections). Here, *muen* butsudan are created. Like other ghosts, they must be treated with respect and caution (see Figure 3.5). Thus the butsudan sometimes avoids its immediate termination; if it is laid to final rest, this is often done in a respectful manner, moving it into the realm of the invisible sainted ancestors. Occasionally it is reborn, when someone is willing to invest it with Buddhist value and perform the necessary labor.

Figure 3.5 *Muen* butsudan linger in a storehouse at Wahiawa Hongwanji Mission in central O'ahu, where they migrated when the Kahuku Hongwanji Mission closed in 2012 due to declining membership. Photograph by the author.

The presence of anti-value in the equation of whether to retain, scrap, or politely turn a butsudan over to a temple is important. As demonstrated by the abandonment of butsudan at temples rather than the dump, negative value can be as powerful a motivator as positive value. Anti-value produces feelings of fear, anxiety, repulsion, or other negative emotions. Though coded negatively by Buddhism, these emotions function effectively to deliver formerly sacred Buddhist objects to the care of temples, from whence they have the possibility of rebirth.

Finally, butsudan as rejected material objects allow us to see how immaterial aspects of Buddhism are changing in the context of American and Canadian society. Asian-American Studies scholar Jane Naomi Iwamura (1996: 162) observes that dominant American culture was a poor fit for Japanese-based ancestor practices, such as those that take place at the typical butsudan: "Ancestor veneration did not fit well with a society which espoused human independence, understood itself spiritually as 'one nation under God,' organised itself according to 'nuclear family' units, and spoke of religious locations mainly in terms of 'churches.'" In the context of the current project, this suggests that the more "Americanized" each generation of Japanese-Americans became, the less space there was for comfortable maintenance of inherited butsudan practices. Therefore, the butsudan themselves were of ever lesser value. From this we can discover that there is a process whereby certain practices and ideas are identified as waste, leftovers from a previous period that are now evaluated as unwanted and to be jettisoned in some fashion. This leads to the transformation of objects associated with those practices and ideas into physical waste. In other words, the accumulation of butsudan as objects at temples is a visible sign indicative of a larger reworking in which invisible concepts and worldviews are examined, altered, and sometimes discarded.

Notes

1 Jōdo Shinshū is represented in the United States and Canada by five denominational organizations; in order of decreasing size they are the Buddhist Churches of America, Hompa Hongwanji Mission of Hawai'i, Jodo Shinshu Buddhist Temples of Canada, Higashi Honganji Hawai'i District, and Higashi Honganji North America District. A handful of independent Jōdo Shinshū temples also exist in the United States.

2 Butsudan are commonly found in conjunction with death registers, spirit tablets, and similar items that convey traceable names and dates. These help to date family butsudan, to an extent. In my temple rummagings, the earliest memorialized

person I found was born in 1823 in Japan and died (date unknown) in Hawai'i. The earliest death date I found was in 1901, for a four-year-old girl who died and was memorialized, also in Hawai'i. Both dates were inscribed on paraphernalia never encountered apart from butsudan. It is possible that the tablet for the 1901 death was not produced until later, as it was found with several other tablets that were clearly produced in the 1930s. Oral history accounts indicate widespread butsudan use by at least the 1920s, if not significantly sooner. Note that here I am focusing only on persons clearly memorialized via butsudan usage. In my exploration of Japanese-Hawai'ian cemeteries I have encountered gravestones that are much earlier than this, but they do not necessarily imply the use of butsudan.

3 Interview, April 18, 2019.

4 Temples are the natural places for people to turn to when they want to get rid of a butsudan in a respectful manner. In Japan, there are additional possibilities, such as butsudan retailers and specialist disposal companies. Lacking such options, Americans and Canadians typically have to interact with religious, rather than secular, organizations. For more on the Japanese companies, see Gould 2019: 197–220.

5 Interview, January 17, 2019.

6 Here I am speaking of inherited butsudan; among the Jōdo Shinshū interviewees for this research, there were no stories of people dropping off their own butsudan because they are no longer Buddhist, but this does happen in some cases. It seems to be particularly common in Sōka Gakkai, which has a high rate of out-conversion, although Sōka Gakkai butsudan are often abandoned because the owner has moved into a more established Buddhist sect, rather than because they have left Buddhism. Among the many elements of Sōka Gakkai that are unique, the group has a very distinctive butsudan design that does not easily accommodate non-Sōka Gakkai images and practices. Such high emphasis is placed on butsudan use that disgruntled ex-members may see rejection of their Sōka Gakkai butsudan as the key action in their severing of ties with the group. A small number of these abandoned Sōka Gakkai butsudan end up at Shin and other temples.

7 Interview, April 17, 2019.

8 Very uncommonly something entirely different is going on, such as an old butsudan being abandoned because a nicer new one has been acquired. Such upgrading used to be a significant phenomenon. As Abe (2017: 245) notes, most second generation Japanese immigrants (Nisei) owned a butsudan, which was generally upgraded twice, sometimes three times, "over the course of several decades." Each time the old butsudan was replaced with a bigger one "with more gold." But that era has long passed, and it is rare now for an older butsudan to be replaced with a newer, more elaborate one. As to what happened to the unwanted cheaper butsudan in earlier periods, at present I have no evidence to confirm their fates. My initial speculation is that most were donated to temples and subsequently burned. Given that most

families upgraded their butsudan, I doubt that there would have been much demand for smaller, used ones. From what I have seen, the enormous number of old butsudan currently in temple back rooms arrived relatively recently, not generations ago.

9 Interview, January 10, 2019a.

10 Interview, June 16, 2019.

11 Interview, April 15, 2019.

12 Interview, April 16, 2019a.

13 Interview, January 28, 2019.

14 Gould and others have already noted similar dynamics in Japan. See Gould 2019: 214.

15 Interview, January 10, 2019b.

16 Interview, April 16, 2019b.

17 Interview, April 16, 2019a.

18 Interview, January 10, 2019b.

19 Interview, April 16, 2019b.

20 However, one minister did say that he is aware that some people have fears of spirits; he reassures them that the temple will handle the butsudan in a way that eliminates any supernatural threat, although he himself dismisses the idea that the brief sutra chanting that he performs has any such actual power or purpose. Interview, April 16, 2019a.

21 Interview, January 10, 2019b.

22 Interview, April 17, 2019a. Juseige is a short sutra extract, often used in North American weekly services and short memorial services. The Amidakyō is used for more formal memorials and the Shōshinge for funerals. Neither is ever used for butsudan.

23 Ibid.

24 Interview, April 17, 2019b.

25 Interview, April 18, 2019.

26 Interview, April 17, 2019a.

27 Interview, April 16, 2019c.

28 Interview, April 18, 2019.

29 Interview, January 10, 2019a.

30 Interview, January 10, 2019b.

31 Interview, April 16, 2019d.

References

Abe, David K. (2017), *Rural Isolation and Dual Cultural Existence: The Japanese-American Kona Coffee Community*, Cham, Switzerland: Palgrave Macmillan.

Ambros, Barbara (2010), "Vengeful Spirits or Loving Spiritual Companions? Changing Views of Animal Spirits in Contemporary Japan," *Asian Ethnology*, 69 (1): 35–67.

"Butsudan Adoption Program," *Guiding Light*, November 2015: 13.

Clark, Brian and Stuart MacDonald (2017), *Leaving Christianity: Challenging Allegiances in Canada Since 1945*, Kingston, ON: McGill-Queen's University Press.

Fujimura, Bunyu (1985), *Though I Be Crushed: The Wartime Experiences of a Buddhist Minister*, Los Angeles: The Nembutsu Press.

Gould, Hannah (2019), "Caring for Sacred Waste: The Disposal of *Butsudan* (Buddhist Altars) in Contemporary Japan," *Japanese Religions*, 43 (1&2): 197–220.

Hirasawa, Caroline and Benedetta Lomi (2018), "Modest Materialities: The Social Lives and Afterlives of Sacred Things in Japan," *Japanese Journal of Religious Studies*, 45/2: 217–25.

Iwamura, Jane Naomi (1996), "Homage to Ancestors: Exploring the Horizons of Asian American Religious Identity," *Amerasia Journal*, 22/1: 162–7.

Juon (2002), [Film] Dir. Takashi Shimizu, Japan: Pionner LDC, Nikkatsu, Oz Co., Xanaduex, in association with Aozora investment.

Qian, Zenchao, Sampson Lee Blair and Stacey D. Ruf (2001), "Asian American Interracial and Interethnic Marriages: Differences by Education and Nativity," *International Migration Review*, 35 (2): 557–86.

Rambelli, Fabio (2010), "Home Buddhas: Historical Processes and Modes of Representation of the Sacred in the Japanese Buddhist Family Altar (*Butsudan*)," *Japanese Religions*, 35 (1&2): 63–86.

Roof, Wade Clark and Mark Silk, (eds) (2005), *Religion and Public Life in the Pacific Region: Fluid Identities*, Walnut Creek, CA: AltaMira Press.

Solomon, Molly (2015), "Why Traditional Japanese Altars are Vanishing with the Times," *Hawai'i Public Radio*, December 31. https://www.hawaiipublicradio.org/post/why-traditional-japanese-altars-are-vanishing-times (accessed January 27, 2019).

Stengs, Irene (2014), "Sacred Waste," *Material Religion*, 10 (2): 235–38.

Unno, Alice (2008), "Growing Up Buddhist," in Peter N. Gregory and Suzanna Mrozik (eds), *Women Practicing Buddhism: American Experiences*, 175–87, Boston: Wisdom Publications.

Williams, Duncan Ryūken (2019), *American Sutra: A Story of Faith and Freedom in the Second World War*, Cambridge, MA and London, England: The Belknap Press of Harvard University Press.

4

The Great Heisei Doll Massacre

Disposal and the Production of Ignorance in Contemporary Japan

Fabio Gygi

The Picture That Never Was

"Don't take any pictures of the dolls in the garbage truck!" It was only this warning from a senior member of the dollmakers' guild that made me aware of what I was waiting for. After the monks who had performed the memorial service for dolls (*ningyō kuyō*) returned to the temple, the few participants and spectators left. I was the only person remaining, curious as to what would happen next. Most helpers were standing around indecisively and I noticed a lot of sideways glances directed toward me, making me quite uncomfortable; I was definitely an undesired presence at this stage. I decided to walk up to the main hall of the temple to create some distance.

Earlier that day I had observed several volunteers of the dollmakers' guild in turquoise *happi*—the colorful overcoats that indicate group identity at Japanese festivals—painstakingly arrange an endless number of dolls on a makeshift table made from cardboard boxes and covered with a large piece of red felt. The effect was quite fetching: the temple gate and its guardian lion were surrounded by a sea of dolls dressed in auspicious red and orange colors. Small groups of dolls from the displays for the doll festival (*hina-ningyō*) consorted with larger, more realistic Ichimatsu dolls, stuffed animals locked horns with the helmets of warrior dolls, elaborately dressed decorative dolls (*ishō-ningyō*) associated with plastic dolls clad in Western ball gowns, and four identical Peko-chans with protruding tongues (mascots for the Fujiya bakery) congregated with a hairdresser apprentice's head. The variety reflected the continuing importance of dolls as

Figure 4.1 Dolls waiting for their memorial service at Mongakuji, October 2019. Photograph by the author.

nationally coded material culture: as toys, decorative objects, paraphernalia for festivals, and markers of local identities, craftsmanship, and tradition.

The occasion was a *ningyō kuyō*, a memorial service for dolls that are no longer wanted. This ritual of disposal is currently practiced at temples and shrines all over Japan, usually in spring and autumn. The Japanese term *kuyō* is derived from the Sanskrit word *pūjā*, and refers to a devotional offering to the Buddha, the Dharma (the Buddhist law), and the Sangha (the community of practitioners). As Ambros (2012: 6) has pointed out, the merit generated through such offerings is dedicated to the spirits of the dead; such rituals are thus closely linked to funerals in Japan. The performance of such rites for inanimate objects poses interesting questions for historians and anthropologists alike. Are such rites proof of an ancient animistic worldview in Japan? Do they indicate that "the Japanese" do not make the same distinctions between humans and nonhumans as Westerners do? While such questions and categories tend to frame discussions around Shinto and techno-animism in Japan (see Allison 2006; Jensen and Blok 2013; Richardson 2016; see also Gygi 2018 for a critique), the historical and folkloristic record shows that most of these memorial rites are a modern innovation, often driven by local craft guilds rather than by ancient beliefs about the soul of things.[1]

What is remarkable about the *ningyō kuyō* is that it involves the use of an established Buddhist ritual[2] to facilitate the disposal of objects that are not apparently "sacred" (in contrast to the objects discussed by Abrahms-Kavunenko; Holmes-Tagchungdarpa; Wilson this volume). This, in fact, works to the benefit of all parties involved: temple priests, considered funerary specialists in Japan, can open up a new stream of revenue; the dollmakers' guilds, who organize the events, acquire added respectability through association with venerable temples; and the participants can rest assured that the disposal is undertaken with the necessary ceremonial flourish. By briefly drawing the dolls into the halo of a religious institution, they can later be disposed of, thus extending Buddhism's dominion over secular material culture.

The aim of this chapter is to investigate the performative functions of these rites: What did they *do* in the eyes of participants, officiating monks, members of the local crafts guilds, and random visitors? How did they facilitate disposal? How did they turn cherished objects into disposable rubbish? It is based on fieldwork carried out in the autumn of 2019, during which I traveled to observe such rites every weekend in the Greater Tokyo area, Osaka, and Kyoto. On one bright autumn morning, I had ventured out into Saitama, the province adjacent to Tokyo, to visit the Mongakuji temple,[3] nestled in the neglected suburbia at the fringes of the capital, among corrugated iron walkways offering vistas of nothing but the endlessly repeating cluttered cityscape typical of such sleeper towns in Japan.

After the priest of the temple had chanted passages from Pure Land Buddhist scripture and the few participants had offered incense on the makeshift altar, the official part of the proceedings was over. A lull followed. The volunteers from the dollmakers' guild idly walked around and commented on different dolls. One white-haired member wound up all the wind-up dolls he could find; melancholic music box melodies filled the air in a last lament, a swansong. When I returned from the main hall, I saw that the volunteers had all taken off their *happi* coats. Did they not want to make the *happi* dirty? Was it simply too hot? Or did they no longer want to be recognizable as members of the dollmakers' guild when disposing of the dolls? Other than two men who were maskless, everybody wore masks and white work gloves. Male volunteers started removing metal horns from warrior dolls. This was the start of the rubbish separation (*gomi bunbetsu*): metal parts were collected separately since they were classed as "resources" (*shigen*) and would therefore be recycled. One of the younger guys suddenly shouted: "Ok, let's do it!" (*dewa yarimashou!*). The volunteers started opening the cardboard boxes that had served as display tables. The red felt was ripped from under the dolls, and they tumbled into the boxes; those that fell off the tables were picked up and thrown in. It took less than thirty minutes for the carefully arranged sea of dolls to disappear. To my surprise, a blue local authority Isuzu rubbish truck reversed up to the temple gate, and two rubbish men helped to tip the boxes in. Each time the compressing mechanism was triggered, an avalanche of doll debris tumbled down the loading maw of the truck. Apart from the volunteers I was the only witness; this is when I was warned not to take a picture.

What follows revolves around the picture that was not taken, that could not have been taken. Although I did not realize it at that moment, my interpretation of the *ningyō kuyō* is drawn more from this interdiction than from the ethnographic description of the rite and my interviews with participants and volunteers. As an ethnographer, I was conflicted between my desire to know the truth about the fate of the dolls, and the volunteers' wish not to divulge that truth. How ethical was it to do ethnographic research that publicly revealed what the participants who had brought their dolls to the rite likely knew but chose to forget? When I wrote my field notes that evening, I returned to this prohibition again and again. What was it that I was not supposed to document? It had been okay to take pictures up to that point. Why had I desired to take a picture of the "forbidden moment"? As I imagined what such a photograph would look like, it was vivid in my mind's eye: the delicate features of a tiny *hina* doll in the process of being destroyed in the maw of a cold, thoughtless machine; the stark contrast between the world of tradition, culture, and refinement, and the category of that which is without value: rubbish, dirt, trash. The particular punctum of such an image is the incommensurability of these two worlds: the world of rubbish that we are happy to distance ourselves from, and the world of dolls, of the home, the familiar, and the beautiful. Such a picture would be incongruous and jarring, inducing feelings of pity, and suggesting violence done to the doll or innocence destroyed. This is precisely why many of my interlocutors said that they could not bear to simply throw away their beloved dolls with the rubbish. The truth that the ritual renders invisible, then, is that the dolls end up simply being thrown away. To show this would make the ritual ineffective as a conduit to disposal. We pay others to do what we do not want to do in order to avoid facing our own cruelty, indifference, and callousness.

The Production of Ignorance

What does the memorial service for dolls do? What purpose does it serve that could explain its popularity since the beginning of the Heisei era (1989–2019)?

My argument in this chapter is that the rite can be fruitfully understood as a new social form that produces ignorance concerning the fate of these dolls, and that this ignorance enables their former owners to maintain certain notions about objects, consumption, themselves, and national culture. Since ignorance is commonly understood to mean the absence of knowledge, it may seem counterintuitive to grasp it as something actively produced. It might also be taken as an affront against ethnographic decency to argue that our informants are actively fostering ignorance when they are supposed to be the "cultural experts" to whom we, as anthropologists, defer. Such an understanding, however, is predicated on the unsustainable assumption that our informants are as interested as we are in the pursuit of some pure form of knowledge (Chua 2009). Mair et al. (2012: 2) make ignorance itself the ethnographic object, starting from the premise that "under certain circumstances, ignorance has a substance of its own, as the product of specific practices, with effects that are distinct from the effects of the lack of knowledge to which the ignorance in question corresponds." As they assert, "sometimes people work to produce these states of ignorance in themselves, sometimes they produce them in other people" (ibid.: 7). This can make itself felt in a variety of registers: it may manifest as "structural ignorance" (Proctor and Schiebinger 2008: 3) on the side of bureaucracies and institutions, or as "strategic ignorance" on the side of individual actors vis-à-vis social and institutional demands (Gershon 2000).

The production of ignorance can be framed as a psychological, cultural, and political phenomenon. In the case of the memorial services for dolls, the psychological aspect of "closure by ignorance" has effects that radiate into the social, cultural, and (finally) political sphere. The ignorance produced is both a desired good and a reflection of wider contradictions in Japanese relations to objects, self-images, processes of consumption, and essentialist ideas about Japanese culture. In Buddhist doctrine, "ignorance" or "unwisdom" is that which actively obstructs insight into the essential emptiness of all phenomena. In the example under discussion the ignorance is similarly productive: it keeps things in place that otherwise would fall apart.

Despite local variations, there is a clearly discernible order of proceedings for a memorial service for dolls, whether it takes place at a temple or at a Shinto shrine. At the latter they are usually called *ningyō kansha-sai* ("Doll Gratitude Festival") or *ningyō shōten-sai* ("Doll Ascension Festival") to avoid the more somber and funerary associations of the Buddhist term *kuyō*. Many of my informants did not distinguish between the two, however, and used *ningyō kuyō* as a general term. For the purposes of this chapter I stick to the

Figure 4.2 Altar at the Mongakuji with paper substitutes (*hitogata*), incense burners, and ritual offerings. Photograph by the author.

Buddhist terminology and to the order of service observed at Mongaku temple. The historical record suggests that the Buddhist form was the model for the corresponding Shinto ceremony, which gained traction only in the 1980s, quite possibly in imitation of the success of Buddhist rites.[4]

The participants bring their dolls, pay the fee (starting from 3,000 Yen or about twenty-eight US dollars) at the makeshift reception marquee, and write their names on small pieces of paper shaped like a rudimentary human silhouette called *hitogata*.[5] These are then put on the altar together and are later burnt by the temple in lieu of the dolls. This substitution is widely practiced for two main reasons: first, it would be difficult to burn all of the dolls given the increase in their numbers since the 1990s; second, many of the more recent dolls contain plastic parts or polyester clothing that releases toxic fumes when burnt. Environmental concerns led to a reshaping of the ritual in the 1980s and

1990s (Tanaka 2005). During my fieldwork it was common practice to burn only a selected number of old dolls made from wood, paper, and silk together with the wooden or paper *hitogata*, while most of the dolls were disposed of via compactor trucks in a landfill. The Doll Burning Ceremony at the Ōi Shrine, held in April in Shimada, Shizuoka Prefecture, was the only rite I observed where all the dolls were burnt. The smell of burning plastic was overpowering and the priest confided to me that they receive complaints from neighbors every year.

Apart from the eighteen volunteers from the dollmakers' guild, who were all wearing the turquoise *happi*, there were only nine other attendants: a mother with her two grown-up children, a woman and a man who offered incense and wandered off, an elderly mother with her grown-up son who brought a large standing doll that looked fairly new, an older man who took pictures on his digital camera, and myself. They waited until their dolls were arranged and looked at the display, most of them taking a last picture. Many of the participants left before the service started at 1:30 p.m.

In front of the arranged dolls stood an altar covered in green felt, the main pieces of which were a memorial tablet (*ihai*) with the inscription *ningyō kuyō-i* written under the Sanskrit syllable AUM, an incense burner, and a metal box with a white banderole inscribed with the six syllables *Namu Amida Butsu* (Hail to Amitābha Buddha). Two burning candles, two incense offering boxes, and offerings of salt, a radish, tangerines, a whole sea bream, and a bouquet of flowers decorated the altar.

The abbot of Mongakuji then appeared in the robes of the Pure Land sect of Buddhism and burned some incense before launching into the Buddhist service (*hōyō*) by intonating a sutra, which contained several passages in Sanskrit. There were two interactive elements: the offering of incense at the altar and the chanting of ten repetitions of the prayer *Namu Amida Butsu*, the core practice of the Pure Land sect.[6] The head of the dollmakers' guild briefly addressed the few stragglers, thanking everyone for participating. He was the first person to offer incense. We all then offered incense in pairs. The crows in the pine trees, as if participating in the chanting, crowed in unison.

What happens during a *ningyō kuyō* in symbolic or cognitive terms? Interviewing participants, members of the dollmakers' guild, and officiating priests at different rites, I collected a range of different, sometimes even contradictory, interpretations. As far as I could observe, the Buddhist services were not specific to the *ningyō kuyō*; that is, the sutras chanted and offerings made were part of a standard repertoire (differing slightly according to sect). The specific connection to the dolls was usually made in a brief address to the congregation by the priest or a ranking member of the local dollmakers' guild, which usually conveyed a sense of gratitude toward the dolls.

Priests were generally quite reluctant to elaborate on the details of the ritual, which was usually a standard Buddhist service with some elements of funerary practice added to it. The priests I talked to were careful to frame the rite as an expression of gratitude to the dolls who had been playmates and companions, without elaborating on its more metaphysical aspects. Participants, on the other hand, sometimes took their cue from the similarity of *ningyō kuyō* to funerary rites and used religious phrasing to explain to themselves and others what happens: "The dolls are burnt and become buddhas."

However, the ritual's emphasis is on orthopraxy over orthodoxy. While many participants told me that they were saying "thank you to the dolls" when bowing, when I asked them about their interior state of mind when offering incense, the majority characteristically answered that they had tried to catch a glimpse of the person before them and to imitate them as closely as possible. Do you bow first and then bring your hands together? Do you bow once or twice?[7] Do you take the incense with the right hand and raise it to your forehead or not?[8] Do you offer incense once or twice?[9] The ritual does not require verbal elaboration, internal states of mind, or, indeed, particular beliefs about what is happening. That is not to say that participants lacked feelings of gratitude or certain beliefs regarding the dolls, but these were not necessary for the ritual to work.

At the heart of the ritual is the act of making the doll disappear. This is achieved in two ways, which I conceptualize here as "vertical" and "horizontal" disposal. In the former, the dolls are burnt and the smoke rises into the sky, whereas the ashes fall to the ground. Implicit in this is the understanding that the emotional aspect of the doll rises with the smoke into heaven in an example of sacrificial logic. The burning is viewed by the former owner in an act of dramatic witnessing; the doll literally ceases to exist in front of their very eyes. As already noted, this is rarely practiced today due to the toxic fumes caused by the burning of plastic and polyester. The horizontal method works by removing the doll from the field of vision of the observer without destroying it. Needless to say, this solution requires niftier footwork than a final and dramatic burning. The contradiction that the ritual must address is that between the wish to get rid of the doll and its enduring presence as a material object. The only way to do this is to obfuscate the materiality of the object. Like mass-produced buddha statues that are mere matter *before* consecration (Brox 2019), the dolls *after* the ritual return to the state of empty vessels. This is achieved by clever manipulation of the temporal and spatial frames of the ritual itself.

It is useful to think of these ritual frames in terms of Goffman's (1974) frame analysis, as constitutive of experience and, thus, of reality. There is a vast literature on ritual frames and framing in anthropology, only a small part of which I can draw on here. Bruce Kapferer (2006: 516) notes that "the framing of [. . .] ritual action is created by the action itself and can operate as an invisible membrane surrounding the action, momentarily setting it off from the ongoing flow of life yet simultaneously pragmatically engaged with it." More abstract elaborations based on Bateson's (1972) take on the frame emphasize the mind and metacognition (see, for example, Handelman 2004; Houseman 2012; Robbins and Sumiala 2016). My analysis moves in the opposite direction toward the concrete materiality of the frame. In this, I am following Goffman's (1974: 250–1) emphasis on the frame as a device that transforms reality:

> Activity framed in a particular way—especially collectively organized activity—is often marked off from the ongoing flow of surrounding events by a special set of boundary markers or brackets of a conventionalized kind. These occur before and after the activity in time and may be circumspective in space; in brief, there are temporal and spatial brackets.

These brackets, also called "transformation devices" by Nelson (2012), mark the ritual frame. The location of the *ningyō kuyō* at a temple or a shrine means that the spatial bracketing uses an already well-established sacred space to operate within, together with a fully developed ritual language that is adapted to the case at hand. There is a particular flow to these proceedings that is marked by temporal brackets: the entering of the priests, often in the form of a procession from the main hall; bells, gongs, and other instruments that indicate the beginning; and ritual incantations that focus the attention of the participants toward what is about to happen. The most important transformation devices for the *ningyō kuyō*, however, are the temporal breaks and the material devices that allow for a "break in presence" (Rettie 2004: 120) in the sense that the involvement of those present is directed away from the material presence of the dolls, which enables a shift of the ritual frame.

Callon (1998) points out that the framing that Goffman envisions can be understood in two diametrically opposed ways: either framing is the norm and creates closed systems of interactions that are isolated from the external world; or framing is ephemeral, and connections to the world outside create overflow that always threatens to disrupt the frame. My understanding here is closer to the latter, since this chapter deals ethnographically with a flow of material objects that have to be carefully hidden or ignored in order for the ritual to "work." As in Callon's (1998) example, the efficacy of the rite is always threatened by the potential return of the things themselves.

To sum up, the ritual frame deals on the one hand with intersubjectivity, the shared meanings and actions that establish the shared frame as a cultural event. On the other hand, it deals with interobjectivity, the fact that the enduring presence of the material world before and after the ritual both enables the framing of ritual action, and harbors the potential for disturbing the frame. Latour (2007), who coined the neologism "interobjectivity" in a paper on primate research, argues that what is intersubjectively co-present in face-to-face interactions is extended in time and space through material agents that both enable and constrain interactions in particular ways. The ritual is thus set up as an act of disappearance, during which breaks of presence are used to mask the fact that the dolls are being shifted horizontally.

Le Grand Escamotage

The main object of the *ningyō kuyō* is to make the dolls disappear, that is, to create the *illusio* in those who brought their dolls that they have ceased to be by rendering the material object absent. The previous owners do not necessarily lack knowledge of what this implies; rather, they choose not to know. The temples and shrines that provide these services aid and abet (that is, collude) in this *illusio*. At each stage, the participants can distance themselves from the act of disposal, both physically and mentally. The manipulation of spatial and temporal frames, as well as visible markers of social identity, is crucial to achieving a smooth, staggered process of disposal.

The temporal structure of the different rites allows for a separation between the more symbolic and the more material aspects of the detachment/disposal process. A strict division of labor obtains: usually there is a temporal interval between the ritual, during which ritual experts perform symbolic actions, and the disposal, during which volunteers or *sagyosha* (manual laborers) do the heavy lifting. These different frames of action are often marked by divergent atmospheres: the ritual frame with Buddhist monks and shrine priests evinces a sense of calm and reverence, even one of compassion, while the frame of manual work often feels quite violent, unceremonious, and unsentimental. These aspects rarely occur together, but when they do, as for example at the Kanei-ji temple in Ueno, the division of labor is upheld; the priests officiate and pray while the lay assistants throw the selected dolls into the fire. More frequently, I observed a strict separation. At the Ōi Shrine in Shimada, for example, the head priest prayed in front of the dolls and then lit the torch, before returning to the shrine building. Only then were the remaining dolls on the altar thrown into the fire. At the Hōkyōji in Kyoto, the entrance of the nuns and the abbess marked the beginning of the rite, but in this special case, the burning of representative dolls took place beforehand and their ashes were presented on the altar.

At the Tennōji in Osaka two completely different crews dealt with receiving the dolls and their final disposal, which occurred after a conspicuous time lapse of three hours. At Mongakuji in Saitama described earlier, the same crew dealt with both processes, but for the disposal they took off their *happi* coats and were mostly wearing uniform black underneath. As they were wearing face masks and gloves, I could not straightaway tell that they were the same people. I felt pressured to leave precisely because my own presence provided a continuity that extended the ritual frame and did not allow for the break in presence necessary to shift from the frame of ritual, in which the dolls were conceived of as carefully handled objects of affection, to a frame in which they were construed as mere rubbish.

The Meiji Shrine, a popular tourist site in central Tokyo, oversees one of the largest and most recent of such events, the "Doll Gratitude Festival" (*ningyō-kanshasai*) established in 1990. Here, they manage to do the escamotage in plain sight. When I attended in October 2019, an estimated thirty thousand dolls were brought in and displayed all along the shrine's perimeter. The event was organized by the Japanese Doll Association (Nihon-ningyō-kyōkai).[10] I talked to several members in attendance, including a former president (who talked about the rite in terms of ancient Japanese culture), the head of the academic section (who thought of the dolls more sociologically in terms of intergenerational links and inheritance), and two of the senior members who were tasked with identifying and separating valuable dolls from the chaff of everyday knickknacks (who emphasized the emotional aspects of dolls). They all professed ignorance as to what would happen to the dolls after the rite had ended. Acting as a hinge between the theoretical and the practical aspects of the ritual was Kitamura-san, the head of a Tokyo-based dollmakers' guild, who directed a group of students working part-time at the shrine. When I asked him what would happen to the dolls afterward, he hesitated and gave me a level look: "They are disposed of (*shobun sareru*)." Tanaka-san, who was in the process of opening her own doll museum, took me over to the small exhibition space where the dolls considered worth conserving were held and displayed. When we walked back, I asked her plainly what would happen to the other dolls, and she too replied that she did not know. The surprise must have been apparent on my face, because she added after a pause: "Well, later in the afternoon, a curtain will be drawn and then . . . . You can only hear an enormous whooshing noise!" Indeed, this is what happened.

Kitamura-san and dozens of student volunteers started to draw ropes across the courtyard from the pillars and hung a large curtain made from baby blue and white-striped fabric called *hanmaku*. This complicated operation took quite a while. Many visitors, foreign and Japanese, lingered on to see what would happen, but the student volunteers formed a cordon around the curtain and asked people not to lift it. Once the yard was concealed from sight, the volunteers disappeared inside, and there was a whooshing noise as thousands of dolls were swept off the tables and thrown into large, unmarked cardboard boxes. After some rain in the morning, the day had started to brighten, and brisk gusts of autumn wind occasionally lifted the curtain to reveal the scurrying of legs as the student-workers ran to get more dolls. Full boxes were sealed and lifted by hand or transported on small handcarts to the perimeter of the shrine and then out through the side gate into the shrine woods. There they ended up carefully stacked in a parking lot. After one side of the shrine precinct was cleared of dolls, the curtain was moved to the other. By now, newcomers no longer linked the boxes to the dolls and even the most obstinate stragglers (apart from myself) had left. After the curtain was removed, the premises looked as before; it was difficult to imagine that thirty thousand dolls had been displayed there only a few hours before. The part-time workers went on to a post-work party. Out in the parking lot, the boxes had been piled three meters high and formed a precise, fort-like rectangle; they were left deserted. I originally planned to wait and see what would happen next, but when the shrine park closed at 4:40 p.m., I was politely ejected by the security staff.

To recapitulate, in order for the dolls to shift from being objects of affection to being mere rubbish, it is important to disrupt the underlying material continuity of the object. This disruption is achieved by a division of labor among different sets of people and by temporal breaks that allow for the switching of the frame. The other transformation device relevant here is the visual barrier that was created by the curtain. Such striped curtains are often used in Japan to demarcate ritual occasions, both religious and secular. At another rite in Kōnosu, a lilac-colored *hanmaku* was used to give the jumbled boxes a more ceremonious look; when I looked more carefully, I saw that the curtain was strung directly around a large metal waste container, thus hiding

Figure 4.3 Volunteers installing the *hanmaku* curtain that serves as a material frame, Meiji Shrine, October 2019. Photograph by the author.

the "true" nature of the event. Or rather, the curtain was mediating between two different frames, both equally true. The waste container is just another framing device; things in it are rubbish because they have been thrown into it. But the "rubbishness" of such things can easily be undone by their removal (their "rescue") from the dumpster.

The same is true for the curtain drawn across the yard. The curtain blocks the gaze of the audience but also acts as a hinge, not concealing reality[11] so much as mediating between two different realities: the reality of the ritual and the reality of the material existence of things. In that sense, it acts as a literal frame that contains and sustains the particular reality—that of the dolls' absence—that the ritual creates. The *hanmaku* is thus the ritual frame that conceals the act of escamotage, that is, the removal of the dolls by sleight of hand. Needless to say, this requires the audience's collusion. From my observations it was fairly clear that those trying to peek behind the curtains were visitors and tourists rather than ritual participants. Those who brought dolls to the Meiji Shrine deposited them at the reception, paid the fee, and waited until the dolls were put out, often taking some pictures; some attended the formal ceremony, but left before the curtain was drawn.

What Is Held in Place by the Ritual

The shift in ritual frames that allows the divestment, and then disposal, of the dolls as rubbish has important implications. Why, one may ask, is the production of ignorance so important for the efficacy of the ritual? The answer lies in the parallelism of ignorance and absence. On an individual, psychological level, the desire not to know what happens to the doll is precisely what enables a sense of closure even though the doll itself is not destroyed. The participants collude with religious institutions to create ignorance in themselves and, to a lesser degree, in others. The ignorance thus produced also keeps in place certain self-beliefs or assumptions that would otherwise be threatened. These self-beliefs form three concentric circles that link individuals with society and the nation in crucial ways. The first and innermost circle contains beliefs that participants hold about themselves: that they are caring, considerate, and sentimental. Female participants often emphasized their emotional ties to the dolls, which they expressed in the language of cuteness (*kawaii*), reflecting the sentimentalization of material culture that went hand in hand with the rise of consumerism in postwar Japan. Participating in such a rite was a way to display these traits to others and thus to manifest them as socially shared values— this is the second circle containing notions of intersubjectivity and sociability shared through practices of concern (Traphagan 2004). As I was particularly interested in the dolls as nonhuman actors, I initially interpreted them as animate entities—as social others in their own right. But while the language used suggested animacy, these answers also conveyed a consideration and care that extended to other humans through the medium of the doll. This was especially true of elderly female participants, who often told me that they had brought their dolls to the *ningyō kuyō* so that their children would not have to do it after their death. Younger men, by contrast, tended to frame their explanations of rites of divestment in terms of "national culture" and *kokuminsei*, the supposedly unique ethnic characteristics of the Japanese, thus linking the individual to the nation state (the third circle). My conspicuous presence as a foreign ethnographer usually triggered a first layer of responses in this frame, meaning that the *ningyō kuyō* would be described as embodying the ancient spirit of Japan and exemplifying the care that the Japanese afforded their possessions. It was often challenging to access the more personal motivations of participants in a brief conversation at the ritual. But my encounter with one participant of the ritual at Mongakuji, where this article began, serves to illustrate the cares and concerns that did sometimes surface.

I met Yoshi (a participant in his fifties) and his mother while I was waiting for the priests of Mongakuji to appear. I had seen them earlier on, checking in at the reception and leaving a large doll in the care of the attendants before strolling around the temple grounds. Yoshi glanced at me with some curiosity and when I smiled, he came over and introduced himself in halting English. We quickly established that Japanese was the easier way to communicate. His mother retreated and hovered in the background. I really wanted to talk to her, too, but Yoshi made it quite clear that he was the spokesperson for both of them and that she was too shy to speak to a foreigner. He was intrigued that I had come all the way from "my country" to observe something as local as this. His first question was "Do you not have anything like this in your country?" When I answered in the negative, he said proudly that the Japanese have a particular proclivity for taking care of things and that this was a national characteristic (*mono wo daiji ni suru nihonjin no kokuminsei*). When I pressed him mildly as to why then, given this proclivity, they wanted to get rid of their dolls, he replied:

> In cases when the grandchildren cannot take possession of dolls one is indebted to (*o-sewa ni natta ningyō*), it's better to let them become buddhas (*jōbutsu shitemoratte*) than to throw them away. The memories will remain, and pictures will also remain. (*In English:*) Hearts of memory! (*In Japanese:*) We keep them in our mind. *Shūkatsu* is popular at the moment; instead of the grandchildren, one throws away one's stuff oneself.

When I asked him which of the displayed dolls were theirs, he was suddenly unsure and did not venture to point them out. I seemed to remember that they had brought the large standing doll very visibly displayed right in front of us. But it looked a bit too new and shiny, contradicting Yoshi's earlier statement that the Japanese are a people that treat objects carefully (rather than throwing away new things carelessly). We looked at it in hesitant silence. Yoshi also seemed to be aware of the contradiction, adding: "Well, we look after things well, that is why they look so new." Listening to the conversations of the dollmaker guild's volunteers over the course of the day, I noticed that many of them pointed out to each other that most of the dolls looked fairly new. When I asked the woman in charge how to tell whether a doll was new or old, she replied that the age was visible predominately in the material and the shape of the face; new dolls look more modern, and their clothes are shiny because they are made mainly from polyester. "Older dolls," she said, "have a more faded look. There are quite a lot of new dolls this time." Indeed, when the golden autumn sunlight directly hit the dolls, I could see the difference; the older dolls seemed to absorb the light, while the new ones glistened and gleamed gaudily.

This brief exchange with Yoshi encapsulates much of the data I gleaned from talking to attendants and participants at similar rites.[12] Yoshi's answer to my question contains in condensed form the emotional economy of the rite: debt, gratitude, attachment, divestment, exchange. The doll that has fulfilled its duty as a companion and as a decoration, in later years is thanked and treated as a real being that can "become a buddha," its essence separated from the physical object and dealt with in the Buddhist grammar of funerary rites.[13] But on another level of this discourse, dolls are mediators between their current owners and other people to whom consideration is also extended: by taking care of emotionally charged objects such as dolls within their lifetime, participants like Yoshi and his mother take an active stance and avoid passing the burden of care on to the next generation, who may not want it. The ignorance produced—in concrete terms, ignorance of the fact that the dolls will end up being unceremoniously thrown into the back of a rubbish compactor truck—helps participants sustain a particular image of themselves as gentle, considerate, and careful people. This is both a self-image and a social perception sustained in others that reflects a nationally inflected understanding of being Japanese and thus part of a long and uninterrupted line of a culture of care and compassion.

The Extermination of the Future

Yoshi's mention of grandchildren being unable to carry on the material culture of their grandparents has another layer of significance. When I asked him whether he had any children of his own, he briefly looked taken aback, then said that he was not married. Clearly, this was an embarrassing, if not painful, topic for him. But it also suggests why he and his mother participated in the rite that day; there was no future trajectory for the doll, no subsequent generation for it to be passed down to. Thus, getting rid of accumulated dolls before one's death can become part of the practice of *shūkatsu*: the socially concerted effort among the aged to retain as much agency for as long as possible in deciding the affairs of their final years. Mladenova (2020: 105), in a paper that addresses *shūkatsu* as a neoliberal technology of the self, argues that "death and dying are discussed with the premise that one has to think about it oneself, organize things and reduce the burden on anyone to a maximum extent." This concern with being a burden or nuisance (*meiwaku*) to one's descendants or unrelated others is consistent with the findings of Kawano's (2014) ethnography of ash-scattering ceremonies: the main motivation for this funerary innovation is that, by "returning to nature," no future caretaker for the grave is required, an ideal solution for the increasing numbers of people who have no children. Mladenova's (2020) material suggests that, in the final analysis, *shūkatsu* is largely a marketing ploy to sell books, workshops, and coaching and that such desperate attempts to wring profit out of the end of life are not taken entirely seriously by the majority of the aging population. Nevertheless, her participants clearly had thought about the implications of their own accumulation of material objects:

> Mrs. Sanda (67), pointed out that they limited their preparations of their end-of-life to a couple of truly necessary activities, like their grave and funeral or by throwing away personally sentimental items, which would otherwise be burdensome for their children to do posthumously. (Mladenova 2020: 118)

Ningyō kuyō can thus be interpreted as part and parcel of a wider cultural innovation in response to demographic shifts (Traphagan and Knight 2003), which have been caused by a life span increase and significant improvements in old age health, a consistently low-fertility rate since the 1990s, and an increasing number of people who remain—whether willingly or not—single throughout their adult life (Ueno 2015). What marks the Heisei era (1989–2019), then, is that together with economic recession and social and demographic change, the stream of material transmission is also thinning out. A dearth of newborn babies translates into a glut of dolls that remain as a painful reminder of the end of family lines (especially the *hina-ningyō* and warrior dolls that are displayed on the annual girls' and boys' days). These dolls are therefore sacrificed on the altar of demographic change. There are indications, however, that the disposal of large numbers of dolls is only a temporary phenomenon. At Mongakuji, I was told that the previous year there had been at least one more row of cardboard boxes, and that the total number of dolls brought to *ningyō kuyō* was decreasing overall. That this is a more general trend was corroborated by my informants at other locations such as the Meiji Shrine. This seems to suggest that while the fertility rate shows no signs of picking up, the thinning out of material culture streams might be slowing as people get rid of their dolls and do not replace them with new ones.

Conclusion: Sacralizing Disposal and Consumption

I called this chapter "The Great Heisei Doll Massacre" to suggest that the last thirty years have foregrounded paradoxes concerning consumption and disposal, attachment and detachment, ignorance, and ritual efficacy. Although first undertaken in the modern era in 1918, the practice of *ningyō kuyō* remained a marginal phenomenon from the 1950s to the 1960s and picked up only during the 1980s, with the number of dolls handed over for disposal increasing exponentially during the 1990s. It is significant that one of the largest events, the Doll Gratitude Festival at the Meiji Shrine, was inaugurated in 1990, the first year of the Heisei era. As this era drew to a close in 2019 with the ascension of a new emperor, many organizers and participants alike told me that the number of dolls, although still substantial, was in decline overall. This suggests that the Heisei era, with its stagnating birth rate and declining number of marriages, has led to a parallel thinning out in the material transmission of heirlooms from one generation to the next.

In this context, the rite's function is to create a conduit of disposal in the face of contradictory and often opposing forces. The wish to get rid of an excess of inherited things that are difficult to accommodate in small dwellings is opposed by the sense of duty toward these inherited objects (of which dolls and mementoes form a large part). Members of the older generation, especially the married women who had to look after one or even two sets of grandparents (their own and their in-laws), are very aware of the burden that their own future frailty may pose to their children and their children's spouses. Those who have recently gone through the pain of sorting through and disposing of parents' or in-laws' accumulated things are often especially keen to start decluttering as part of their own final preparations. But how to get rid of these sentimental treasures without feeling heartless and cruel? The ritual provides an answer: by obfuscating the transformation of cherished objects into waste, people can bid farewell to their and others' possessions without incurring feelings of guilt. By providing a ritual frame that creates the illusion that the dolls simply disappear, their disposal is enabled and accelerated. The act of making the dolls disappear has its psychological equivalent in a double forgetting: those who bring the dolls choose to forget that they will be disposed of like rubbish; those who handle them after the ritual must forget that they were emotionally charged objects of affection. It is through this double forgetting that the doll is freed from human attachment and returns to being merely a thing. The "massacre" of a large number of dolls is thus enabled by allowing participants to claim ignorance of what is happening. As a result, material accumulations become unstuck: dolls who have been waiting in alcoves for decades are on the move again.

These domestic struggles are mirrored on a larger scale in the contradictions of consumption in the contemporary global market economy. The imperative to be mindful of the environment and to keep, mend, and cherish things rather than to just throw them away is pitted against the promise of consumerism—that to get rid of old things (which may or may not "spark joy"; see Gould in this volume) makes space for the new, the exciting, and the joyful. What the rite does on this level is to sacralize and thus legitimize disposal in the face of both the demands of sentimentality and the strictures of waste consciousness. In negotiating these contradictory attitudes toward things and opening a channel for disposal, the production of ignorance proves to be its own kind of wisdom.

Notes

1 See, for example, the scholarship on rites for aborted foetuses (Takeda and Hoshino 1987), shoes (Matsuzaki 1996), scissors (Ōsaki 1997), needles (Kretschmer 2000; Guth 2014), animals (Nakamaki 1995), pets (Ambros 2012), and corporate *kuyō* (Nakamaki 2005).

2 As I will discuss, some Shintō shrines also organize ceremonial disposals, but the Buddhist form has probably served as the model (see also note 5).

3 All names used in my description and discussion of this particular ritual, including that of the place ("Mongakuji"), are anonymized.

4 The Kada Awashima Shrine in Wakayama has an association with dolls that goes back to the early modern period, but dolls were left there as votive offerings rather than for disposal (see Gygi, forthcoming).

5 *Hitogata* (lit. "human shape") is the native Japanese reading of the Chinese characters for doll 人形 (Japanese: *ningyō*; Chinese: *renxing*).

6 Pure Land Buddhism was founded by the ex-Tendai monk Hōnen (1133–1212) who brought elitist Buddhism to the masses by simplifying meditative practice and elaborate rituals to the repetition of the *nembutsu* prayer, which in the age of declining dharma is thought to be enough to guarantee salvation.

7 At Buddhist temples it is customary to bow once, while bowing and clapping twice to attract the deities is standard Shinto practice.

8 In True Pure Land Buddhism, also called Shin Buddhism, the most widespread religious affiliation in contemporary Japan, the incense is directly strewn on to the embers rather than being lifted to the forehead as in other sects such as Zen, Tendai, and Shingon.

9 The Shingon and Nichiren sects of Buddhism offer incense three times, others only two.
10 The Meiji Shrine and the name of the association are correctly identified, but I have anonymized all participants and disguised their positions.
11 "Concealing reality" would suggest a simple dichotomy between the "false" surface and the "deep" truth, a problematic rhetoric that has frequently been used to describe Japan as a place of smoke and mirrors. See Robertson (2005) on the adjacent metaphors of the mirror and mask.
12 I observed ten such rites at temples and shrines from 2013 to 2019, most of them between September and late November 2019.
13 There is some doctrinal basis for this, especially in Shingon Buddhism (Rambelli 2001), but the version I describe here was a Pure Land Buddhist rite. However, such theological points of contention often leave little impression on practitioners who find the ritual language too obscure to follow.

References

Allison, Anne (2006), *Millenial Monsters: Japanese Toys and the Global Imagination*, Berkeley: University of California Press.

Ambros, Barbara R. (2012), *Bones of Contention: Animals and Religion in Modern Japan*, Honolulu: University of Hawai'i Press.

Bateson, Gregory (1972), "A Theory of Play and Fantasy," *Psychiatric Research Reports*, 2: 39–51.

Brox, Trine (2019), "The Aura of Buddhist Material Objects in the Age of Mass-Production," *Journal of Global Buddhism*, 20: 105–25. doi: 10.5281/zenodo.3238213.

Callon, Michel (1998), "An Essay on Framing and Overflowing: Economic Externalities Revisited by Sociology," *The Sociological Review*, 46 (1): 244–69. doi: 10.1111%2Fj.1467-954X.1998.tb03477.x.

Chua, Liana (2009), "To Know or Not to Know? Practices of Knowledge and Ignorance among Bidayuhs in an "Impurely" Christian World," *The Journal of the Royal Anthropological Institute*, 15 (2): 332–48. doi: 10.1111/j.1467-9655.2009.01556.x.

Gershon, Ilana (2000), "How to Know When Not to Know: Strategic Ignorance When Eliciting for Samoan Migrant Exchanges," *Social Analysis: The International Journal of Anthropology*, 44 (2): 84–105. https://www.jstor.org/stable/23166535

Goffman, Erving (1974), *Frame Analysis: An Essay on the Organization of Experience*, Chicago: Northeastern University Press.

Guth, Christine M. E. (2014), "Theorizing the Hari Kuyō: The Ritual Disposal of Needles in Early Modern Japan," *Design and Culture*, 6 (2): 169–86. doi: 10.2752/175470814X14031924627068.

Gygi, Fabio (2018), "Robot Companions: The Animation of Technology and the Technology of Animation," in Miguel Astor-Aguilera and Graham Harvey (eds), *Rethinking Relations and Animism: Personhood and Materiality*, 94–111, London: Routledge.

Gygi, Fabio (forthcoming), "The Afterlives of Dolls: On the Productive Death of Terminal Commodities," *Ars Orientalis* 52.

Handelman, Dan (2004), "Re-framing Ritual," in J. S. Kreinath, C. Hartung, and A. Deschner (eds), *The Dynamics of Changing Rituals: The Transformation of Religious Rituals within their Social and Cultural Context*, 9–20, Berne: Peter Lang.

Houseman, Michael (2012), "Pushing Ritual Frames Past Bateson," *Journal of Ritual Studies*, 26 (2): 1–5. https://www.jstor.org/stable/44368852

Jensen, Casper B. and Anders Blok (2013), "Techno-animism in Japan: Shinto Cosmograms, Actor-network Theory, and the Enabling Powers of Non-human Agencies," *Theory, Culture & Society*, 30 (2): 84–115. doi:10.1177/0263276412456564.

Kapferer, Bruce (2006), "Dynamics," in J. S. Kreinath and M. Stausberg (eds), *Theorizing Rituals: Issues, Topics, Approaches, Concept*, 507–22, Leiden: Brill.

Kawano, Satsuki (2014), "'Who Will Care for Me When I Am Dead?' Ancestors, Homeless Spirits, and New Afterlives in Low-Fertility Japan," *Contemporary Japan*, 26 (2): 49–69. doi: 10.1515/cj-2014-0003.

Kretschmer, Angelika (2000), "Mortuary Rites for Inanimate Objects: The Case of Hari Kuyō," *Japanese Journal of Religious Studies*, 27 (3–4): 379–404. https://www.jstor.org/stable/30233671

Latour, Bruno (2007), "Une sociologie sans object? Remarques sur l'interobjectivité [A Sociology Without Objects? Remarks on Interobjectivity]," in O. Debary and L. Turgeon (eds), *Objets & Mémories*, 37–57, Paris: Éditions de la Maison des sciences de l'homme.

Mair, Jonathan, Casey High, and Ann H. Kelly (2012), "Introduction: Making Ignorance an Ethnographic Object," in Jonathan Mair and Ann H. Kelly (eds), *The Anthropology of Ignorance: An Ethnographic Approach*, 1–32, London: Palgrave Macmillan.

Matsuzaki, Kenzō (1996), "Kibutsu no kuyō kenkyū josetsu: Kutsu no kuyō o chūshin ni," *Mingu Kenkyū*, 112: 23–32.

Mladenova, Dorothea (2020), "Optimizing One's Own Death: The Shūkatsu Industry and the Enterprising Self in a Hyper-Aged Society," *Contemporary Japan*, 32 (1): 103–27. doi: 10.1080/18692729.2020.1717105.

Nakamaki, Hirochika (1995), "Memorial Monuments and Memorial Services of Japanese Companies: Focusing on Mount Kōya," in Dolores P. Martinez and Jan van Bremen (eds), *Ceremony and Ritual in Japan: Religious Practices in an Industrialized Society*, 146–160, London: Routledge.

Nakamaki, Hirochika (2005), "Memorials of Interrupted Lives in Modern Japan: From Ex Post Facto Treatment to Intensification Devices," in Tsu Yun Hui, Jan Van Bremen, and Eyal Ben-Ari (eds), *Perspectives on Social Memory in Japan*, 44–57, Leiden: Global Oriental.

Nelson, Timothy J. (2012), "Transformations: The Social Construction of Religious Ritual," in John P. Hoffman (ed), *Understanding Religious Ritual: Theoretical Approaches and Innovations*, 9–30, London: Routledge.

Ōsaki, Tomoko (1997), "Hasami-kuyō o megutte: Tokyo-to Minato-ku Shiba Zōjōji [The Memorial Service for Scissors at the Shiba Zōjōji Temple in Minato Ward]," *Mingu Mansurī*, 30 (1): 14–24.

Proctor, Robert N. and Londa Schiebinger (2008), *Agnotology: The Making and Unmaking of Ignorance*, Stanford: Stanford University Press.

Rambelli, Fabio (2001), *Vegetal Buddhas: Ideological Effects Of Japanese Buddhist Doctrines On The Salvation Of Inanimate Beings*, Kyoto: Cheng & Tsui.

Rettie, Ruth (2004), Using Goffman's Frameworks to Explain Presence and Reality, [Conference paper] 7th Annual International Workshop on Presence, Valencia, Spain, October 2004.

Richardson, Kathleen (2016), "Technological Animism: The Uncanny Personhood of Humanoid Machines," *Social Analysis*, 60 (1): 110–128.

Robbins, Joel and Johanna Sumiala (2016), "Ritual Intimacy—Ritual Publicity: Revisiting Ritual Theory and Practice in Plural Society," *Suomen Antropologi: Journal of the Finnish Anthropological Society*, 41 (4): 1–5.

Robertson, Jennifer (2005), "Introduction: Putting and Keeping Japan in Anthropology," in Jennifer Robertson (ed), *A Companion to the Anthropology of Japan*, 3–16, Oxford: Blackwell.

Takeda, Dōshō and Eiki Hoshino (1987), "Indebtedness and Comfort: The Undercurrents of *Mizuko Kuyō* in Contemporary Japan," *Japanese Journal of Religious Studies*, 14: 305–20. https://www.jstor.org/stable/30233996

Tanaka, Masaru (2005), "Ningyō-kuyō ni miru ningyōkan no shosō [Aspects of Dolls as Seen Through Memorial Services for Dolls]," *Ningyō-Gangu Kenkyū*, 16: 262–68.

Traphagan, John W. (2004), *The Practice of Concern: Ritual, Well-Being, and Aging in Rural Japan*, Durnham, NC: Carolina Academic Press.

Traphagan, John W. and John Knight (2003), *Demographic Change and the Family in Japan's Aging Society*, Albany, NY: State University of New York Press.

Ueno, Chizuko (2015), *Ohitorisama no saigo [The End-of-Life of Single Women]*, Tokyo: Asahi Shimbun Shuppan.

5

Reincarnating Sacred Objects

The Recycling of Generative Efficacy and the Question of Waste in Tibetan and Himalayan Buddhist Material Cultures

Amy Holmes-Tagchungdarpa

In recent years, different Buddhist communities have taken to recycling with great enthusiasm.[1] In Taiwan and Japan, major Buddhist organizations coordinate recycling initiatives (Hsiao et al. 2019; Lee and Han 2015; Williams 2010); in Thailand, the monastics of Wat Chak Deang make monastic robes out of recycled plastic bottles (Tanakasempipat and Kuhakan 2020); in Sikkim and Bhutan in the eastern Himalayas, monasteries encourage their patrons to provide donations without plastic packaging; and two monasteries in Malaysia and Thailand are made from glass bottles (Sunkara 2018; Wisman 2017). Buddhist philosophers and ethicists depict these activities as part of normal Buddhist behavior and as logical extensions of Buddhist concepts in practice. For example, popular American Buddhist teacher Thubten Chodron states that: "Taking care to recycle our cans, jars, bottles and paper is part of the practice of mindfulness in our homes! Compassion and concern for others should motivate us to minimize the use of disposable, nonrecyclable materials in temples and Dharma centers and to recycle the materials we can" (Chodron 2001: 105). The association that she draws between recycling and Buddhist teachings of mindfulness and compassion shows that she, like many other contemporary Buddhist authors, considers concern for spiritual liberation and concern about the planet to be interconnected. Buddhist practitioners should therefore see environmentally concerned behaviors such as recycling as a part of their practice. Author Rosemary Roberts' Buddhist book for general audiences *What Would Buddha Recycle?* extends this point even further, outlining an entire ethos for "seeing your involvement in the planet in a new light" as a way to attain Buddhist soteriological goals (Roberts 2009: 1). Covering topics as diverse as clothing, transport, and consumption choices and connecting them with Buddhist ideas, she argues that ". . . mindfully caring for the Earth and its inhabitants can be done by making small changes and coming to simple realisations about your lifestyle—which is just how Buddha made his way to Nirvana" (ibid.: 1–2). Such examples represent manifestations of the "greening of Buddhism," a trend that took off in the 1960s with the contemporaneous popularization of Buddhism and rise of environmental movements and countercultural ideas. This trend has been widely critiqued by scholars as ahistorical (Harris 1991) and positioned as an example of broader Orientalist histories of misrepresenting Buddhism. However, associations between Buddhism and the environment, and especially "green activities," should not be quickly dismissed. Different Buddhist groups have embraced these environmentalist stereotypes, and used them to generate new forms of engagement and organization in response to contemporary environmental challenges (Elverskog 2020; Huber 1991; Yeh 2014).

Are Buddhist recyclers examples of these new forms of engagement? Or is there historical precedent for their activities? Scholarship on early Indian Buddhism suggests that there is a history of recycling in Buddhist communities, citing the example of the Buddha encouraging his monks to recycle their old robes and to use "bed covers, pillowcases, foot towels, and floor mops" mixed with mud to plaster their cells (Singh 2012: 76–7). However, as historian Johan Elverskog (2020) has recently argued, Buddhism, from its very beginnings in India, can also be seen as a "prosperity theology" that has conceptualized wealth as an unproblematic indication of good karma. Generally speaking, neither laypeople nor monasteries were chastised for accumulating wealth, and the monastic law code (*Vinaya*) regulated an array of economic activity, including "landholding, lending and borrowing on credit, investment of perpetual endowments, dealing in commodities, and even the ownership of servants and slaves" (ibid.: 42). Given the "deep entanglements" of Buddhists with "money, wealth, production, and status" (ibid.: 42), it could be argued that, historically, there was no impetus for recycling material culture in Buddhist communities. In fact, the donation and sponsorship of new sacred objects and sites provided opportunities for monastics and laypeople to gain merit. Canonical literature and local practices that developed throughout Buddhist societies have extolled luxury goods as symbols of spiritual purity and encouraged the donation of precious materials to monasteries and for the making of sacred objects (see Caple in this volume).

What role, then, has old, worn out, or replaced material culture played in Buddhist communities? Given the liberating potential of Buddhist material culture, can the recycling extolled by contemporary Buddhist teachers and authors be seen in action in Buddhist communities? How does thinking about the disposal and recycling of the most valued sacred objects allow us to complicate assumptions regarding soteriologically productive elements of material culture? In this chapter, I will consider these questions directly through exploring sacred waste. Anthropologist Irene Stengs (2014: 235) has defined sacred waste as

> material residues and surpluses that cannot be disposed of as just garbage (or rubble), but neither can be kept or left alone. Its ambiguous nature, charged with a religious, moral, or emotional value on the one hand, but at the same time a kind of leftover for which no proper destination exists, makes sacred waste precarious matter, and hence often a ground for conflict and contestation.

Stengs (2014) emphasizes that sacred waste is not necessarily connected with specific religious traditions or objects. The examples of recycling with which I opened this chapter demonstrate how the sorting, disposal, or recycling of seemingly mundane waste can be seen by Buddhist communities as activities that generate merit. In this chapter, I will explore the question of what communities do with sacred waste by considering how people negotiate the disposal or recycling of "power objects" (*rten*)[2] (Gentry 2019) in Tibetan and Himalayan Buddhist communities—and whether they are actually ever considered waste at all. James Gentry (2019) refers to Buddhist artifacts in the Himalayas as "power objects" since these materials can "enable unmediated access to the powerful sources of the Buddhist tradition for a range of pragmatic and transcendant goals" to the extent that they may be "promoted as viable complements or substitutes for the study and cultivation of the Buddhist doctrine." Power objects are myriad, and include ritual tools such as bells, drums, and vajra (*rdo rje*); depictions of the Buddha's body (in the form of paintings and statues), speech (in the form of books), and mind (in the form of stupas); and basically any object associated with enlightened energy (which means that the clothing, household implements, and bodily fluids of Buddhist masters can be power objects). The potential for objects to be generative depends on their histories, which means that material culture and objects in general must be approached with care and consideration of their biographies. Given the efficacy that these objects generate, disposing of them, or changing their status, needs to be undertaken with great care. I will demonstrate how these negotiations often lead to the reincarnation of sacred objects through recycling. The idea of reincarnation is a prominent one in Tibetan and Himalayan Buddhism, due to the institution of the incarnate lama, or *trülku* (*sprul sku*), a teacher identified at a young age who is held to be the manifestation of an awakened master who transmitted his wisdom on to another (or several others) at the time of death. Here, I will argue that objects can also be like *trülku* in their ability to maintain continuity of blessings or *jinlap* (*byin rlabs*) across different lives and changes in their physical manifestations over time.

At the outset, a significant challenge in this chapter is how to define sacred waste in Tibet and the Himalayas. In many ways, power objects in Vajrayana Buddhism never transition into the state of waste (understood here as something left over or of no further use). Instead, once they are acknowledged as sacred objects, or "supports" (*rten*), they remain as animate living beings activated through consecration (*rab gnas*) rituals. Once consecration awakens the power present in these objects, turning them into agents of transformation, they become capable of generating desirable forces for human flourishing and capable of changing their form. As seen in other chapters in this volume (e.g., Abrahms-Kavunenko; Gould; Wilson), this state of animation complicates the disposal of sacred objects. Instead, in many contexts, they are repurposed, or reincarnated, into new forms. This chapter will outline the process through which sacred objects are created and how Buddhist practitioners negotiate their wear and use. Through case studies based on fieldwork and historical research in areas throughout the Himalayas that practice Buddhism, including eastern parts of the Tibetan plateau in contemporary China, northern West Bengal and Sikkim in India, and Nepal,[3] I will demonstrate how the aging of objects makes them all the more efficacious. Buddhist communities in these regions do not conceptualize recycling as a "green" process to help the environment in an instrumentalist way. Instead, they see it as a spiritually charged, important process that assists with the generation of merit through interaction with the forces of blessings or *jinlap*, pollution or *drib* (*sgrib*), and prosperity or *yang* (*g.yang*). The practice of transforming rather than disposing of sacred objects, and the acknowledgment of their rejuvenated state, means that these Buddhist communities remain open to including myriad old and used substances in their offerings and interactions with sacred objects. Since the disposal of power objects is often fraught with complications, their recycling is preferable and common. In Tibetan and Himalayan contexts, recycling is therefore a complex and multilayered process.

Jinlap: How Sacred Objects Become Living and Generative

In Tibetan and Himalayan Buddhist communities, Buddhist sacred objects are not inanimate—mere representations of the Buddha or other powerful people or deities. They are also capable of transmitting the blessings of these beings and other powerful figures who have interacted with the objects. Objects that correspond to the Buddha's speech (texts, *dhāraṇīs*), body (statues, paintings), and mind (stupas, *tsha tsha* or clay votives) (Bentor 1996: xx) are all considered to be receptacles of blessings, or *jinlap*. Buddhist studies scholar Holly Gayley (2007: 466) defines *jinlap* as "a potency or power localized in a sacred object that is understood to transform its immediate environment and those who come into direct contact with it." She argues that these blessings may have an "apotropaic effect, conferring worldly blessings (such as protection from illness, obstacles, and malignant spirits), as well as a soteriological effect, geared toward salvation in subsequent rebirths or alternative release from cyclic existence." This potency is the reason why practitioners choose to create amulets and medicinal pills out of book pages and dust, mud, plants, or rocks collected from sacred sites (Huber 1991), and why they wear cords and amulets blessed by lamas who generate *jinlap* through their extensive practice.

Objects and places become sacred or powerful through a process. This process may be through association (such as the presence of a buddha, deity, or great practitioner) or through a consecration ritual (*rab gnas*). There are many forms of consecration ritual in Tibetan and Himalayan Buddhism, but all involve the ritual transformation of sacred objects, spaces, and human practitioners themselves, into buddhas (Bentor 1996: xvii). Once an object has been thus transformed, it not only represents its associated buddha or Buddhist figure, but is understood to *become* that object. For that reason, even if objects age and wear out, they retain that efficacy and must be treated accordingly.

Before the ritual process begins, sacred objects are prepared to become repositories of these blessings. Statues and stupas, which are empty objects, must be filled up to prevent any malignant spiritual interference from taking residence in their hollow cores. In ancient Indian Buddhism, *dhāraṇī* formulas and relics were put inside objects to prepare them for ritual awakening. In contemporary Tibetan and Himalayan Buddhism, the contents are known as *zung* (*gzung*). They are complex in their composition and need to be assembled after their collection from various sources, and then prepared before insertion, to increase the *jinlap* of the support that is waiting to be consecrated.

Zung act as an example of the recycling of sacred objects (the receptacles of already established *jinlap*) through their integration into new objects. Historically, *zung* needed to be procured from artisans and lamas who had collected *jinlap*-laden materials and assembled them for preparing objects that were to be consecrated. A widely regarded contemporary lama who continues this practice of *zung* preparation is Lama Jamyang, a Bhutanese Nyingma practitioner in his late eighties resident in Kalimpong, northern West Bengal, whom I interviewed in 2015. Lama Jamyang originally moved from Bhutan to Kalimpong in the 1960s to study with Dudjom Rinpoche (1904–1987), one of the most renowned Nyingma teachers of the twentieth century, who founded Zangdrok Paldri, a large monastery in Kalimpong in the 1950s. Lama Jamyang studied the art of *zung* assembly and preparation during his meditation and ritual studies in Kalimpong, where he settled with his family. This art includes the expectation that the *zung* specialist will be a practitioner who undertakes meditation, and practices visualization and prayer as part of their process of preparation. There is also an important component of material expertise. Preparing *zung* entails being something of a spiritual magpie, since it can incorporate all sorts of items that need to be collected from various sources. Many of these objects are recycled, as they have already been consecrated or are associated with powerful masters and/or places. When Lama Jamyang is assembling *zung* he includes:

1. Handwritten *dhāraṇī* and mantra and mandala charts—especially for buddhas and dharma protectors associated with compassion, healing, and protection. These are wound into bundles so that a greater number can be fitted in, and are often painted with a water and saffron concoction known as *tri* (*khrid*), made for consumption after an empowerment or *wang* (*dbang*).
2. Small paintings and images of buddhas, bodhisattvas, and dharma protectors.
3. *Rilbu* (*ril bu*), medicinal pills made from crushed plants and other *jinlap*-rich substances rolled into balls.
4. Incense.
5. Minerals, such as turquoise and coral that are valued in the Himalayas.
6. Mud, plants, and water collected from sacred sites.
7. Relics from sacred people, including their ashes, teeth, fragments of bone, hair, and nail clippings. This is an example of the recycling of forms of sacred waste that cannot be disposed of easily due to their *jinlap*.
8. Objects that have *jinlap* from their prior use. Lama Jamyang is famous for including dismantled pieces of Dudjom Rinpoche's robes, for example, and also beads from Dudjom Rinpoche's mala.

Lamas and artisans such as Lama Jamyang gain their reputation through assembling *zung* from reincarnated, recycled materials—that is, materials that have already been held to be efficacious and powerful. Lama Jamyang recommends repairing or reusing older sacred objects in new ones instead of destroying them, since even old, well-used objects generate *jinlap*; indeed, the older, or the more frequently they were used by someone with a lot of *jinlap*, the better. Such repurposing is not unusual, and, instead, demonstrates that sacred objects never really cease to be sacred. While a support can be desacralized through inappropriate use, it can still be reinstated through reconsecration—in fact, it should be, in order to prevent it from accumulating problematic energy. Materials that have been used in *zung* preparation which are subject to decay or disintegration, such as dairy products or incense, may be periodically replaced through renovation, or packaged and repackaged to prevent the contamination of other contents.

There is a set process for preparing and inserting the *zung* into a statue or stupa. Lama Jamyang will first insert a *tsokshing* (*tshogs shing*) or life force stick, which functions as a spinal cord within the statue. This contains the life force of the deity and is covered in mantras. He then inserts the other items, seals the case on the base of the object, and then paints on mantra syllables. If the object is a statue, he paints in the eyes and the *dzöpu* (*mdzod spu*; Sanskrit: *urna*) on the forehead. Before he hands back the item to be awakened through consecration, he will put a mask on the statue to prevent any malicious energies or spirits from taking up residence within it. The support is then handed off to the next set of ritual specialists, the lamas or monastics who will perform the consecration ceremony that awakens it.

New technologies and connections are leading to modifications of this tradition. Lama Jamyang now frequently uses photocopied *dhāraṇī* and modelling glues for his painting. In China, it has become common for people to purchase goods that have already been consecrated or for consecration to be very brief, and mass-produced *zung* are made in factories for sale in shops or for bulk purchase. Any lama, even one passing a shop on the street, may be invited to perform a brief prayer, as opposed to a longer consecration (Brox 2019). In Chengdu, you can now also buy your own do-it-yourself *zung*-making kit, containing pre-printed mantras, a small *tsokshing*, and a bag of incense. This type of consumer-tailored, mass-produced product leaves out older forms of recycled and repurposed materials, and what they signified: that supports never really go to waste because they are reincarnated into new forms. Lama Jamyang also follows this recycling process for older statues that need to be renewed in order to purify them from any pollution they may have accumulated.

Reincarnating Generative Efficacy: What to Do with Decaying Sacred Objects

The recycling of *jinlap*-laden objects is not without controversy. Twentieth-century Tibetan scholar Gendun Chöpel (1903–1951) remarked on the concern he felt when seeing people throw away old and defective texts from their homes and from monasteries, but was also critical of people taking these same texts to eat, to make amulets to wear, or to put into statues and stupas as *zung*, as was popular in his day (dGe 'dun chos 'phel 2009: 12–14) and remains so. Philosopher Dorji Wangchuck has expressed concern that such practices can lead to the loss of important historical and intellectual culture, and are part of broader patterns of biblioclasm and libricide in Tibetan-language societies (Wangchuck 2015: 536).

What is the alternative to these practices lamented by the above-mentioned scholars? As the Buddha said, all objects are eventually subject to decay. What should Buddhists do with these power objects? Tibetan and Himalayan communities have several responses to this conundrum. Here I will discuss two that represent alternative types of reincarnation: first, maintenance to prevent decay, which is still a form of reincarnation since it may lead to a change in the form of an object, and second, repurposing of objects into new contexts. Both of these responses suggest that sacred waste is rarely considered to be waste.

Throughout Buddhist history, there have been traditions of venerating certain types of material that would, in other contexts, be considered as waste. Buddhist relics (*ring bsrel*) may be made up of corporeal remains of Buddha himself and other advanced practitioners, including their ashes, bones, fingernails, and hair; they may also be material items, including clothing or ritual objects, texts that hold Buddhist teachings, or any number of "a wide spectrum of other items believed to derive from, emulate, represent, or incarnate a Buddha's presence . . ." (Germano 2004: 52). The connection with the Buddha, and with practitioners who have actualized his teachings (known as *rten 'brel*), is, of course, what transforms this waste into sacred objects. Stupas are often repositories for these objects (Strong 2004), and in Tibet and the Himalayas there are well-documented traditions of building and, more importantly here, renovating stupas. This strategy prevents decay through the objects' reincarnation in a new body—the stupa. Aged or worn-out objects never, therefore, become waste in the conventional sense of the word; they are seen as perpetually capable of generating efficacy. When they do wear out, as Stengs has written, sacred objects are in an ambiguous state (Stengs 2014), their recycling through the renovation of a site using a combination of old and new materials, or their reincarnation in a new form, allows for the removal of this ambiguity and the objects' continued use.

The processes involved in the renewal of sacred sites are illustrative of how objects can be recycled, or reincarnated, into new forms while retaining their *jinlap*. Many sacred sites have gone through multiple renovations, the histories of which reveal the entanglements between social, political, economic, and religious forces. Patrons often undertake such restorations to create an association with and a connection to these sites, which are receptables of blessings and power. They therefore intentionally recycle and retain elements of old objects from the sites' previous iterations. One vivid example of an often renovated and reincarnated sacred site is the Svayambhū stupa ('Phags pa shing kun), one of the oldest, most iconic stupas in the Kathmandu Valley, Nepal. The tales around its foundation date back to when the Kathmandu Valley was a great lake. According to Tibetan traditions, the previous Buddha Vipaśyin planted a lotus seed in the middle of the lake, which sprouted into a grand lotus. The bodhisattva Mañjuśrī found the lotus so beautiful he wanted to make it a shrine to inspire all sentient beings, so he slashed a gorge through the mountains between India and Nepal and drained the lake. Under the Valley dwelled the great cosmic turtle that holds up the world. The draining of the lake eased the turtle's burden, and a huge piece of timber was erected on his back to allow for the construction of a new shrine. Earth and stone were placed around the central axis, and this became the stupa, topped by the lotus. Mañjuśrī is attributed with the founding of a new civilization in the Valley, as he enthroned a new king to care for the people living around the shrine (Holmes-Tagchungdarpa 2014: 107–8). Although sources do not agree on the date when the stupa was first created, there exists abundant documentary evidence of its periodic renovation. Historian Alexander von Rospatt (2013: 276) has found that between 1370 and 1817 there were at least eleven complete rebuilds of the stupa; since then, major renovations were carried out in 1918 and between 2008 and 2010.

Why have so many resources been expended on this specific sacred site in its various recycled iterations? As von Rospatt (2013: 277–8) has pointed out, since the Buddha's relics cannot age, it is important that they be enshrined safely and securely. The Svayambhū stupa is home to the power of the Buddhist deities, and therefore renovations need to be undertaken with utmost care and with acknowledgment of the stupa's agency. According to the Newar tradition, the mantras that charge the stupa, which are "infused in the course of their construction, and at the time of their consecration," are renewed daily with rituals and worship and in annual reconsecrations and life cycle rituals (ibid.).

This also explains why the physical container of the relics needs to be renewed periodically. The incorporation of the "divine essence" (Sanskrit: *nyāsa*) from the older stupa into the restored one is a representation of reincarnation, as it uses older forms to affirm the continuing efficacy of the stupa (ibid.). It can also be seen as a form of recycling, as the old form is transformed to allow it to continue to generate efficacy. In my study of the 1918 renovation of the stupa by eastern Tibetan teacher Tokden Shakya Shri (1854–1919), I found that the Tibetan renovation team and their sponsors from throughout the Himalayas shared these concerns. In particular, Tokden Shakya Shri's biography notes that his community hoped to inspire sentient beings by keeping the stupa well presented, and saw the renovation as an occasion to attain merit and form a connection with the buddhas and deities resident in the stupa (Holmes-Tagchungdarpa 2014: 108–9).

The association between powerful historical narratives and sacred histories connects to another way that worn sacred objects are recycled or reincarnated in Tibet and the Himalayas. In many cases, objects in monastic storehouses and on shrines that are aged or in a state of decay due to age and wear are called "treasures" or *terma* (*gter ma*), which are retained due to their ability to continue to generate *jinlap*. This term also has another level of significance in how it relates to distinctive *terma* lineages. These lineages are promulgated by *tertön* (*gter ston*), treasure discoverers, practitioners who are held to rediscover teachings and objects that have been hidden in the Tibetan and Himalayan landscape by Guru Rinpoche, the famous saint attributed with establishing Tantric Buddhism in Tibet in the eighth century CE, and his Tibetan consort Yeshe Tsogyal. *Tertön* have karmic connections with Guru Rinpoche as they are often considered to be reincarnations of his students. At preordained times they receive prophecies or visions that lead them to discover texts and objects that inspire their recovery of remembered teachings from Guru Rinpoche (Doctor 2005; Thondup 1997). Texts are often found in esoteric *ḍākinī* script and are decoded into Tibetan language through tantric practice (Gyatso 1998), while objects come in many forms, including statues, ritual implements, conch shells, and rocks (Germano 1998).

These rediscovered texts and images are considered to be from another time. Their attributed purpose is to inspire and guide meditative and ritual practice, but they can also have additional purposes after being rediscovered, which depend on the situation in which they are found. After these treasures are discovered, *tertöns* go through a process of presenting them for the contemporary context, which represents a form of recycling, as old forms are presented in new ways. Since the revitalization of religion in Tibetan cultural areas of the

People's Republic of China in the late 1970s, following roughly twenty years of suppression, *terma* have served to reinspire and galvanize Tibetan identity and cultural practices. Influential recent *tertön* Khenpo Jikmé Phuntsok (1933–2004) founded Larung Gar, a teaching and practice center that is now home to thousands of monastic and lay residents from Tibetan and Chinese ethnic communities. His students Khenpo Sodargye and Khenpo Tsultrim Lodrö are internationally known for their teachings on contemporary themes including intersections between Buddhism and science, and the environment and ethics; they and other students from Larung Gar now lead Buddhist centers and give talks around the world.

Khenpo Jikmé Phuntsok's life and activities made important bridges between historical forms of charisma and legitimacy, and the contemporary political and cultural context. For example, while he found many texts and objects in visions and the landscape of eastern Tibet, Khenpo Jikmé Phuntsok's *terma* discoveries (or rediscoveries) included his identification of a site in northeastern Tibet as having historical significance. This led to an archaeological dig that found building stones and treasure chests that demonstrated the historical significance of the site, which had been forgotten (Germano 1998: 77). This example of the correspondence between *terma* rediscovery and archaeology gestures toward the myriad levels of value that *terma* have in contemporary Tibetan communities and how *terma* allow for old sacred objects to be reincarnated and then recycled through their transformation for use in new contexts.

The Problem of Pollution

While many objects can move on to new lives through reincarnation and recycling, what about completely worn-out objects? Pollution is an important force that influences the options available for the disposal of sacred objects (see also Abrahms-Kavunenko, this volume). In some contemporary Tibetan and Himalayan Buddhist communities, pollution is the reason that students are often instructed to burn any Buddhist texts or objects that are worn out or no longer needed. Lama Zopa Rinpoche, the head teacher for the international organization Foundation for the Preservation of the Mahayana Tradition (FPMT), instructs his students to

> not incinerate such materials with other trash, but alone, and as they burn, recite the mantra om ah hum. As the smoke rises, visualize that it pervades all of space,

> carrying the essence of the Dharma to all sentient beings in the six samsaric realms, purifying their minds, alleviating their suffering, and bringing them all happiness, up to and including enlightenment. (Zopa Rinpoche 2012: 239)

Why is burning preferable? Burning allows for the merit of the texts to spread through the atmosphere with the smoke, thereby benefiting more beings. Another explanation is that other means of disposal may lead these sacred texts, which are understood to be manifestations of the Buddha and capable of generating blessings, to accumulate defilement or pollution. This pollution is a source of great spiritual anxiety and a significant reason why recycling as a practice can be seen as problematic and complicated.

In a paper about recycling in India, Frank Korom (1998: 200) argues that a significant impediment to the collection of waste is religious concern related to pollution. More specifically, he explains that "contact with polluting agents threatens the ritual purity of twice-born castes. . . . Because the upper castes fear substance pollution, the onerous task of dealing with human-produced garbage falls on the so-called service castes or on the *dalits*, the former untouchables." While caste systems take on diverse and different iterations throughout the Himalayas and do not always map on to the Indian system, the concern for ritual pollution connected to objects is a common one and has impacted waste management initiatives in Tibetan and Himalayan Buddhist communities. Political ecologist Elizabeth Allison's research in Bhutan has revealed the disconnection between technocratic waste management strategies developed by the state and local worldviews connected to waste—particularly anxieties about ritual pollution (Allison 2014, 2016, 2019). In fieldwork related to waste management around the sacred mountain of Khawa Karpo (Kha ba dkar po) in Yunnan, China, anthropologist Bo Wang discovered complex and competing ideas relating to the definition of and interaction with waste and ritual pollution among Tibetan pilgrims and Han Chinese tourists (Wang 2017, 2019). In both the Bhutanese and Sino-Tibetan contexts, these differing perspectives have led to problems and challenges in the implementation of waste management policies.

These difficulties have arisen because Buddhist community members are concerned about ritual pollution (as with *jinlap*) for both worldly and soteriological reasons. Anthropologist Christian Schicklgruber (1992: 724) explains that during his research in late twentieth-century Khumbo, northeast Nepal, the local community considered ritual pollution to "denote the realm outside their religiously and socially ordered world." They saw it as a form of chaos that a person is born into and comes out of only by entrance into their clan's social order through a naming ceremony. Both death and sexual activity outside the bounds of regulated clan exonamy were also connected to a state of ritual pollution, since they challenge the social order. Birth, sex, and death are also dangerous events in Buddhist soteriological terms, as they represent the inextricable events that lead individuals to become further embroiled in samsara. Anthropologist Geoffrey Samuel (1993: 161) elaborates that this kind of pollution or *drib* is

> the prime cause of misfortune in everyday life, and [it] has to be remedied by appropriate ritual action to the gods. In addition, *drib* makes an individual vulnerable to attack by malevolent spirits of various kinds. Some degree of *drib* is almost unavoidable in everyday life and the attacks of offended deities and of malevolent spirits have to be ritually combatted on a regular basis.

Since so many daily behaviors can lead to pollution, sacred objects can be especially threatening. Through their use they may have picked up pollution and an association with malevolent spirits from a variety of sources. They may also attract further pollution for the person who interacts with them. Recycling can therefore be a complex process and is in need of careful mediation. This mediation may take place through reconsecration, restoration followed by consecration, or through rehousing or changing the location of an object.

Pollution can be dispelled through consecration, along with a number of other rituals including smoke offerings (*bsang*) and *chö* (*gchod*). These purification rituals are essential; without them, sacred objects attract only obstacles and malevolent spirits that bring illness and misfortune—including loss of financial stability and property or social disharmony—to humans who live near them or interact with them. These objects can be resuscitated through new consecrations, or may be reincarnated through their relocation or incorporation into other objects as *zung*, as described earlier.

Yang: Countering Pollution, Generating Positive Forces

Another type of rituals that facilitate the installation of reincarnated, recycled sacred objects into ritual spaces are "summoning of prosperity" (*g.yang 'gugs*) rituals. These rituals are designed to invite *yang* (*g.yang*), translated variously as prosperity, fortune, wealth, and affluence, into the home. *Yang* is a sought after, essential life force that is positive, but also tricky and slippery, subject to "leak[ing], flee[ing], and be[ing] predated on by other human or non-human beings" (Da Col 2012: 175). Lamas and ritual practitioners are commissioned by patrons to perform rituals where they summon *yang* into residential shrine rooms, or restore *yang* that may have been lost after significant events (e.g., death, marriage), leading to a depletion of *yang* in a family (Balikci 2008: 154, 157). This loss of *yang* can lead to the entrance or increase of pollution, which then needs to be cast out through ritual means.

Sacred objects with *jinlap* act as magnets for *yang*. This is another reason why these objects cannot be disposed of easily and why people prefer to recycle reincarnated sacred objects rather than to burn them. As sacred objects are awakened for deities to take residence, *yang* is invited in to bring auspiciousness and favorable circumstances. When objects are reincarnated or recycled, *yang* is once again invited in. An example of this process can be found in Sikkim in the eastern Himalayas, where domestic shrine rooms are incomplete without a *yangdrom* (*g.yang 'grom*), a prosperity chest. The sponsoring family is responsible for preparing the *yangdrom*, inside which they place a variety of objects associated with prosperity and auspiciousness, including

> precious minerals, such as gold, silver, diamond, turquoise, coral, and other precious stones; jewelry; and money, ideally from around the world to represent the fortunes of Dzambuling (this present world in Buddhist cosmology). Other objects are more specific to the Sikkimese context, representing local regimes of value. These include grains (such as rice, barley, and mustard seeds), dry fruits, ocean water, dirt, grass, and stones from holy sites. Chinese tea is also a sought-after item. (Bhutia and Holmes-Tagchungdarpa 2019: 166)

While families also frequently include objects with contemporary connections to wealth (such as sugar, foreign alcohol, and Coca-cola), the inclusion of older objects and family heirlooms such as jewelry, coins, and precious minerals is significant. These items have been repurposed from their original use and when families rejuvenate their prosperity chests in subsequent years (ideally every three years), the items remain in the chest. Over time, the *jinlap* and *yang* become more efficacious; therefore, the older, the better. Objects that have decayed past reuse (specifically, consumable items such as butter) are removed from the *yangdrom*, taken outside to a clean place, and burned as offerings.

Local community members also offered family heirloom jewelry and precious stones for the creation of *zung* to fill the large, 137-foot Avalokitesvara statue built in Pelling, western Sikkim, which was consecrated in 2018. I saw many people pull off their rings made from gold, silver, and other precious metals, and offer earrings, pearl necklaces, rosaries, and gold accessories to be included in the *zung*. Several people told me that doing so would create a favorable karmic connection between themselves and Avalokitesvara that would last for lifetimes. This connection would be further reinforced through ritual interaction, such as circumambulation and incense offerings.

This recycling of significant objects to attract and trap *yang* in the prosperity chest and a large statue is designed to capture *yang* for the family unit and the community. It demonstrates again that older objects have their own unique form of *jinlap* that cannot be easily thrown away. Instead, it needs to be acknowledged lest it seep from an object or the object attract malevolent energy. At the *yangdrom* ceremonies I have witnessed between 2007 and 2020, objects encased in packaging that was beginning to disintegrate were not discarded, but were, instead, put into new forms of wrapping. Ironically, this wrapping was often plastic, suggesting that in this instance, the "zombie-like" long life and anti-entropic qualities of plastic may actually be desirable, in contrast with Mongolian concerns (Abrahms-Kavunenko, this volume), since plastic will make the objects—and their *jinlap*—last longer.

Conclusion

The question of how to dispose of sacred waste in Buddhist communities in Tibet and the Himalayas pushes us to consider whether sacred waste actually exists for Buddhists in this region. Here, once a sacred object is awakened through consecration, its generative ability to produce *jinlap* remains. Even as it ages, is worn down, or in other ways succumbs to the inevitability of impermanence and change, a sacred object remains powerful and venerated as a reincarnating agent capable of granting blessings. Instead of disposal, sacred objects are often repurposed and reincarnated as *zung* to fill other sacred objects, become treasures to be cared for in residential shrines or monasteries, or are renovated or refreshed. In this way, although their outer form might change, these sacred objects are reincarnated through recycling, and continue to hold the same efficacy as in their earlier lives. The recycling of sacred objects is thereby actively encouraged and sought after, though recycling here differs from environmentalist processes and goals; instead of just caring for the earth, this recycling ensures the continuity of positive spiritual forces such as *jinlap* and *yang*. This respect for and awareness of the continued efficacy of objects also helps us to understand how and why monasteries made from old bottles may be seen as efficacious. Following consecration, they become as powerful as monasteries made from gold—or even more powerful if the bottles already have *jinlap* through association with a sacred site or great masters. It also helps us to see how recycling projects may be a meritorious activity if undertaken with both the motivation to benefit beings *and* awareness of the respective *jinlap* or *drib* of different objects.

Sometimes a radical change in the form of an object or the location of its residence leads to the opportunity for unforeseen types of transformation. While I was visiting a monastery in Arunachal Pradesh in the eastern Himalayas in 2016, the lamas informed me that they had recently moved their woodblocks of the Buddhist canon due to space constraints. They were no longer in the monastery, and had not been used for *zung* in a stupa. Instead, they had been deposited in a river. A conservationist might cringe at the loss of these important sacred objects; however, as von Rospatt (2013) argues in his discussion about renovating Buddhist sites, Buddhist concepts and perspectives can allow us to think about these actions in new and enriching ways. From the point of view of the lamas, the woodblocks were not cast out as trash, but, instead, were able to perform their role as generators of merit and as guides for Buddhist practitioners even more effectively in their new locale. The river would carry their prayers and *jinlap* far away and around the world, transforming all sentient beings who came in contact with the water. This would suggest that sacred waste (to the extent that it can be considered waste at all) is in a constant cycle of reincarnation, taking on new forms and being recycled to create new opportunities for awakening.

Notes

1 My deep appreciation for all of the Tibetan and Himalayan teachers and members of Buddhist communities who have discussed issues related to materiality and waste with me, especially the late Sindrang Yab Gomchen Pemayangtse Dorje Lopen Chewang Rinzin and Lama Jamyang and his family, as well as people who must remain anonymous. I also thank Trine Brox, Elizabeth Williams-Oerberg, Jane Caple, Kalzang Dorjee Bhutia, Saskia Abrahms-Kavunenko, and Ven. Chuehruey for their insightful feedback, additional information, and editing suggestions that have benefited this chapter. Research for this chapter was funded by Grinnell College, Occidental College, and the "Mapping Religious Diversity in Modern Sichuan" project led by Stefania Travagnin and Elena Valussi that has been generously sponsored by the Chiang Ching-Kuo Foundation for International Scholarly Exchange.

2 I provide the popular Wylie transliteration for key Tibetan terms that are translated, such as "power objects" (*rten*). For terms in Tibetan and Himalayan languages

that are not translated (e.g., *trülku*), I have followed the "THL Simplified Phonetic Transcription of Standard Tibetan" (Germano and Tournadre 2003) and provide the Wylie transliteration (e.g., *sprul sku*) in parentheses where the terms first appear.

3 Common forms of Buddhism connected through the use of classical Tibetan texts, institutional and lineage forms, and shared histories are practiced in parts of contemporary India (including in Ladakh, Himachal Pradesh, Sikkim, West Bengal, and Arunachal Pradesh), Bhutan, Nepal, China (including in the Tibetan Autonomous Region, Sichuan, Yunnan, Gansu, Inner Mongolia, and Qinghai), and Mongolia. To be concise, in this chapter I will refer to these forms of Buddhism as Tibetan and Himalayan Buddhism, since I will not address Mongolian examples in my discussion. On Mongolian Buddhist material culture, see Abrahms-Kavunenko in this volume.

References

Allison, Elizabeth (2014), "Waste and Worldviews: Garbage and Pollution Challenges in Bhutan," *Journal for the Study of Religion, Nature and Culture*, 8 (4): 405–28. doi: 10.1558/jsrnc.v8i4.25050

Allison, Elizabeth (2016), "At the Boundary of Modernity: Religion, Technocracy, and Waste Management in Bhutan," in Megan Adamson Sijapati and Jessica Vantine Birkenholtz (eds), *Religion and Modernity in the Himalaya*, 163–81, New York: Routledge.

Allison, Elizabeth (2019), "The Reincarnation of Waste: A Case Study of Spiritual Ecology Activism for Household Solid Waste Management: The Samdrup Jongkhar Initiative of Rural Bhutan," *Religions*, 10 (9): 1–19. doi: 10.3390/rel10090514

Balikci, Anna (2008), *Lamas, Shamans and Ancestors: Village Religion in Sikkim*, Leiden: Brill.

Bentor, Yael (1996), *Consecration of Images and Stūpas in Indo-Tibetan Tantric Buddhism*, Leiden: Brill.

Brox, Trine (2019), "The Aura of Buddhist Material Objects in the Age of Mass-production," *Journal of Global Buddhism*, 20: 105–25. doi: 10.5281/zenodo.3238213

Bhutia, Kalzang Dorjee and Amy Holmes-Tagchungdarpa (2019), "A Spot of Enlightenment: Tea as a Fuel for Connectivity in Himalayan Buddhist Cultures," in Lipok Dzüvichü and Manjeet Baruah (eds), *Objects and Frontiers*, 157–73, Delhi and New York: Routledge.

Chodron, Thubten (2001), *Buddhism for Beginners*, Boston: Snow Lion.

Da Col, Giovanni (2012), "The Poisoner and the Parasite: Cosmoeconomics, Death and Hospitality among Dechen Tibetans," *Journal of the Royal Anthropological Institute*: 175–95. doi: 10.1111/j.1467-9655.2012.01771.x

Doctor, Andreas (2005), *Tibetan Treasure Literature: Revelation, Tradition, and Accomplishment in Visionary Buddhism*, Ithaca: Snow Lion.

Elverskog, Johan (2020), *The Buddha's Footprint: An Environmental History of Asia*, Philadelphia: University of Pennsylvania Press.

Gayley, Holly (2007), "Soteriology of the Senses in Tibetan Buddhism," *Numen*, 54 (4): 459–99. doi: 10.1163/156852707X244306

Dge 'dun chos 'phel (2009), "Rgyal khams rig pas bskor ba'i gta rgyud gser gyi thang ma," in Dge 'dun chos 'phel (ed), *Mkhas dbang dge 'dun chos 'phel gri gsung 'bum*, vol. 1, 3–480, Khreng tu'u: Si khron dge skrun tshogs pa and Si khron mi rigs dpe skrun khang.

Gentry, James (2019), "Tibetan Buddhist Power Objects," in *The Oxford Research Encyclopedia of Religion*, New York: Oxford University Press. doi: 10.1093/acrefore/9780199340378.013.657

Germano, David (1998), "Remembering the Dismembered Body of Tibet," in Melvyn Goldstein and Matthew Kapstein (eds), *Buddhism in Contemporary Tibet*, 53–94, Berkeley: University of California Press.

Germano, David (2004), "Living Relics of the Buddha(s) in Tibet," in David Germano and Kevin Trainor (eds), *Embodying the Dharma: Buddhist Relic Veneration in Asia*, 51–92, Albany: State University of New York Press.

Germano, David, and Nicolas Tournadre (2003), "THL Simplified Phonetic Transcription of Standard Tibetan," *The Tibetan & Himalayan Library*. https://www.thlib.org/reference/transliteration/#!essay=/thl/phonetics.

Gyatso, Janet (1998), *Apparitions of the Self: The Secret Autobiographies of a Tibetan Visionary*, Princeton, NJ: Princeton University Press.

Harris, Ian (1991), "How Environmentalist is Buddhism?" *Religion*, 21 (2): 101–14. doi: 10.1016/0048-721X(91)90058-X

Holmes-Tagchungdarpa, Amy (2014), *The Social Life of Tibetan Biography: Textuality, Community and Authority in the Lineage of Tokden Shakya Shri*, Lanham, MD: Lexington.

Hsiao, Hsin Yi, Hsun-Ta Hsu, Debra Boudreaux, and Alice Ting (2019), "Global Grassroots Green Movement Drive by Tzu Chi Foundation's Recycling Volunteers," in Alice M. L. Chong and Iris Chi (eds), *Social Work and Sustainability in Asia: Facing the Challenges of Global Environmental Changes*, 61–82, Milton: Routledge.

Huber, Toni (1991), "Traditional Environmental Protectionism in Tibet Reconsidered," *Tibet Journal*, 16 (3): 63–77. http://www.jstor.org/stable/43302228

Korom, Frank J. (1998), "On the Ethics and Aesthetics of Recycling in India," in Lance E. Nelson (ed), *Purifying the Earthly Body of God: Religion and Ecology in Hindu India*, 197–223, Albany: State University of New York Press.

Lee, Chengpan and Ling Han (2015), "Recycling Bodhisattva: The Tzu-Chi Movement's Response to Global Climate Change," *Social Compass*, 62 (3): 311–25. doi: 10.1177/0037768615587809

Roberts, Rosemary (2009), *What Would the Buddha Recycle? The Zen of Green Living*, Avon, MA: Simon and Schuster.

Samuel, Geoffrey (1993), *Civilized Shamans: Buddhism in Tibetan Societies*, Washington, DC: Smithsonian Institution Press.

Schicklgruber, Christian (1992), "Grib: On the Significance of the Term in a Socio-religious Context," in Shōren Ihara and Zuihō Yamaguchi (eds), *Tibetan Studies: Proceedings of the 5th Seminar of the International Association for Tibetan Studies, Narita 1989*, 723–34, Narita: Naritasan Shinshōji.

Singh, Arvind Kumar (2012), "Economic Management: An Interpretation from the Buddhist Perspective," *Sri Lanka International Journal of Buddhist Studies*, 2: 74–87.

Stengs, Irene (2014), "Sacred Waste," *Material Religion*, 10 (2): 235–8.

Sunkara, Lavanya (2018), "This Thai Temple Was Built Using 1.5 Million Beer Bottles," *Architectural Digest*, October 9. https://www.architecturaldigest.com/story/this-thai-temple-built-using-millions-beer-bottles (accessed September 15, 2020).

Strong, John (2004), *Relics of the Buddha*, Princeton: Princeton University Press.

Tanakasempipat, Patpicha and Jiraporn Kuhakan (2020), "Bottles for Blessings: Thai Buddhist Temple Recycles Plastics into Robes," *Reuters*, February 6. https://www.reuters.com/article/us-thailand-environment-temple/bottles-for-blessings-thai-buddhist-temple-recycles-plastics-into-robes-idUSKBN2000LI (accessed September 15, 2020).

Thondup, Tulku (1997), *Hidden Teachings of Tibet*, Boston: Wisdom Publications.

von Rospatt, Alexander (2013), "Buddhist Strategies of Keeping its Sacred Images and Shrines Alive: The Example of the Svayambhū-caitya of Kathmandu," in David Park, Kuenga Wangmo, and Sharon Cather (eds), *Art of Merit: Studies in Buddhist Art and its Conservation*, 275–85, London: Archetype Publications.

Wang, Bo (2017), "Waste and Sacredness: Nature and Cultural Conceptions of Solid Waste in Tibetan Southwest China," Ph.D. dissertation, University of Wisconsin-Madison.

Wang, Bo (2019), "Sacred Trash and Personhood: Living in Daily Waste-Management Infrastructures in the Eastern Himalayas," *Cross-Currents: East Asian History and Culture Review*, 30: 101–19. https://escholarship.org/uc/item/49c2f6qt

Wangchuk, Dorji (2015), "Biblioclasm/Libricide in the History of Tibetan Buddhism," in Olaf Czaja and Guntram Hazod (eds), *The Illuminating Mirror: Tibetan Studies in Honor of Per K. Sorensen on the Occasion of His 65th Birthday*, 527–39, Wiesbaden: Dr. Ludwig Reichert Wiesbaden.

Williams, Duncan Ryuken (2010), "Buddhist Environmentalism in Contemporary Japan," in Richard K. Payne (ed), *How Much Is Enough? Buddhism, Consumerism and the Human Environment*, 17–37, Somerville: Wisdom Books.

Wisman, Anne (2017), "Buddhist Temples Made from Recycled Glass Bottles," *Buddhistdoor Global*, August 1. https://www.buddhistdoor.net/news/buddhist-temples-made-from-recycled-glass-bottles (accessed September 15, 2020).

Yeh, Emily T. (2014), "The Rise and Fall of the Green Tibetan: Contingent Collaborations and the Vicissitudes of Harmony," in Emily Yeh and Chris Coggins (eds), *Mapping Shangrila: Contested Landscapes in the Sino-Tibetan Borderlands*, 255–78, Seattle: University of Washington Press.

Zopa Rinpoche, Lama (2012), *How to Practice Dharma: Teachings on the Eight Worldly Dharmas*, Boston: Lama Yeshe Wisdom Archive.

6

Zombie Rubbish and Mummy Materiality

The Undead and the Fate of Mongolian Buddhist Waste

Saskia Abrahms-Kavunenko

In Mongolia before the socialist purges of the late 1930s, Buddhist religious offerings were made from items that could decompose. Prayer scarves were made from silk and offerings to deities were made from edible items such as barley grains and dairy products. When they were made of enduring materials, such as the rocks placed upon sacred cairns (*ovoos*) that stand upon high mountain passes, they discoursed with invisible beings who could assist in the procurement of good fortune for all those who passed. In the postsocialist period (which began in 1990), however, some products used as ritual offerings are mass-produced and are cheap to purchase. Differing from the things used for Buddhist rituals in the presocialist period, these items are made from materials which do not easily biodegrade. Unlike the sacred rocks whose stability marks the sanctity of the landscape, store-bought items, such as polyester prayer scarves and food offerings wrapped in plastic, take on a new kind of materiality that lingers problematically.

Although Buddhism is often imagined in popular culture to run counter to materialism and the consumptive practices of capitalist societies, lay Buddhists and Buddhist institutions are very much entangled in the processes of wealth generation and consumption patterns that produce waste. Items used in Mongolian Buddhist rituals are often generated by large-scale industrial processes that function within the logic of global capitalism and, like other consumables, they can be cheap and easy to buy. These ritual items are made from materials which are easily broken, yet their material properties linger beyond their short life span as wanted things. They can be difficult to discard and can contribute to pollution problems at pilgrimage sites. Used Buddhist items, as this volume shows, do not always behave like ordinary discarded things. They can pose difficulties for those who seek to get rid of them (Gould; Gygi; Wilson this volume) and their potency can be powerfully carried from one ritual use to be repurposed for another (Brox; Holmes-Tagchungdarpa this volume).

Reno (2014: 20) describes how the enduring materiality of contemporary consumables and the development of mass waste disposal systems have created an environment in which discarded items enter a condition wherein they are neither "dead nor alive." Our rubbish, he argues, enters a kind of "zombie state" (ibid.), neither able to decompose, nor be fully alive. This chapter extends Reno's idea of undead waste as an analogy for contemporary problems with discarded items. It will explore the undead qualities of used Mongolian Buddhist ritual items that do not easily reintegrate into biotic systems. Mongolian Buddhist waste can take on the undead materiality of other kinds of garbage, yet it can differ qualitatively from every day "zombie" rubbish. If a ritual item is discarded it can become materially ambivalent *and*, like the anti-entropic bodies of mummies, energetically and spiritually ambivalent. In resisting physical atrophy sacred items can exact new kinds of obligations.

This chapter will utilize the "undead" as a way of analyzing the differences between ordinary and sacred waste, while foregrounding their material properties. Specifically, it will look at what zombies and mummies, as two different classes of the "undead," can tell us about the materiality of discarded items. The cinematic development of zombie films reflects unfolding concerns about mass-consumer culture and its attendant generation of garbage, while mummies, in both Hollywood films and in Inner Asia, instantiate concerns about the disturbance of animate materials and the desire to avoid curse-like qualities. Just as cinematic zombies and mummies create different kinds of problems that need to be solved, there are distinctions between the kinds of problems that mundane rubbish and Mongolian Buddhist ritual waste create. Both ordinary waste and Buddhist ritual waste resist entropy. However, while ordinary rubbish can be seen as having zombie-like qualities, discarded materials from Mongolian rituals instantiate a kind of "mummy materiality" wherein items are charged with potency and exact extra-mundane responsibilities.

Undead Waste

Monsters are often formed from the crossing of categories, beings that are not quite one thing or another, or the possession of a characteristic to an "unnatural" degree (Musharbash 2014). The undead, as a subclass of monster, are animate beings that are neither alive nor dead. In contemporary Euro-American cinematic tropes zombies have human bodies without a human mind, mummies have supernatural powers which are awakened when they are disturbed, and vampires feed off the living to maintain their own extra-normal life span. Changing portrayals of the undead can give form to popular anxieties. Early cinematic representations of zombies discoursed with colonial race anxieties (McAlister 2012), while the first depictions of mummies in horror films dialogued with contemporary discomforts surrounding European scientists unearthing the long-entombed bodies of the dead. Although monsters can represent or instantiate what we fear in any given epoch, they cannot be reduced to their symbolic forms (Musharbash 2014). They create, in their host populations, real affects and real actions. Just as a haunted house will dissuade people from moving in, Mongolian vampiric imps (*chötgör*)[1] can cause people to break up households and move to other parts of the country (Swancutt 2008).[2] The fear that monsters produce in us affects us in physically tangible ways (Musharbash 2014).

Pollution and rubbish, likewise, cross categories. Discussing food taboos in *Leviticus*, Douglas (2002 [1966]) argues that certain foods were avoided because their exceptionalism rendered them to be perceived as polluting. Pigs, for example, pollute because they do not conform to the categories that were accorded to the kinds of things that humans eat. It is not just human subjectivities that define what is and what is not polluting. Due to the enduring materials with which we now create things to use and discard, contemporary rubbish crosses categories, not just because it does not conform with the symbolic ordering of human subjectivities, but also because of the materials from which it is made. In Mongolia the increasing consumption of throwaway items over the past couple of decades has coincided with growing concerns about spiritual decline (Abrahms-Kavunenko 2019a). As the country has transitioned from socialism to capitalism, the ability to purchase goods has become a marker of development. Basic items such as food are bought covered in disposable packaging to ensure freshness and hygiene, and disposable items are cheap and easy to buy. However, the rubbish that this consumption produces, especially when carelessly discarded, has come to indicate moral and spiritual degeneration.

With the expansion of large-scale urban settlements and the relatively recent mass production and consumption of petroleum-based products, human relationships to waste have changed. Items are now made to be obsolete (Hawkings 2019) and the new materials with which we make these products mean that unwanted materials now linger in new ways, unable to transform again into life-generating soil and other forms of organic matter. In most places around the world, including Mongolia, people now use and discard products with unprecedented rapidity (ibid.). The development of mass waste, an invention of eighteenth- century European urbanization processes, means that waste disposal systems now place even compostable refuse out of the cycles in which they could break down through ordinary semi-biotic processes (Reno 2014). As Reno (ibid.: 20) writes:

> Through incineration and conventional landfill, it could be argued that mass waste deposits appear *undead*, life-like and yet unable to generate new ecological possibilities. One can think of environmental, technical, and regulatory approaches to mass waste as the *zombie model*. Mass waste must be contained forever, encased in a landfill, because it is thought threatening to everything it comes into contact with and yet it cannot die.

In large urban landfills biodegradable materials, mixed with plastics and other items which cannot decompose, are unable to reenter organic cycles, becoming, instead, a hazardous source of excess methane. In these new waste trajectories, the animals, plants, and fungi that normally decompose materials are either stopped from doing so because human activity has rendered these materials imperishable before they are disposed of, or do so in a manner that leads to further ecosystemic disequilibrium. Mass waste becomes "undead," taking on a new status as a kind of *zombie* rubbish.

The term "zombie" in the cinematic genre owes its genesis to Afro-Haitian ritual practices in which *zonbi* refers to the souls of the recently deceased whose living essences are trapped and whose bodies are made to work enslaved for the living (McAlister 2012). There are similar practices in South Africa where people accused of witchcraft are said to enslave the dead to labor and toil on the witches' behalf (Comaroff and Comaroff 1999; Niehaus 2005). The first cinematic imaginings of the zombie, in films such as *White Zombie* (1932) and *I Walked with a Zombie* (1943), are set in Haiti and discourse with colonial anxieties and curiosities regarding Afro-Haitian ritual practices. Later cinematic renderings of the zombie in North America shifted radically from these initial inspirations. Contemporary film zombies, rather than being the dead entranced to work for the living, are ravening quasi-beings infected and infectious with some obscure, radically transformative affliction. Instead of being productive for those who have entranced them, they indiscriminately seek out the living to feast on their flesh and/or brains, and in the process dissolve the distinction between the living and the dead. Beginning with Romero's *Night of the Living Dead* (1968) and *Dawn of the Dead* (1978), the zombie film genre has transformed to form a critique of modern consumer society and "mindless" consumption. The genre has also shifted in its scale of threat, from targeting specific families or individuals for thralldom to apocalyptic-scale societal breakdown, wherein zombies now threaten to destroy the entire fabric of civilization (Newbury 2012: 99). A key feature of millennial zombie films such as *Shaun of the Dead* (2004) and *28 Days Later* (2002), not found in Romero's seminal undead trilogy, is the centralization of fast food culture and the endlessly proliferating rubbish which it produces (Newbury 2012). While in *Night of the Living Dead*, Romero envisions zombies wandering through empty fields in an agricultural district, the contemporary zombocalypse stumbles or flees through the Styrofoam cups and happy meal cartons of the urban refuse of a rampant consumer society.

While the post-1968 cinematic zombie can and should be killed, sometimes fairly easily, it is their mass effect that creates problems. Zombies, in this way, are like plastic waste. Individually they are a problem, as a massing they overwhelm. Our accelerated consumptive practices have led to a situation in which rubbish now fills the air, the land, and the seas. Plastic detritus, from large items down to microplastics, are now found ubiquitously, from the deepest oceans (Choy et al. 2019) to the heights of Everest. So pervasive are plastics that some commentators have suggested that instead of calling the new geological era dominatingly affected by human behaviors the Anthropocene, it should be termed the "Plasticene" ('Editorial': Notes from the Plasticene Epoch' 2014). Entering our food chain at every point, we are not sure what this plastic will do to human bodies and minds, and to other life on the planet. What we do know is that the threat lies, like that of zombies, in the sheer quantity of waste.

The Morality of Waste

When I first arrived in Mongolia's capital Ulaanbaatar to do fieldwork at Buddhist temples and Dharma Centers for thirteen months in 2009 and 2010, the sight of informal rubbish collectors, who collect recyclables to be sold on to China, rummaging through waste piles and carrying bottles through the city was a notable feature of city life. Recycling, up until the ban on rubbish exports to China in 2018, happened only in this informal sector, partly accounting for why Mongolia's rubbish output is so high (Byamba and Ishikawa 2017). In the neighborhoods containing *gers* (nomadic felt tents) inside fenced areas, waste collection can occur as infrequently as once a month (ibid.). In these *ger* neighborhoods in winter, which made up around 83 percent of Ulaanbaatar's built area in 2015 (World Bank 2015: 1), the generation of ash from coal-fired stoves accounts for more than the total of the rest of the city's household waste combined (Byamba and Ishikawa 2017: 6). To keep *ger* residents warm at all times against the winter cold, urban stoves must run day and night, and are a major cause of the chronically bad levels of air pollution in the city (Abrahms-Kavunenko 2019a).

In Ulaanbaatar, urban waste disposal is a noticeable aspect of city life. It is estimated that in the city, urbanites create over one kilogram of waste per person per day (not including recyclables), meaning that the city's waste output is well above the global average (Byamba and Ishikawa 2017: 6). The regular movement of garbage trucks around the city is accompanied by piercing music blasted from loudspeakers. The trucks display emblems proudly announcing the generosity of their Japanese donors. Rubbish is either collected from communal waste piles outside the buildings, or in the *ger* neighborhoods, or by apartment personnel from the landings on the stairways between apartments. When I returned to Ulaanbaatar to do further fieldwork in 2013, and again for another eight months in 2015 and 2016, complaints about the presence of rubbish in the countryside and in the Tuul river that runs through the southern section of the city had increased. Indeed, from 2009 to 2019 the Asia Foundation reports that the amount of garbage that the city produces has increased to seven times its 2009 rate (The Asia Foundation 2019). On top of this waste output it is estimated that an additional 15 percent of this amount is illegally dumped (Byamba and Ishikawa 2017). For people in poorer areas, who struggle to afford coal or the new high- efficiency briquettes to burn, rubbish and old tires are burned to provide heat and fuel for cooking, adding to air pollution problems.

This sevenfold increase in rubbish over the last decade is related to changing consumption practices in the city, a trend which has not gone unnoticed by urbanites. It was common for friends and acquaintances to tell me stories of a previous time in which people desired or needed less things to be happy. During an interview with retired ecologist Dr. Bold in 2015, he told me that during the socialist period people had few material things and their *setgel* (mind, emotion, spirit) was good. The focus has changed, he told me, to acquiring more and more material things. Likewise, a Buddhist lama, whose marriage had ended, argued in an interview in 2016 that the core problem with the contemporary period in comparison with the socialist period was that people needed a lot of things to be happy. His wife and child, in his opinion, needed more than a lama's salary to be content. As a consequence he had chosen to continue his vocation rather than to stay married. This sense of declining happiness linked to increased consumerism was quite common in conversations and interviews with friends, acquaintances, lay Buddhists, and monastics. While most people also emphasized the positive aspects of freedom of religion and the opportunities for the youth (providing they had enough money), people often told me that capitalist motivations had replaced more communitarian motivations.

Some monastic and lay Buddhists described to me how increasing financial motivations in the city meant that the quality of Buddhist practice was declining. Following the Democratic Revolution in 1990 and the lifting of restrictions on religion there was a blossoming of Buddhist practices as the old men who had been lamas before the purges of the 1930s started to revive old temples and create new Buddhist communities. Having a living connection to the presocialist past, this early postsocialist period was characterized by generous support from the laity who, despite the broader financial hardships of the time, often gave generous donations to new congregations. In a comprehensive survey of temples in 2007, Majer and Teleki found that only half of these temples survived the initial renewal of the 1990s (Teleki 2009). As Teleki reports, the new temples struggled to recruit and retain young lamas and after the old lamas died the novice lamas found it difficult to generate consistent support from the local laity. Many of my interlocutors discussed the early postsocialist period, even in 2009, as a kind of golden period. The lamas' living links to the past and the perceived purity of their motivations were often compared to the lax morality and financially driven intentions in the present (see also Abrahms-Kavunenko 2015; Caple, this volume).

In an interview with a friend, Ankha, after we had been on a trip to the nearby national park Terelj in 2015 and seen piles of mixed plastic and biodegradable garbage left by visiting tourists, she told me that (mostly internal) tourism was causing pollution in the countryside. She then went on to link the presence of rubbish to moral degeneration in the city:

> I think the atmosphere is polluted as well as the Mongolian population. They are polluted inside. . . . More and more Mongolians want to be rich . . . . Too much ambitious behavior isn't good for the country . . . . So that's why we have to have some balance . . . . Mongolian politicians aren't so loyal. They only want to eat. They only want to improve their life. They don't want to improve the lives of the Mongolian population. So I think pollution is everywhere in Mongolia. Especially inside . . . . People throw out their rubbish from their car window. And they make a lot of garbage and a lot of mess on the bank of the Tuul river. Even

> though they understand that the Tuul river is the main resource of our water. It means their motivations are polluted.

For Ankha, spiritual pollution (*buzarlal*) and the pollution of landscape and air (*bokhirdol*) are connected (see also Abrahms-Kavunenko 2019a). If people's intentions are polluted, as many people told me, then the environment becomes polluted. Rampant consumerism and improper waste disposal are connected with a lack of shared consideration for other people. These bad actions are underscored by bad intentions which, in turn, are often thought to cause bad effects in the future through the mechanism of karma (ibid.).

Other friends and acquaintances linked the increasing rubbish problem to the growing disconnection from the countryside caused by too many years of urban living and the excessive items that people use in the city. In Mongolia the relative lack of consumerism and the simplicity of nomadic herders' lifestyles tend to be romanticized by urbanites. When middle-class friends saw plastic rubbish littering the countryside, they assumed (perhaps correctly) that this waste was coming from urban tourists. I heard complaints that the increasing consumerism in the city was being met with a flood of poor-quality products. As a couple of friends described, as soon as these products were bought they needed to be thrown in the bin, contributing to new and unending waste production and disposal. Given the rather dramatic increase in rubbish over the last decade, these are more than just perceptions of consumption patterns. As people use and throw away more and more items, these items find their way into urban landfill being suspended in a zombie-like state, unable to decompose. Like cinematic zombies, this rubbish poses a problem of scale, rather than in the biographies of specific items. More and more consumption creates more and more waste.

Animate Materials

In Ulaanbaatar, the biography of an item affects whether or not it may contain hidden potencies. As has been documented in North America (Kilroy-Marac 2016, 2018; Newell 2014), a person's belongings can be thought to carry with them the energy of the person to whom they once belonged. Højer (2012) discusses how pawnshops in Ulaanbaatar can be places of spiritual danger due to the presence of belongings that have been reluctantly separated from their owners in ways that may have caused them to carry the energetic residues of loss and anger. Due to perceived difficulties in completely alienating these things from their previous owners, pawnshop employees must be careful in navigating their exchanges, remaining mindful not to mistreat the commodities, which could carry with them dangerous potentials (ibid.).

Mongolian Buddhist items, like ritual offerings elsewhere, are more likely than mundane items to contain potent energies. In an article describing the hazardousness of ritual waste in Cuban popular religion, Wirtz (2009) describes how ritual offerings, even though discarded, can carry with them hidden dangers. Some ritual offerings left on the street are identifiable only through their ritual biographies and can appear to be almost identical to ordinary rubbish. Even though they can be difficult to recognize, tampering accidentally with ritual items is believed to cause ill effects for those who interfere with them (ibid.). In Mongolia, ritual items, sacred texts, or mundane items that are imprinted with sacred symbols are more likely to contain hidden potentials than ordinary materials.

During the socialist period in Mongolia (1921–90) people were actively discouraged from keeping religious artifacts. The socialist purges of the late 1930s were accompanied by the destruction of public ritual life, including in its physical forms. Sacred items, including mummified lamas, were burned, temples were destroyed, and around a fifth of the monastic population were killed (Kaplonski 2014). Despite the difficulties and considerable dangers of harboring illicit items, many Mongols saved valued ritual items and texts from destruction. When I spoke to people about whether their family practiced Buddhism during the socialist period, many people discussed ritual items that were handed down within their family. In one interview with lay Buddhist Dawaatsuren, an IT worker who was thirty-nine in 2015, he told me of how his grandfather, who had been a lama in the 1930s in Hovd province, had practiced in secret throughout the socialist period. As he described, in the late 1930s:

> There was a big temple in our village. They destroyed the sutras and books. Most of them were burned. But during the night-time my grandfather brought a camel and loaded as much as he could on the camel and then hid them in a cave . . . during the daytime he herded sheep around there and, without anyone knowing what he was doing, he brought out the sutras and practiced. . . . He [later] sent one carload of Buddhist sutras and statues to Gandan monastery. He saved most of the scriptures and sutras from that temple. . . .That is what my grandma said.

Like Dawaatsuren's grandfather, many people risked their own safety to keep Buddhist texts and artifacts safe. These items have often been passed down through families who now keep these sacred items or texts on their household shrines. However, the remembrance of where exactly an item has come from or what the family is supposed to do with it is not always clear. This can be a source of anxiety, and some families, unsure of what to do with sacred items because of their potency, have given these items to temples (see Højer 2009). As the head librarian from Gandan told me in an interview in 2016, Gandan Khiid is struggling with the huge collection of texts that families have given the temple. Without the resources to properly store the texts, they have developed problems with mold, dust, insects, and rodents.

The improper treatment of sacred items by lay families is believed by some to lead to blockages in fortune, illness, or even death. As Oyunbat, a middle-aged professional described to me in 2009:

> When I was a child my younger sister had a problem. She was one year old but she had a serious illness. My parents went to many hospitals many times for about one year. But she wasn't well. One time my aunt went to a Buddhist lama who *mereglekh* [divines]. You use coins. This lama said that they had some Buddhist *burkhan* [Buddha, deity, god] at home but that the *burkhan* was not in a suitable place. After my aunt came to my home she said that to my parents. We found a *burkhan* picture. About two years before my grandmother died and she had some *burkhan*, some pictures. But we didn't have any religion, so after she died, we put them in there [gesturing to indicate a cupboard]. We searched and we found them and we relocated and renewed them. After that my younger sister was well. I was young, about ten years old, but I thought that this is not ordinary. This is not simple. The lama has powers. The lama knew about this.

Oyunbat's family's pictures representing Buddhist deities are a source of both faith and dangerous potential. Not treated in the correct way, one of them had caused the illness of the family's youngest child. Treated correctly, the pictures are generative of religious devotion. The image of a buddha or Buddhist deity has resonance beyond its material appearance. It is imbued with potency that can either help or hinder. For those who feel they cannot properly look after a religious item, the potency of a ritual item may lead to avoidance rather than engagement (see also Højer 2009). Yet, it can be difficult to discharge one's responsibility for the item once it is no longer wanted.

For some Buddhists, the presence of a Buddhist image on a mundane object can cause even ordinary objects to become spiritually ambivalent. When chatting with a middle-aged lay Buddhist friend in 2009, she complained to me about the printing of the Buddha's image on a box of matches. This, she told me, made the object difficult to dispose of after use. After all, she asks me, how could a person place the Buddha's image in the rubbish? If the matchbox is placed in the rubbish bin in Ulaanbaatar it will end up mixed in with other refuse on the floor, then being taken to one of the city's landfill sites. In printing the Buddha's image on the box the matchbox becomes a potential site of disrespect.

Buddhist ritual waste in Mongolia can become problematic as it mixes with mundane materials, discarded and suspended part way between life and decomposition. In this form, discarded ritual items cannot be correctly treated as alive, and cannot have a proper death or decommissioning. This problem does not generally occur for perishable offerings, though this depends on whether or not they are packaged when offered. Religious store owner Gerelmaa tells me that, along with prayer scarves, the main item she sells is dirty barley (*khaltar arvai*). This offering is made when people return to their birthplaces and visit sacred pilgrimage sites. It is also used in other rituals such as the *dallaga* ceremony, which calls prosperity into the home (Abrahms-Kavunenko 2019b). The barley, due to its dark color, as Gerelmaa tells me, has properties that purify. As a seed it is able to generate and multiply positive results. When eaten by birds it spreads and furthers the multiplication of good results.

Dairy products are thought to be sacred in Mongolia offering purification and referencing the maternal bond from infant to child (Thrift 2014). Many Mongols in the city and in the countryside make offerings from their first cup of milk tea to the four directions for purification. Offering milk while circumambulating sacred sites is a common part of ritual activities in both the country and the city. Many people, when traveling, stop their cars to circumambulate *ovoo*s (sacred rock cairns) and leave some offerings. As milk is seen as a good offering for the local spirits, one often sees milk cartons on *ovoo*s, left in tetra packaging. What will happen to this milk carton, bloated in the sun? Will someone remove it as it, mixed with other packaged and unpackaged offerings, becomes increasingly unsightly?

On Facebook in early 2020 a friend shared a post about the ritual offerings made at *ovoo*s. Accompanying it was a picture of an *ovoo* completely covered in offerings of bread, milk products, and sweets, some of them packaged and others not. While the author's main complaints were about how much money was being spent on ritual offerings all around the country, he also scolded fellow Mongols for leaving items such as prayer scarves on the *ovoo*s, writing that Chinese nylon cloth can pollute the environment for 200 to 300 years.[3] It was, and is, better, he wrote, to offer small amounts of milk and grains which can be eaten by birds. Placing perishable offerings in volumes that can be eaten by birds can multiply the blessings, but leaving items wrapped in plastic or mixed in with imperishable items restricts this process, causing pollution problems at the site.

Figure 6.1 An *ovoo* covered in offerings. Photograph by the author.

Figure 6.2 Offerings of milk, prayer scarves, and an image of Yamāntaka on an *ovoo*. Photograph by the author.

As many people in Ulaanbaatar were born in the countryside (the population of the city has more than doubled over the last thirty years), they feel a disjunct between the multiplication of disposable, yet enduring, objects and the life-generating movement of materials in nomadic life (Abrahms-Kavunenko

2019b). Contemporary ritual objects when discarded present new challenges. Many ritual items and offerings now resist atrophy. They are trapped in an enduring, undead state. Yet, unlike ordinary zombie waste, which threatens as a collective, discarded ritual items are more akin to the materiality of Inner Asian mummies. In not dispersing through organic processes and thereby distributing the blessings and intentions they contain, such items become stuck. In a liminal status between offering and trash, these items demand ongoing respect, exacting continuing obligations and threatening potential ill effects if treated improperly.

Mummy Materiality

Mummies in Inner Asia are sacred relics that are often associated with spiritual attainments. In some ways they share characteristics with Euro-American cinematic tropes. Due to their anti-entropic materiality, both must be treated correctly in order to avoid the awakening of curse-like qualities. In Hollywood, mummy films are generally about the proper treatment of human remains and respect for bodies that resist deterioration. Unlike zombies, which have dramatically transformed since their cinematic inception from slow-moving entranced ladies, to the running/screaming infected undead, mummies have not changed much since they were first portrayed on the screen (save an improvement in special effects). Mummy films, such as *The Mummy* (1932) and the more recent *The Mummy* (1999) begin with the awakening of a curse through the disturbance of an interred body. The body itself, characteristically wrapped in linen cloth, becomes animated and follows those who have disturbed it, embodying the inescapable logic of the curse. In order to avoid their demise, the protagonists of the film must perform a magical remedy. The resolution is not in the killing of the undead (as it is in zombie films) but, rather, a magical undoing of an original wrong. Like zombie films, mummy films have changed in the scale of the disturbances the film imagines. Both were initially about curses or problems for the individuals in the story who had disturbed the peace, and were fairly local in their reach. Now, mummy and zombie films speak to broader anxieties of a coming global apocalypse. The Mummy, no longer content with visiting its curse on those who disturbed it, now presages universal destruction. Mummy films are about proper treatment of materials that exist beyond their life span. This proper treatment reflects the specific biographies of individual mummies. Zombie materiality, in contrast, overwhelms.

In 2015 the global media paid brief attention to a stolen mummified Mongolian lama that was found seated in the lotus position and covered in animal skins in the possession of someone living in Ulaanbaatar. For a brief period, there was some conjecture among the Mongolian public about whether or not the lama was in a deep state of meditation and hence alive, or whether the body had been intentionally mummified. The police were prosecuting a forty-five-year-old man for stealing the mummy and trying to sell it on the black market. The theft of religious items for sale in illegal markets in Mongolia is not uncommon in the postsocialist period. Temples and religious centers are often poorly guarded and thefts of statues and other sacred items have occurred in the capital city and other parts of the country. What was particularly brazen about this theft was that it was the theft of an entire human body. The improper treatment of such a body could have dire consequences for the thief, made worse by the conjecture over whether or not the mummy, rather than being dead, was in a state of deep meditation. These questions were hotly debated by Mongolian lamas and scientists for a brief period, with some people suggesting that this mummy might be as miraculous as the "incorruptible" body of Lama Itigelov further north in one of Siberia's Mongolian cultural regions, Buryatia (Jonutytė 2019: 53).

The body of Lama Itigelov is a popular site of pilgrimage for Mongols who travel north to Buryatia, to the east of Lake Baikal in Russia, to visit the body on the eight days per year that he is displayed. Lama Itigelov died before the socialist purges in Russia in 1927. Before his death he instructed the lamas of his monastery to exhume and then rebury his body thirty years after he had passed away. When he was exhumed in secret in 1955 the excavators were amazed to find that his body had not decayed. As per his wishes and due to the danger of keeping his body above ground during the period, his body was again interred. In 2002, when he was dug up again, his body had still not deteriorated. Unlike the linen-wrapped cinematic mummy, Itigelov's skin is visible and he has a waxy appearance. Important as an attestation of Buryat sovereignty and as a sacred relic to inspire faith, the body of Itigelov is believed by some to be meditating, neither fully alive nor quite dead (Bernstein 2012: 270, Jonutytė 2019). Others believe that after becoming enlightened, Itigelov left behind an "imperishable body" to inspire faith in the postsocialist era (Quijada 2012; see also Bernstein 2012: 270). As scientific discourses have failed to come up with a convincing story of how the body has avoided decomposition, Itigelov is now a site of faith, prayer, and curiosity for visitors who believe that contact with the sacred body can yield positive effects (Bernstein 2012; Quijada 2012).

By the time I arrived in Mongolia in the late spring of 2015, the popular consensus was that, unlike Itigelov, the stolen mummy in Ulaanbaatar had been intentionally mummified by skilled embalmers. The body was certainly sacred, but lacking a miraculous story of its spontaneous mummification, the body has not become a site of pilgrimage. Mummification is not an unusual practice among Buddhists—it is still carried out by Tibetans in exile (Bernstein 2012), Buddhists in Taiwan (Gildow and Bingenheimer 2002), and in other parts of the Buddhist world. Preserving the body of a deceased person who has reached spiritual attainment is believed to enable the body to impart teachings and blessings after they die (ibid.: 270).

A year later in 2016, I was sitting drinking tea with a Tibetan Rinpoche in Ulaanbaatar. He is the son of the Ninth Javzandamba, the most important reincarnation lineage in Mongolia, and had been living in Mongolia for six years. At the time we met, he was residing in small quarters on the second floor of a temple in Ulaanbaatar's Gandantegchenliin Khiid (or Gandan), the largest temple compound in Mongolia. As I was being led in by a friend to be introduced, he told me that the door to this section of the temple must be locked at all times. This place, he said, is where the mummified remains of the Ninth Javzandamba are kept.

The first in the Javzandamba lineage was the renowned artist Zanabazar (1635–1723). His beautiful sculptures of Tārā and other buddhas and bodhisattvas, which survived the socialist purges, are now among Mongolia's most prized artworks. The nomadic temple that was once his habitation eventually settled along the banks of the Tuul River and formed the basis for what is now Ulaanbaatar (Campi 2006). Due to the tumultuous history of the region, the Ninth Javzandamba's life was spent mostly in obscurity. After the Eighth Javzandamba's death in 1924, the Mongolian socialist government outlawed searches for the rebirths of high lamas. Despite this decree, the Ninth Javzandamba was recognized as a child in Tibet. His identity was kept secret to avoid the religious persecutions that were occurring in the newly socialist Mongolia. Although a householder at the time, the Ninth Javzandamba fled Tibet to India in 1959 during Chinese incursions, fearing that his high status would be revealed. After a life in exile, and difficulties in being granted permission to visit Mongolia (Abrahms-Kavunenko 2019a; Jadamba 2018), the Ninth Javzandamba died in Mongolia in 2012, shortly after he had been granted Mongolian citizenship and ritually enthroned in 2011.

The Javzandamba's son lamented to me that his father had been unable to make the best use of his precious human life. Wasting a human life, he explained, was as if you had a piece of gold in your house that you did not know was there.

His mummified body, as the Javzandamba's son told me, must be prayed over every day. The decision to mummify his body, rather than have it cremated, he explained, was not his. Mummifying the body brings with it responsibility. Rituals must be carried out daily to avoid disrespecting the sanctity of the mummy. The human body is sacred, in both its living capacities and beyond. By rendering the body imperishable through intentional chemical processes, the Ninth Javzandamba's special human remains endure with power and potency beyond his death. Perhaps reflecting the fact that consciousness itself is an anti-entropic force, by transforming a body once endowed with special capacities of mind into a state which resists entropy, the suspended state of the body accords it with special capacities and exacts attendant responsibilities from those who keep it. Although mummies in Inner Asia are not discarded as such, the responsibility of their enduring materiality shares similarities with discarded Buddhist ritual items that cannot decompose.

Due to the enduring material properties of certain kinds of ritual waste, some items take on the same kinds of anti-entropic qualities of mummified lamas. Like other kinds of ordinary rubbish they become undead, unable to fully die and reintegrate into biotic systems. Unlike ordinary zombie rubbish in whose collectivity a threat is posed, these items individually carry with them hidden potencies that exact extra responsibilities, even after they have been discarded. Their biographies are interwoven into their imperishable materiality, containing potentially hidden threats if not correctly treated.

Enduring Materiality

Many Buddhist items used in home offerings, at temples, and on pilgrimages are now made from enduring materials. In 2016, Gerelmaa told me that one of the most popular items that she sells in her shop were prayer scarves (*khadag*s), which are used for rituals in Buddhist, shamanic, and other rituals, such as visiting one's birthplace (*nutag*) in the summer months. *Khadag*s can be bought from small stores like Gerelmaa's that specialize in religious items or from places such as the Naran Tuul market. Sky blue (*tsenkher*) *khadag*s are one of the more iconically Mongolian aspects of Buddhist, shamanic, and other rituals. The characteristic blue color speaks to the Mongolian relationship to the sky (*tenger*), the expansiveness and clarity of which is worshipped and respected across the Mongolian cultural region. Before the socialist period these scarves were made from silk. Today these, like other religious items, are mostly mass-produced in China and the generation of the characteristic blue color causes significant amounts of environmental pollution at the places where they are dyed (Peter Marshall, textiles specialist, personal communication).

The proper treatment and disposal of *khadag*s has been a public concern of monastics, lay Buddhists, and others. Linked to nationalistic imaginings, the image of a young Mongolian woman holding a *khadag* placed in palms facing up with the fold toward the recipient and an offering of milk in a silver cup is a common symbol of hospitality. *Khadag*s are offered during the arrival of high lamas in Buddhist ceremonies, often to be returned, with the blessings of the lama. Circled three times during prosperity ceremonies (*dallaga*), they are used to gather good fortune (Abrahms-Kavunenko 2019b). Tied onto trees, they have been used as a conservation tool to discourage illegal logging. While visiting sites of ritual significance or of pilgrimage, they are offered as a sign of respect to the local spirits.

Since the lifting of religious restrictions following the Democratic Revolution there has been a growth in ritual practices in both the city and the countryside and, consequently, an increase in ritual leftovers. In the 2000s, discoursing with the potentials of Buddhist organizations to encourage environmentally sustainable practices, the Netherlands Mongolia Trust Fund on Environmental Reform–II funded a project titled *Mongolian Buddhists Protecting Nature* (Chimedsengee et al. 2009). On the basis of this research the *Mongolian Buddhist Eight-Year Conservation Plan* (Alliance of Religions and Conservation 2010) was produced. The Eight-Year Conservation Plan, with forewords by the two of the most important Buddhist figures in Mongolia, the then living Ninth Javzandamba and Gandan's Abbot Ven. Choijamts, laid out strategies for Buddhist temples and practitioners to encourage good conservation practices. As well as advising specific strategies for encouraging sustainable practices, this short booklet centralizes two special initiatives: one relating to water and mining and another focusing on the proper usage of *khadag*s. In the special initiative describing *khadag*s, it details their importance for both Buddhist practice and Mongolian culture more generally. The booklet outlines the need to discourage people from tying the *khadag*s to light poles, bridges, and around trees, where they could stunt their growth or "catch on bird's feet and hurt them" (ibid.: 26). The plan makes note of the problem with the enduring materiality of the nylon prayer scarves, and suggests that temples should, along with encouraging people to leave food offerings at pilgrimage sites without plastic packaging, support the use of biodegradable *khadag*s and factories that were creating these kinds of scarves. Perhaps due to the difficulties of making *khadag*s that could compete financially with mass-produced nylon materials, I have not noticed the generation of biodegradable *khadag*s for sale, nor a replacement of the bright blue nylon scarves at sacred sites.

On pilgrimages and during Buddhist rituals the volume of these scarves made as offerings can be considerable. At many pilgrimage sites or ritual events leaving or gifting a *khadag* is a sign of respect to the place, local spirits, deities, or people. In 2009 on a trip to sacred Mother Rock (Eej Khad) it was customary to leave a *khadag* on the sacred rock before whispering three wishes under her arm. On the spring weekend that I visited her in the central Töv aimag there were so many visitors that I stood in line for almost three hours. By the time I reached her she was completely covered in prayer scarves. These *khadag*s can become problematic for people tending sacred sites in two ways: made of nylon they can become problematic if they are tied to trees or respected landmarks, and, as they carry with them the intentions of the person who had offered them, they cannot easily be recycled (see also Makley 2018). Highlighting this problem with disposal in 2015, an American friend told our language teacher that she had bought some *khadag*s during a trip to Naran Tuul to take back to friends in North America as she thought it would make a good gift. Our teacher, horrified, told her that the scarves were sacred and should always be treated with respect. "What will your friends do with it?" she asked, "They will just throw it in the bin!" A waste bin is the appropriate place for items that no longer have any use for city consumers. But it is not what one is supposed to do with sacred items. In landfill they will be mixed with the refuse of ordinary living. Some ritual items used in Buddhist and other ceremonies decompose or are eaten by birds, while others linger on, taking on special kinds of problems for disposal. Like mummies, the anti-entropic components of contemporary *khadag*s transform them to generate extraordinary responsibilities. While other forms of rubbish can be thrown into landfill (posing a threat as a collectivity), each individual *khadag* carries with it specific potency and can generate problems for those who discard them improperly.

Conclusion

Contemporary ideas of economic success are often measured by a person's or a nation's capacity to consume goods, the end point of which is the production of waste. Lower-middle-income countries like Mongolia are often flooded with cheap products, made from materials that break easily, yet whose material properties persist beyond their short life spans as belongings. The perception of moral decline that comes with incorrect rubbish disposal, which is thought to pollute the countryside, reflects broader narratives about capitalism and urban consumption. Just as everyday waste found in the rivers and the pollution of the air can be thought to be caused by poor motivations, ritual items discarded improperly may carry their own kinds of spiritual pollution.

Extending Reno's analogy of the undead to discuss different categories of waste enables us to distinguish between different kinds of discarded materials. Zombie-like rubbish, unable to die, poses its own set of problems. This zombie rubbish is a source of contamination and as collectivity it has the potential to overwhelm. Mongolian ritual waste, on the other hand, poses a different set of challenges. It, like zombie rubbish, resists atrophy. Yet, unlike mundane rubbish which can be thrown into landfill, each individual ritual item may contain powerful hidden potentials that relate to its own specific biography. These items, like the mummified remains of the Ninth Javzandamba or Lama Itigelov, enact continuing obligations for those who offer them and present challenges for those who tend pilgrimage sites.

Discarded items which resist entropy present a challenge to Buddhists, not just because they do not conform to the symbolic order of where things should and should not be, but also because they remain physically suspended in an imperishable state, or break down into smaller units of inassimilable, potentially poisoning materiality. They have their own undead materiality, related to, but distinct from, the undead characteristics of ordinary refuse. Like the bodies of mummified lamas, Mongolian Buddhist items are unable to decompose, yet continue to expect respectful treatment. Instantiating the force and obligation of the sacred, they contain within them the threat or curse that comes with neglect or violation. Unlike Inner Asian mummies, mummy-like discarded ritual offerings rarely receive this esteemed treatment, cast as they are into monstrous molds, and generally find themselves discarded, left to contaminate ritual sites or to be mixed with ordinary rubbish, suspended interminably in landfill.

Notes

1 All italicized words are transcribed from Mongolian (Cyrillic) unless otherwise indicated.

2 In Ulaanbaatar I did not come across any discussions of vampiric imps, though there are thought to be many kinds of energy and invisible other-than-human beings that

affect the unfolding of people's fortunes, such as (but not limited to) ancestral spirits, ghosts, Bodhisattvas, and water and mountain spirits.

3 See Abrahms-Kavunenko 2020 on the importance of a ritual item's origins.

References

28 Days Later (2002), [Film], Dir. Danny Boyle. UK: Fox Searchlight Pictures.

Abrahms-Kavunenko, Saskia (2015), "Paying for Prayers: Perspectives on Giving in Postsocialist Ulaanbaatar," *Religion, State and Society*, 43 (4): 327–41. doi: 10.1080/09637494.2015.1118204.

Abrahms-Kavunenko, Saskia (2019a), *Enlightenment and the Gasping City*, Ithaca: Cornell University Press.

Abrahms-Kavunenko, Saskia (2019b), "Mustering Fortune: Attraction and Multiplication in the Echoes of the Boom," *Ethnos*, 84 (5): 891–909. doi: 10.1080/00141844.2018.1511610.

Abrahms-Kavunenko, Saskia (2020), "Tenuous Blessings: The Materiality of Doubt in a Mongolian Buddhist Wealth Calling Ceremony," *Journal of Material Culture*, 25 (2): 153–66. doi: 10.1177/1359183519857042.

Alliance of Religions and Conservation (2010), *Mongolian Buddhist Eight-Year Conservation Plan*. http://www.arcworld.org/news.asp?pageID=451 (accessed April 20, 2020).

Bernstein, Anya (2012), "More Alive than all the Living: Sovereign Bodies and Cosmic Politics in Buddhist Siberia," *Cultural Anthropology*, 27 (2): 261–85. doi: 10.1111/j.1548-1360.2012.01143.x

Byamba, Bolorchimeg and Mamoru Ishikawa (2017), "Municipal Solid Waste Management in Ulaanbaatar, Mongolia: Systems Analysis," *Sustainability*, 9 (896): 1–22. doi: 10.3390/su9060896

Campi, Alicia (2006), "The Rise of Cities in Nomadic Mongolia," in Ole Brunn and Li Narangoa (eds), *Mongols from Country to City: Floating Boundaries, Pastoralism and City Life in the Mongol Lands*, 21–59, Copenhagen: NIAS Press.

Chimedsengee, Urantsatsral, Amber Cripps, Victoria Finlay, Guido Verboom, Ven Munkhbaatar Batchuluun, and Ven Da Lama Byambajav Khunkhur (2009), *Mongolian Buddhists Protecting Nature: A Handbook on Faiths, Environment and Development*, Bath: The Alliance of Religions and Conservation.

Choy, C. Anela, Bruce H. Robison, Tyler O. Gagne, et al. (2019), "The Vertical Distribution and Biological Transport of Marine Microplastics Across the Epipelagic and Mesopelagic Water Column," *Science Report* 9: Article no. 7843. doi: 10.1038/s41598-019-44117-2.

Comaroff, Jean, and John Comaroff (1999), "Occult Economies and the Violence of Abstraction: Notes from the South Africa Postcolony," *American Ethnologist*, 26 (2): 279–303. https://www.jstor.org/stable/647285

Dawn of the Dead (1978), [Film] Dir. George A. Romero, USA: United Film Distribution.

Douglas, Mary (2002 [1966]), *Purity and Danger: An Analysis of Concepts of Pollution and Taboo*, New York: Routledge.

"Editorial: Notes from the Plasticene Epoch" (2014), *New York Times*, June 15. https://www.nytimes.com/2014/06/15/opinion/sunday/from-ocean-to-beach-tons-of-plastic-pollution.html (accessed July 15, 2019).

Gildow, Douglas and Marcus Bingenheimer (2002), "Buddhist Mummification in Taiwan: Two Case Studies," *Asian Major* 3, XV, part 2: 87–128. https://www.jstor.org/stable/41649866

Hawkings, Gay (2019), "Disposability," https://discardstudies.com/2019/05/21/disposability/?fbclid=IwAR0GBlNGfYViBt0yTsbVllzR9gipGf0UJ3JTBW_QNlpKi1N-Ql4Ec5WjeO0 (accessed May 28, 2020).

Højer, Lars (2009), "Absent Powers: Magic and Loss in Post-socialist Mongolia," *Journal of the Royal Anthropological Institute*, 15: 575–91. doi: 10.1111/j.1467-9655.2009.01574.x.

Højer, Lars (2012) "The Spirit of Business: Pawnshops in Ulaanbaatar," *Social Anthropology*, 20 (1): 34–49. doi: 10.1111/j.1469-8676.2011.00188.x.

I Walked with a Zombie (1943), [Film] Dir. Jacques Tourneur, USA: RKO Pictures.

Jadamba, Lhagvademchig (2018), "Double Headed Mongolian Buddhism," *CESS Blog*. http://thecessblog.com/2018/02/double-headed-mongolian-buddhism-by-lhagvademchig-j-shastri-visiting-researcher-university-of-shiga-prefecture/ (accessed April 22, 2019).

Jonutyte, Kristina (2019), "Beyond Reciprocity: Giving and Belonging in the Post-Soviet Buddhist Revival in Ulan-Ude (Buryatia)," PhD diss., Martin-Luther-Universität, Halle-Wittenberg.

Kaplonski, Christopher (2014), *The Lama Question: Violence, Sovereignty and Exception in Early Socialist Mongolia*, Honolulu: University of Hawai'i Press.

Kilroy-Marac, Katie (2016), "A Magical Reorientation of the Modern: Professional Organizers and Thingly Care in Contemporary North America," *Cultural Anthropology*, 31 (3): 439–58. doi: 10.14506/ca31.3.09.

Kilroy-Marac, Katie (2018), "An Order of Distinction (Or, How to Tell a Collection from a Hoard)," *Journal of Material Culture*, 23 (1): 20–38. doi: 10.1177/1359183517729428.

Makley, Charlene (2018), *The Battle for Fortune: State-Led Development, Personhood, and Power among Tibetans in China*, Ithaca: Cornell University Press.

McAlister, Elizabeth (2012), "Slaves, Cannibals and Infected Hyper-Whites: The Race and Religion of Zombies," *Anthropological Quarterly*, 85 (2): 457–86. https://www.jstor.org/stable/41857250

Musharbash, Yasmine (2014), "Introduction: Monsters, Anthropology, and Monster Studies," in Yasmine Musharbash and Geir Henning Presterudstuen (eds), *Monster Anthropology in Australasia and Beyond*, 1–24, London: Palgrave Macmillan.

Newbury, Michael (2012), "Fast Zombie/ Slow Zombie: Food Writing, Horror Movies, and Agribusiness Apocalypse," *American Literary History*, 24 (1): 87–114. doi: 10.1093/alh/ajr055.

Newell, Sasha (2014), "The Matter of the Unfetish: Hoarding and the Spirit of Possessions," *HAU: Journal of Ethnographic Theory*, 4 (3): 185–213. doi: 10.14318/hau4.3.013.

Niehaus, Isak (2005), "Witches and Zombies of the South African Lowveld: Discourse, Accusations and Subjective Reality," *Journal of the Royal Anthropological Institute*, 11: 191–210. doi: 10.1111/j.1467-9655.2005.00232.x.

Night of the Living Dead (1968), [Film] Dir. George A. Romero, USA: Walter Reade.

Quijada, Justine Buck (2012), "Soviet Science and Post-Soviet Faith: Etigelov's Imperishable Body," *American Ethnologist*, 39 (1): 138–54. doi: 10.1111/j.1548-1425.2011.01354.x.

Reno, Joshua (2014), "Toward a New Theory of Waste: From "Matter out of Place" to Signs of Life," *Theory, Culture and Society*, 31 (6): 3–27. doi: 10.1177/0263276413500999.

Shaun of the Dead (2004), [Film] Dir. Edgar Wright, France, UK, USA: Universal Studios, Studio Canal, and Working Title Films.

Swancutt, Katherine (2008), "The Undead Genealogy: Omnipresence, Spirit Perspectives, and a Case of Mongolian Vampirism," *Journal of the Royal Anthropological Institute*, 14: 843–64. doi.org/10.1111/j.1467-9655.2008.00534.x.

Teleki, Krisztina (2009), "Building on Ruins, Memories and Persistence: Revival and Survival of Buddhism in the Mongolian Countryside," *The Silk Road* 7: 64–73.

The Asia Foundation (2019), "Ulaanbaatar Household Waste Composition Study: Report 2019," Ulaanbaatar: The Asia Foundation.

The Mummy (1932), [Film], Dir. Karl Freund, USA: Universal Pictures.

The Mummy (1999), [Film], Dir. Stephen Sommers, USA: Universal Pictures.

Thrift, Eric (2014), "'Pure Milk': Dairy Production and the Discourse of Purity in Mongolia," *Asian Ethnicity*, 15 (4): 492–513. doi: 10.1080/14631369.2014.939332.

White Zombie (1932), [Film] Dir. Victor Halperin, USA: United Artists.

Wirtz, Kristina (2009), "The Semiotics of Ritual Hygiene in Cuban Popular Religion," *The Journal of the Royal Anthropological Institute*, 15 (3): 476–501. doi: 10.1111/j.1467-9655.2009.01569.x.

World Bank (2015), *Land Administration and Management in Ulaanbaatar, Mongolia*, Washington, DC: World Bank.

7

Something Rotten in Shangri-La

Green Buddhism, Brown Buddhism, and the Problem of Waste in Ladakh, India

Elizabeth Williams-Oerberg

On a warm sunny day in July 2017, in the northwest Indian Himalayan region of Leh, Ladakh, I joined a crowd of a few hundred Ladakhi Buddhists gathered to celebrate the release of a new initiative headed by Thuksey Rinpoche (b. 1986), a high-ranking young Buddhist leader of the Drukpa Kagyü order of Himalayan Buddhism. At the assembly, Thuksey Rinpoche revealed a new item the Drukpa Kagyü organization had designed in order to help reduce the problem of waste in Ladakh: garbage holders to be hung on the back of taxi drivers' car seats. To celebrate this innovation, the Young Drukpa Association (YDA) planned a clean-up drive beforehand as a form of *pad yatra*, or walking pilgrimage. Monks, nuns, volunteers from the YDA, and children who attended the Druk Padma Karpo School run by Thuksey Rinpoche all walked in a long line picking up garbage along the entire eight kilometers from the town of Choglamsar to the Leh polo grounds. Before setting out, the YDA president, Rinchen Wacher, declared during an interview: "We are doing *pad yatra*, where 300 people are in a queue and wherever we find garbage, we can just clean that up. It is just to send a message to the people. It is very important to clean up the environment!"[1] All of the garbage collected was placed in large piles on the polo grounds where the Indian Independence Day celebrations had been held earlier that day. The heaps of garbage worked as a backdrop for the celebration of this Drukpa Buddhist initiative, which brought together political and religious leaders with the shared aspiration to raise awareness about the environment and to help solve the problem of waste in Ladakh. Not only was the event attended by Thuksey Rinpoche, who gave a motivational speech about the environmental impact of tourism and the importance of cleaning up the environment, but also by the

Chief Executive Councilor (CEC), Dr. Sonam Dawa, who was this autonomous region's leading political figure.

This cold desert, high-altitude region of northwest India has seen a massive increase in the tourism industry throughout the past few decades. The garbage bags to be slung on the back of taxi drivers' car seats were on their way to popular tourist destinations such as Buddhist monasteries, the Khardong-La pass—the highest motorable road in India—and Pangong Lake. Pangong Lake is a beautiful, crystal blue glacial lake that served as the backdrop for the immensely popular Bollywood movie *3 Idiots* (2009) which has been the highest grossing Bollywood movie of all time. The popularity of this movie has reached beyond India, with dedicated fans in Southeast Asia who are increasingly taking the Bollywood pilgrimage to Ladakh to visit the picturesque lake where Amir Khan and Kareena Kapoor danced their hearts away. These tourists also stop by the Druk Padma Karpo School, run by the Drukpa organization and Thuksey Rinpoche, which was showcased in the movie as a model of sustainable education. Following the release of *3 Idiots,* the number of tourist arrivals in Leh increased dramatically from 28,273 in 2003 (15,315 foreign; 12,958 domestic) to 181,301 in 2014 (59,305 foreign; 121,996 domestic),[2] 235,698 in 2016 (38,005

Figure 7.1 Monks, nuns, and volunteers picking up garbage along the road to Leh, Ladakh, as part of the Young Drukpa Association (YDA) clean-up drive and *pad yatra.* Photograph by Jakob Williams Oerberg, used with permission.

foreign; 197,693 domestic) (Palkit 2017), and 277,000 in 2018 (Kashmir Reader 2018). Whereas previously the bulk of tourists who came to Leh were foreign, domestic tourists now far outnumber them.

With this sudden increase in tourists, there has been a dramatic increase in garbage and a drain on the region's limited resources. Leh town has turned into a bustling marketplace with congested traffic from all of the cars, taxis, and buses used to transport these tourists around Ladakh. As one article puts it bluntly, "Ladakh is fast approaching its breaking point" (Bardi 2016). The air is polluted, and so are the streams and mountainsides. Garbage is everywhere. Roadsides are lined with plastic bottles and litter; makeshift piles of trash are a common sight in neighborhoods and open fields; and streams have turned into stinky, grey muck, clogged with plastic bags, old clothes, and laundry detergent. Yangchan Dolma, the vice president of the Women's Alliance in Leh lamented in a newspaper article: "[We] used to drink from the streams—now you wouldn't even want to put your hand in them, let alone your mouths" (Bardi 2016).

Waste disposal has become an immense problem in Ladakh, similar to other Himalayan regions (Allison 2014). While glacial recession, scarcity of water resources, water pollution, and cloudbursts cause considerable environmental challenges, the most threatening environmental issue in Ladakh is waste (Dar et al. 2018: n/a). Solid waste management has become particularly problematic in

Figure 7.2 Open dumping area near Choglamsar, Ladakh. Photograph by Kunzang Angmo, used with permission.

the summer months because of mass tourism, and the absence of proper landfill and sewage treatment systems (ibid.). Tourism-generated waste often winds up in streams and along roadsides, blowing across the vast cold mountainous desert terrain. During the tourist season Leh city collects 16–18 tonnes of waste per day, compared to only 3–4 tonnes in the "lean season" of November through February (Wangchuk 2018). According to the former District Commissioner of Leh, Avny Lavasa, "among the 15 tonnes of garbage that is generated daily in Leh, 90 per cent of it comes from tourists" (Karelia 2018). In essence, the Leh district of Ladakh has a "waste menace" (Dar et al. 2018): there is something rotten in Shangri-La.

Throughout this chapter, I examine the role that Buddhists have played in relation to the "waste menace" in Ladakh. While Buddhist-led organizational efforts to address the "brown agenda" and deal with waste in Ladakh, such as picking up trash, have become more common, it is their "green" initiatives, such as tree-planting and wildlife conservation, that have attracted global attention and awards. Global green environmental campaigns are slightly more palatable and attractive than those addressing the problems of stinky brown waste. As Elizabeth Allison (2014) points out, waste disposal problems and pollution have become an important brown agenda in the Himalayas, yet initiatives to address these brown pollution problems receive considerably less attention than green initiatives. Moreover, while Buddhist leaders champion green initiatives, they tend to cloud over the role that Buddhists have played in producing waste and contributing to Ladakh's brown environmental problems. While tourism has most frequently borne the blame for the region's waste problem, Buddhist consumption and the amount of waste produced at large Buddhist festivals has rarely come into focus. Tibetan Buddhist leaders living in exile stage large Buddhist festivals in Ladakh, leaving large quantities of waste in their wake when they return to their homes in other parts of India. However, what I term Brown Buddhism, by which I mean both Buddhist waste and Buddhist efforts to combat the problem of waste, has not drawn as much global attention as Green Buddhism.

Green and Brown Buddhism

Since the 1970s, Buddhists have reaped the benefit of being deemed a "green religion" in contrast to Christianity (Taylor 2010). Buddhism, as an Eastern tradition, has been aligned with environmentalism as having a close relationship with nature when compared with Christianity as a Western tradition (Obadia

2013: 313). The idea that the West has lost its respect for nature, while Eastern religions such as Buddhism have preserved a spiritual relationship with the natural world has pervaded Euro-American popular culture since at least the 1960s and 1970s (Stoll 2012: 266). "Ecological Buddhism" had its start in Western urban societies, gaining momentum in the 1950s with the influence of counterculture movements such as the Beat and hippie movements (Obadia 2013: 314). Bron Raymond Taylor (2010) points to the influence of the Beat poet Gary Snyder in aligning Buddhism with green movements and as a defining figure for what he terms "Dark Green Religion," in which "nature is sacred, has intrinsic value, and is therefore due reverent care" (10). Often, Buddhism is positioned as green due to a particular "Buddhist worldview" that emphasizes the interconnectedness of all beings (James and Cooper 2007: 93).

Buddhist-led environmentalism, however, frequently has more to do with practical efforts, such as garbage collection, that are related to a larger movement of engaged Buddhism, than with asserting doctrinal justifications for environmental alignment (Obadia 2013; Williams 2010: 21). Buddhist approaches to the environment through beliefs and practices related to nonhuman beings may at first glance seem to correlate with more global environmentalist movements that emphasize vegetarianism, animal rights, and minimization of environmental destruction. But quite often in practice these correlations do not withstand examination, and stark divergences appear (Allison 2015; Yonnetti forthcoming). For instance, Himalayan beliefs and practices related to nonhuman beings who inhabit mountainous landscapes[3] do not automatically lead to a minimization of environmental destruction, as any visit to a Himalayan Buddhist area experiencing vast economic growth and development such as Ladakh will attest to (Allison 2014, 2015). Moreover, the correlation between global environmental activism and local beliefs related to nonhuman beings is rarely invoked in green and brown Buddhist environmental campaigns. This points to how Buddhist ecological activism perhaps has more to do with local practices and global politics than with religious beliefs.

This chapter does not debate whether or not Himalayan Buddhism might be deemed a "Dark Green Religion" (viewing nature as sacred, of intrinsic value, and due reverent care) (Taylor 2010). Rather, it pays attention to the global aspirations within Buddhist environmental activism and the politics inherent in the "ecologization" of Buddhism. According to Lionel Obadia, there is a distinction between the "ecologism" of Buddhism, which relates to Buddhist beliefs about the environment, and the "ecologization" of Buddhism, through which correlations are made between Buddhist beliefs and modern global environmentalist approaches (Obadia 2013: 314). Obadia argues for the importance of taking into consideration the vastly influential political dimension of contemporary "eco-Buddhist" demands. As Buddhism has become ecologized in Ladakh, what might be the underlying political dimension of contemporary Green Buddhist demands and Brown Buddhist initiatives to tackle waste?

Brown Buddhist initiatives, such as the clean-up drive, have become a regular occurrence in Leh, with various organizations—religious and otherwise—leading volunteers throughout the city to pick up the trash that litters the fragile landscape. Both within and beyond Leh, so-called clean-up drives have been arranged for locals and tourists alike to collect garbage. For example, in May 2018, "The Himalaya Clean-up" was organized in Leh district with the theme "Let's make Ladakh plastic free" (Himalaya Clean-up Drive 2018). The aim of this initiative was to pick up the plastic waste that had accumulated in streams and fields across Leh. It was organized by Rural Development, Leh, in collaboration with the Young Drukpa Association (YDA), Leh's Education Department and Municipal Committee, the Nehru Yuva Kendra youth organization, the Integrated Mountain Initiative, and the World Wildlife Fund for Nature (WWF). Afterward, at an awareness program commemorating the clean-up drive, the Buddhist leader Geshes Thubstan Phuntsog is reported to have stated: "To have inner peace and happiness it is compulsory to have a clean environment . . . [a] clean environment is important for other living beings to survive and it is the responsibility of humans to keep the environment clean" (ibid.). Thubstan Phuntsog positions picking up trash as a Buddhist practice, as a practice that creates the conditions through which to obtain inner peace and happiness, as well as ensuring the survival of other living beings. Statements such as these turn Brown Buddhism into Green Buddhism. By picking up garbage (brown) one can have inner peace and a clean environment (green). This alignment of Buddhism and modern environmentalism is similar to what Obadia (2013) refers to as the "ecologization" of Buddhism.

Internationally renowned Himalayan Buddhist leaders have increasingly turned toward Green Buddhist initiatives to help promote their Buddhist organizations globally. For example, the exile-Tibetan leader of the Drukpa Buddhist order, Gyalwang Drukpa (b. 1963), has become a leading figure of Himalayan Buddhism, including in India, Nepal, Bhutan, and Tibet, which has had much to do with his large campaigns to raise awareness about the environment. As stated on a Drukpa website, the Gyalwang Drukpa is "a world-renowned humanitarian, author, environment[al] A-list[er] and champion of gender equality."[4] Most of the environmental initiatives that the Gyalwang

Drukpa sets in motion are funded by the international Live to Love foundation, the secular organizational arm of the Drukpa organization.[5] Live to Love has a wide, international appeal. Its celebrity ambassadors include the Academy Award-winning actress Susan Sarandon, the Malaysian actress Michelle Yeoh from *Crouching Tiger, Hidden Dragon* (2000), and the immensely popular Bollywood star Amir Khan from *3 Idiots* (2009). The YDA, which led the above-mentioned garbage bag inauguration, heads the practical running of the environmental campaigns that the Gyalwang Drukpa promotes. As the ambassador of Waterkeeper Alliance,[6] the Gyalwang Drukpa is involved in green initiatives such as the cross-border clean water programs. He also helped to build the Druk Padma Karpo School in Shey, Ladakh, which won an award for "Best Sustainable Development of the Year" for its environmentally friendly architecture.[7] The Druk Padma Karpo School, which was showcased in the movie *3 Idiots*, has since become a major tourist stop along the Bollywood pilgrimage route in Ladakh. The Gyalwang Drukpa is moreover reported as declaring: "I am more of a community leader who believes in working for and with the people and to that extent see more merit in opening schools and dispensaries and planting trees."[8] He has also led other award-winning green initiatives, such as twice breaking the Guinness World Record for "simultaneous tree-planting" in 2010 and 2012.[9] He has been duly recognized for his environmental championing in Ladakh, receiving the United Nations Millennium Development Goals (MDG) Award and India's Green Hero Award for his work in sustainable development. He has also been awarded with two commemorative stamps in South Asia—one in India and the other in Sri Lanka.[10]

Among the Gyalwang Drukpa's global followers from places such as the US, South America, Europe, East Asia, and Bhutan, the annual "eco *pad yatra*" or walking pilgrimage with an environmental education perspective has become highly popular.[11] Similar to the *pad yatra* that took place before the garbage bag inauguration ceremony, these annual eco *pad yatras* combine pilgrimage and garbage collecting, but they are much longer events with a participation fee, and more emphasis on visits to Buddhist sites along the way. Here Green Buddhism and Brown Buddhism are again combined: the Brown Buddhist engagement of picking up trash becomes more palatably enshrouded in a Green Buddhist pilgrimage that helps one get back in touch with nature. As stated on the Drukpa *pad yatra* homepage, the intent of the eco *pad yatras* is to remedy some of the ailments of the modern era: "Modern lifestyle with conveniences has resulted in a disconnection with the natural science and beauty. A *Pad Yatra* helps us to return to the basics."[12] Wendy J. N. Lee, sister of the Live to Love foundation's previous president, Carrie Lee, directed a documentary on the eco *pad yatra*, *Pad Yatra: A Green Odyssey* (2013), which was narrated by the actress Daryl Hannah and produced with the help of Michelle Yeoh. It is curious that the color green hardly appears in the movie. Ladakh is mostly a brown place, especially along the pilgrimage routes in the mountains. Yet, "A Brown Odyssey" does not have the same ring to it and would be unlikely to attract the same global acclaim. Brown Buddhism does appear in the movie—the participants collected half a ton of plastic on the route—but its focus is on the Green Buddhist activities that were conducted along the way, namely the planting of 50,000 trees and the educating of villagers about maintaining the natural environment (THR 2013).

The Gyalwang Drukpa is not the only Green Buddhist champion among the Himalayan Buddhist leaders who visit Ladakh regularly. The exile-Tibetan leader of the Drikung Kagyü Himalayan Buddhist order, Chetsang Rinpoche (b. 1946), has also turned his sights toward Ladakh to feature his green initiatives. In 2013, he inaugurated "Go Green, Go Organic" in Ladakh. According to Chetsang Rinpoche:

> Go Green directly deals with global issues such as weather calamities, ecological imbalances, global warming and so forth, which are some of the biggest issues facing us in this highly developed modern world. So Go Green is intended globally, to take care of our world by planting trees for birds, animals, insects, and all living beings on this planet.[13]

Go Green, Go Organic clearly has a Green Buddhist focus with its planting of trees and promotion of organic agriculture. The organization is a nonprofit foundation financed mostly by Chetsang Rinpoche's followers in Taiwan,[14] and works to create sustainable agricultural initiatives, mostly in the far-flung regions of Ladakh, such as Changthang. It is also involved in tree plantation initiatives near Leh town, such as in the village of Phyang. One of the more well-known environmental projects Chetsang Rinpoche is associated with is the Ice Stupa project in Phyang. The Ice Stupa is an artificial glacier in a conical form that somewhat resembles a Buddhist stupa.[15] The purpose of this project is to gather water particles from the air, collect them, and turn them into a frozen glacial form that melts gradually in the spring rather than merely evaporating. The water created from this melting ice formation is then used to water newly planted trees in an effort to "green" brown Ladakh. The Ice Stupa has received a great deal of media attention and has become a popular tourist destination.[16]

Chetsang Rinpoche, similar to the Gyalwang Drukpa, has a large international following. But instead of overseeing the Kagyü institutes he founded in Dehra

Dun, India, or going on global teaching tours, since 2019 he has preferred to spend his summers in Ladakh, at Phyang monastery, working in his kitchen garden.[17] As he declared:

> Some people may wonder, why is this Dharma teacher doing all these earthly works: the reason is that nowadays, when global warming and many other problems are arising and threatening the people and all other living beings, we cannot just stay at the monastery and relax. We should go into society and help the people with what is needed for this 21st century.[18]

For Chetsang Rinpoche, the most important issue facing the world is the problem of global warming, an environmental issue which demands attention from Buddhist leaders and monastics.

Exile-Tibetan leaders of prominent Buddhist organizations in Ladakh have thus initiated widely publicized Green Buddhist initiatives, such as the Drukpa organization's record-breaking simultaneous tree planting two years in a row, and the Drigung Kagyü organization's Go Green, Go Organic initiative and the Ice Stupa. However, the need of the day in Ladakh is not green, it is brown. The dramatic mountainous landscape that attracts tourists is a vast brown desert. Green Buddhist initiatives such as tree planting can, in practice, be problematic. Newly planted tree plantations often turn into cemeteries for dead saplings; when they do survive, they take away precious water resources from villagers who need the water for their kitchen gardens. Yet, such Green Buddhist initiatives receive much greater global attention and more awards than brown ones.

Almost every Buddhist organization in Ladakh currently has a focus on the environment. As Dorje,[19] a young Ladakhi friend, put it to me frankly when I asked why this was the case, "they have to, otherwise no one will listen to them."[20] Or rather, they do so in order that they will be listened to by not only Ladakhis but, perhaps more importantly, the global public. Ladakh has gained international attention both for its magnificent landscape, Buddhist monasteries, and connection to Bollywood, and for being a place that needs international donors' help and support if it is to be sustained. Pretty much since the advent of its tourism economy, Ladakh has become a showcase Himalayan region "in need." In 2017, there were over 700 registered nonprofit organizations in Ladakh. International humanitarian projects address issues such as education, health, architectural preservation, and the environment. The humanitarian organizations that run them are very visible, as they often advertise their work with large signs adorned with their logos. Fundraising campaigns to "help save the Himalayas" with accompanying billboards and brochures are splattered throughout the landscape of Ladakh, vying for the attention of tourists who visit the region and might perhaps become future sponsors of these philanthropic initiatives (see Williams-Oerberg 2020b). These fundraising campaigns have turned into a lucrative effort to funnel funds from Europe, the US, and East Asia to Ladakhi Buddhist organizations.

In short, saving the environment can be big business. For Buddhist leaders, it is a cause that helps draw focus toward their religious institutions as slightly disguised "secular" organizations. Both the Gyalwang Drukpa (Drukpa) and Chetsang Rinpoche (Drikung) deem their humanitarian organizations and initiatives such as Live to Love and Go Green, Go Organic to be secular. At the same time, they promote the importance of preserving and expanding their particular Buddhist lineage and religious organization. However, with so much focus on the environment, and even on the specific problem of waste through eco *pad yatra*s and clean-up drives, the lack of initiatives to address the environmental impact of Buddhist-related tourism is remarkable. A telling example is the waste created at the large Buddhist festivals held by these same Buddhist environmentalist leaders, which have come to permeate the Ladakh Buddhist tourism landscape in the past few years. Hence, while Buddhists seem to focus on tackling the problem of waste in Ladakh, they do little to consider how they may be one of the major contributors to creating this problem in the first place.

Buddhist-Generated Waste

The Buddhist waste problem in Ladakh can be traced back to 1974, when the borders opened and tourists were allowed entry into the region, marking the advent of the tourism economy. At this time, most of the tourists were foreigners interested in catching a glimpse of "Little Tibet" or the "Last Shangri-La"—what is often referred to as the last remaining bastion of Tibetan Buddhism (see Williams-Oerberg 2020a).[21] After the borders to Tibet closed with the Chinese occupation, international tourists interested in traveling to Himalayan Buddhist regions turned their sights to Ladakh, where a living and thriving Himalayan Buddhist culture has existed since at least the tenth century (Singh 2010). Tourism brochures and websites continue to market the region as a Buddhist "Shangri-La," with picturesque monasteries and smiling monks inviting tourists to visit and experience their living Himalayan Buddhist culture. Even the government of the State of Jammu and Kashmir, of which Ladakh was previously a part, once recognized Buddhism as the Unique Selling Point (USP) that distinguishes the region from other tourist destinations in India and in the world (Williams-Oerberg 2020a).

The main tourism sites in Ladakh are situated in the Leh district, which has a Buddhist majority, compared to the other district in Ladakh, Kargil, which has a Muslim majority and very few tourist arrivals.[22] In Leh, Buddhist monasteries have opened their doors to tourists and built tourist-related businesses to support them, such as restaurants and cafés, souvenir shops, hotels, guesthouses, and museums. Most of the main monasteries in Leh have what is termed "monastery festivals" or *tsé chu*,[23] which are advertised widely to draw an increasing number of tourists. The Drukpa Kagyü Hemis Monastery festival is the most renowned of these and draws a large crowd of Ladakhis and tourists from all over the world. Previously, most of these festivals took place in the winter. Due to the advent of the tourism industry, many of these festivals have been moved to the summer to attract more visitors (Jina 1994: 186). Ladakhi Buddhist leaders have not shied away from tourism; rather, they have actively promoted their monastery festivals to draw tourists to the region to witness colorful ritual performances that provide a stark contrast to the surrounding dull brown yet spectacular mountainous landscape. Buddhist festivals celebrated in Leh district draw crowds ranging from hundreds to hundreds of thousands, depending on the occasion and the particular star power and global network that the Buddhist leaders who head them possess.

Since the 1990s, Buddhist tourism has increased with the visits of renowned Buddhist leaders. The Dalai Lama visits Ladakh almost every summer, attracting large numbers of Ladakhis and tourists who attend his annual teaching program at his summer palace in Choglamsar. In 2014, he conferred the 33rd Kalachakra empowerment in Leh, attended by over one hundred thousand participants, demanding a massive organizational effort with a large number of volunteers as well as considerable resources to support such a large crowd. If we consider that the total population of Leh district is around 133,487 with an area of 45,110 square kilometers,[24] and that the area is a high-altitude, arid, cold desert region, the strain on the natural resources, including water usage and waste removal, is significant to say the least. While Ladakhis are aware that tourism puts a strain on the natural environment, this has not halted or altered the holding of large Buddhist festivals. The waste they produce is mostly due to the enhanced consumption that takes place alongside Buddhist ritual performances.

Other large Buddhist festivals that have produced a considerable amount of consumption-driven waste include those held by the Drukpa Kagyü and the Drikung Kagyü organizations. In 2016, the Drukpa Kagyü organization held a spectacular event celebrating the millennial anniversary of Naropa, an eleventh-century Indian mahasiddha who is a leading religious figure in the Kagyü Buddhist order. The main focus of the "Naropa 2016" was on the Gyalwang Drukpa, who is recognized as the reincarnation of Naropa. A new three-story tall Naropa palace (*naro phodrang*) was built especially for the occasion. The main event was the Naro Gyan Druk ritual, which involves the Gyalwang Drukpa ceremoniously wearing the Six Ornaments of Naropa while sitting on a golden throne in front of the palace. Afterward, these ornaments were on display so that pilgrims could receive blessings from them throughout the entire six-day festival.

The festival was widely advertised, especially among Drukpa followers worldwide, to attract a larger audience. The Gyalwang Drukpa, the environmental champion discussed previously, has a very large international following with over 27 million followers worldwide, all of whom he urged to come to Ladakh to participate in this important Buddhist ritual (Williams-Oerberg, 2020c).[25] According to the Naropa festival website, more than 500,000 people attended.[26] In 2018, the Naropa Palace was again used as a site for a Naropa festival, this time as a reminder or commemoration of the successful Naropa 2016, albeit with a smaller audience.

Figure 7.3 Naropa palace at Hemis Zhing Skyong built for the Naropa 2016 festival. Photograph by the author.

Another large Buddhist festival, this time held by the Drikung Kagyü Buddhists, took place in July 2018, led by Chetsang Rinpoche, the Green Buddhist champion of Go Green, Go Organic and the Ice Stupa. It commemorated the 800+ anniversary of the parinirvana (death after attaining Enlightenment) of Jigten Sumgön (1143–1217), the founder of the Drikung Kagyü order, but was also an occasion to inaugurate the new construction of Tserkarmo monastery in Tingmosgang where the festival took place. Chetsang Rinpoche presided over the occasion, giving multiple tantric initiations, along with other prominent Drikung Kagyü leaders with a large global following, such as Nupa Rinpoche and Paljin Tulku Rinpoche. This festival was again widely advertised but drew a smaller crowd of thousands, instead of hundreds of thousands.

For each of these festivals, the leaders of Himalayan Buddhist orders—the Dalai Lama (Gelukpa), Gyalwang Drukpa (Drukpa Kagyü), and Chetsang Rinpoche (Drikung Kagyü)—presided over ritual ceremonies that drew large crowds from among not only local Ladakhis but also their global following. Leaving aside the carbon footprint left by those who traveled from around the world to Ladakh, imagine the waste that such festivals produce. The aftermath of the consumption practices of so many visitors not only includes the garbage accumulated from the packaging and leftovers of the snacks they consumed and the plastic cups and paper plates provided by the organizing committees, but also the festival brochures, flyers announcing other Buddhist fundraising projects, and souvenirs produced to commemorate the occasion. At the Naropa festival, a plethora of souvenirs were produced with the Naropa logo, including various wide-brimmed hats to help shield attendees from the blistering sun, tea thermoses, bags, t-shirts, phone covers, umbrellas, books, and CDs published by the Drukpa organization. Sellers from across the Himalayas came with goods ranging from wool sweaters and shawls to plastic housewares, and colorful plastic toys and balloons to entertain the children present. Just below the market was a makeshift restaurant area where small tents served fried noodles and spicy rice dishes—all in disposable paper and plastic containers. Even with the Naropa 2016's purported focus on environmentalism and the presence of Robert F. Kennedy as the spokesperson for Waterkeeper Alliance, very little was done to reduce the environmental impact of bringing 500,000 people to attend this massive Buddhist festival. This brown impact that Buddhists have had in Ladakh, contributing to the problem of waste, is overlooked as Buddhist leaders vie for global attention for the green initiatives that they advocate.

Hence, Buddhist-produced waste, related to consumption at monasteries, by monks and nuns, and by Ladakhi and tourist visitors, as well as that produced at large Buddhist festivals, has contributed a great deal to the waste problem in Ladakh. Some kinds of Buddhist waste are more visible than others, such as the construction of new buildings and infrastructure to house commemorative Buddhist events. The Naropa Palace today stands as a reminder of this waste. The roads that were built and the water and electricity that were re-directed in order to supply what was previously a dry, dusty brown field, now service a Ladakhi Buddhist ruin that stands alone, unused, and deteriorating day by day. In an interview with Norbu, a Ladakhi journalist, he expressed his discontent in the following statement: "I feel that people are coming with huge structures like Naropa Photang, this palace. So then, okay, in twelve years, you do a festival there, then what after that? Who will take care of it? I don't know. They will have to spend lakhs of money for the maintenance of the palace."[27] For Norbu, the palace is evidence of the amount of waste that the festival produced—a structure that requires "lakhs" to maintain, money that might have been better allocated elsewhere, such as roads and schools in remote villages. The palace represents both wastefulness and waste: the Buddhist waste of allocating resources to the building of a structure that is used only once (a wastefulness), and a monument that is left to waste away, unused (a transformation into waste). As the president of the YDA frankly stated, the palace was built under the instruction of Gyalwang Drukpa for only the three days of the festival. "Now," he said, "it has become useless. Holiness [the Gyalwang Drukpa] wants us to make it shine forever. So, we wanted to use that [place for] a cultural workshop."[28] The palace stands empty, used only for the occasional event such as the Kung Fu Nuns self-defense workshop,[29] the annual YDA work retreat, and the 2018 commemoration of Naropa 2016. Hence, the palace represents the multiplicity of Buddhist waste: the moral evaluation of the wastefulness of using valuable resources to build a Buddhist structure that is used only once; and the waste of a Buddhist structure that is "useless" and stands there only as a ruin, unused, deteriorating, and polluting the landscape as a mere remnant of its previous usefulness (see also Abrahms-Kavunenko; Caple this volume). This waste and the waste produced at such large Buddhist festivals, however, was not the focus of the clean-up drive organized by Thuksey Rinpoche and the Young Drukpa Association in Leh on the Indian Independence day in July 2017.

Conclusion

For all of the environmental activism focused on "greening" Ladakh, achieving world records, and receiving global recognition and commemorative stamps, there is a lack of environmental awareness (or recognition) of the waste produced by Buddhists themselves. This raises the question that Malcolm David Eckel asked in 2010: "Is 'Buddhist environmentalism' a contradiction in terms?" Or rather, how contradictory is Green Buddhism? Exile-Tibetan leaders of Himalayan Buddhist institutions in India, such as the Dalai Lama of the Gelukpa, the Gyalwang Drukpa of the Drukpa Kagyü, and Chetsang Rinpoche of the Drikung Kagyü, are highly attuned and connected to contemporary global concerns about the environment. Where Buddhists have been aligned by the Western intelligentsia as intrinsically "green," this has not hurt the Tibetan cause by any means. As Toni Huber has pointed out, the precedents for Tibetan identity projections such as "green" and "peaceful" have been set by Buddhist modernists and international Buddhist movements that position an Eastern religious outlook as one that can save the West (Huber 2008: 363; see also Huber 1997). The allegiance of these exile-Tibetan leaders, who visit Ladakh sporadically in the summer months to preside over large communal rituals and work in their monastery kitchen gardens, lies with Tibetan Buddhist exile communities, more so than with Ladakh. They have a large following across the world—a following which also sponsors the various projects headed under their leadership. The Himalayas is a place which captures the global imaginary not only as a "Shangri-La" and spiritual resource that can perhaps save the West (Bishop 1989), but also as a place that needs "saving." "Save the Himalayas" campaigns enshroud the brown problem of waste within green environmental initiatives such as tree planting and sustainable schools to reach a wider audience, potentially also helping to expand the Buddhist organizations that initiate them. While mass tourism stands as the primary culprit for environmental degradation, the impact that Buddhist-related tourism has had on the problem of waste has been overlooked. Tourists come to Ladakh not only to visit Pangong Lake and take the Bollywood *3-Idiots* tour, but also to visit monasteries in this place where Buddhism has been declared the Unique Selling Proposition (USP) (Williams-Oerberg 2020a).

While Ladakh faces a brown "waste menace," the environmental platforms upon which these Buddhist leaders stand seem to focus more on global media attention and awareness than on local initiatives to reduce waste beyond collecting it in garbage bags. This is evident in the holding of large communal rituals and the waste that they generate. Ladakh has become a place to showcase to the world the importance of particular Himalayan Buddhist lineages through festivals such as the Kalachakra, Naropa 2016, and the commemoration of

Jigten Sumgön, and through the green environmental campaigns forged by these same leaders. Ladakh is also a political battleground for these Buddhist organizations—a place where increasing sectarianism and competition between exile-Tibetan-led Buddhist organizations have become manifest (Patil 2018, see Williams-Oerberg, forthcoming).

Taking a close look at the "ecologization" (Obadia 2013) or greening of Buddhism in Ladakh, and the Buddhist-run initiatives that address issues related to the environment, reveals the political dimension of these contemporary "eco-Buddhist" movements. Efforts to expand Buddhist organizations globally through Green Buddhist initiatives, as well as through spectacular Buddhist rituals staged in "Little Tibet," are perhaps at the cost of the local environment. The local Buddhist environment in Ladakh is not only permeated with growing sectarianism, but also increasingly beset with doubts as to how environmentally friendly these Green Buddhist initiatives might be. Does obtaining the Guinness World Record for simultaneous tree planting benefit Ladakh, an arid, cold-desert mountainous region that does not have the water levels to sustain an increasing number of trees? In addition, some Ladakhis are concerned that the "greening" of Ladakh might lead to increasing rainfall, which is detrimental to the traditional mud buildings, not to mention a cause of mudslides and their disastrous effects. In 2010, a great cloudburst in Leh caused tremendous damage and loss of life. While Buddhism might be considered by some as a green religion, greening Ladakh does not necessarily help save the environment. It might also have significant socio-economic and political consequences for Ladakhis. If water is to be diverted to nourish the newly planted trees, from where is it to be diverted? Many households already face a significant water shortage. And what of the geopolitical ramifications if water is diverted away from the Indus river which leads into Pakistan? Relations between India and Pakistan are already tense. In essence, there is something rotten in Shangri-la, and it is not only the waste produced by tourists and collected in garbage bags during clean-up drives.

Notes

1 Recorded interview, Leh, July 2018.

2 http://leh.nic.in/pages/handbook.pdf (accessed February 6, 2017).

3 These nonhuman beings (*mi ma yin pa)* are often referred to by Ladakhis as simply *lha* or *yul lha* and reference a triad of deities associated with the earth (*sa*

bdag), water *(klu)*, and rocks/trees *(gnyan)* (Butcher 2013; Dollfus 1999; Yonnetti forthcoming).

4 http://www.naropafestival.org/naropafestival/cms/the-gyalwang-drukpa.html (accessed May 1, 2019).

5 Live to Love is the "global humanitarian movement" founded in 2007 by the Gyalwang Drukpa "in his effort to use Buddhist approaches to solve modern day problems." It consists of "an international consortium of secular, non-profit organisations" and focuses on the five aims of education, environmental protection, health services, relief aid, and cultural preservation. See http://www.livetolove.org/about-us/ (accessed May 15, 2019).

6 Waterkeeper Alliance is a large, international nonprofit organization, which focuses on clean water. In 2013, Waterkeeper Alliance named the Gyalwang Drukpa the "Guardian of the Himalayas." See https://www.prnewswire.com/in/news-releases/waterkeeper-alliance-names-gyalwang-drukpa-guardian-of-the-himalayas-225230142.html (accessed April 26, 2019).

7 https://www.arup.com/projects/druk-white-lotus-school (accessed May 7, 2019).

8 http://www.naropafestival.org/naropafestival/cms/the-gyalwang-drukpa.html (accessed May 1, 2019).

9 https://www.tribuneindia.com/2012/20121202/spectrum/main6.htm (accessed May 7, 2019).

10 On the commemorative stamp in Sri Lanka for the *pad yatra*, see http://www.drukpa.com/shop/commemorative-stamps/262-drukpa-pad-yatra-stamp-by-sri-lanka-government (accessed May 1, 2019); on the commemorative stamp in India 2014, see the pinned tweet to twitter account https://twitter.com/drukpa?lang=en (accessed May 1, 2019).

11 http://www.padyatra.org/about (accessed September 27, 2018).

12 Ibid.

13 http://www.drikung.org/81-featured-articles/240-inauguration-of-go-green-go-organic- (accessed May 1, 2019).

14 Personal communication with a Ladakhi monk who helps run Go Green, Go Organic in Ladakh.

15 The form and structure of the so-called Ice Stupa has also been a popular global media topic featuring in *The Guardian* and the *New Yorker*. See https://www.theguardian.com/environment/2017/apr/22/the-ice-stupas-of-ladakh-solving-water-crisis-in-the-high-desert-of-himalaya (accessed May 15, 2019); https://www.newyorker.com/magazine/2019/05/20/the-art-of-building-artificial-glaciers?fbclid=IwAR2t0Wb90_pR90gem3TKG2PrGAeyGcERBsQ%E2%80%A6 (accessed May 15, 2019).

16 https://economictimes.indiatimes.com/industry/miscellaneous/unique-Ice-stupa-cafe-attracts-tourists-in-lehs-village/restaurant-inside-an-ice-stupa/slideshow/68477928.cms (accessed May 7, 2019).

17 Personal communication with the same Ladakhi monk I refer to in note 14.
18 http://www.drikung.org/81-featured-articles/240-inauguration-of-go-green-go-organic- (accessed May 1, 2019).
19 All names in this chapter are anonymized, except for those of highly public religious and political leaders.
20 Personal communication, Leh, August 2017.
21 For a critical discussion on how Buddhism in Ladakh has become subsumed under the umbrella term "Tibetan Buddhism," see Williams-Oerberg, forthcoming.
22 Ladakh is an autonomous region in India that consists of two autonomous districts, Leh district with a Buddhist majority and Kargil district with a Muslim majority.
23 The *tsé chu* is an annual monastery festival typically held on the tenth day of the month in commemoration of Padmasambhava.
24 https://leh.nic.in/about-district/ataglance/ (accessed May 7, 2019).
25 http://www.naropafestival.org/naropafestival/cms/the-gyalwang-drukpa.html (accessed May 7, 2019).
26 http://www.naropafestival.org/naropafestival/album/naropa-2016.html (accessed May 7, 2019).
27 Recorded interview, Bedlewo Poland, May 2017. Lakh is the equivalent of 100,000. One lakh rupees is equivalent to around US$1400.
28 Recorded interview, Leh, July 2018.
29 The "Kung Fu Nuns" are from the Druk Gawa Khilwa nunnery in Nepal, which houses Drukpa Kagyü nuns from across the Himalayas. A promotional brochure for the Kung Fu Nuns states that they "are trained not only in spiritual development, in the complex practice of higher Tantric yoga, but also in humanitarian work . . . . In an effort to promote self-empowerment, the Gyalwang Drukpa introduced Kung Fu in 2009, for health improvement and for self-defense." These nuns accompany the Gyalwang Drukpa on his bicycle and walking tours or *pad yatras* throughout the Himalayas where he promotes gender equality and environmental awareness. ("The 1st Women's Self-Defense Workshop by Kung Fu Nuns Celebrating Self-empowerment" August 16–20, 2017, Hemis Naro Photang, Ladakh, India [brochure]).

References

3 Idiots (2009), [Film], Dir. Rajkumar Hirani, India: Reliance Big Pictures.

Allison, Elizabeth (2014), "Waste and Worldviews: Garbage and Pollution Challenges in Bhutan," *Journal for the Study of Religion, Nature and Culture*, 8 (4): 405–28. doi: 10.1558/jsrnc.v8i4.25050.

Allison, Elizabeth (2015), "Waste and Worldviews: Garbage and Pollution Challenges in Bhutan," *Journal for the Study of Religion, Nature and Culture*, 8 (4): 405–28. doi: 10.1558/jsrnc.v8i4.25050.

Bardi, Ariel Sophia (2016), "How '3 Idiots' Destroyed Ladakh," *BuzzFeed News*. https://www.buzzfeed.com/arielbardi/what-has-3-idiots-done-to-ladakh.

Bishop, Peter (1989), *The Myth of Shangri-La: Tibet, Travel Writing, and the Western Creation of Sacred Landscape*, Berkeley, CA: University of California Press.

Butcher, Andrea (2013), "Keeping the Faith: Divine Protection and Flood Prevention in Modern Buddhist Ladakh," *Worldviews*, 17 (2): 103–14. https://www.jstor.org/stable/43809481

Crouching Tiger, Hidden Dragon (2000), [Film], Dir. Ang Lee, Taiwan: Sony Pictures Releasing.

Dar, Sajad Nabi, Muzafar Ahmad Wani, Shamim Ahmad Shah, and Safiya Skinder (2018), "Identification of Suitable Landfill Site Based on GIS in Leh, Ladakh Region," *GeoJournal*, 84: 1499–513. doi:10.1007/s10708-018-9933-9.

Dollfus, Pascale (1999), "Mountain Deities Among the Nomadic Community of Kharnak (Eastern Ladakh)," in Martijn van Beek and Kristoffer Brix Bertelsen (eds), *Ladakh: Culture, History and Development between Himalaya and Karakoram*, 92–118, Aarhus, Denmark: Aarhus University Press.

Eckel, M David (2010), "Is Buddhist Environmentalism a Contradiction in Terms?," in Richard K. Payne (ed), *How Much Is Enough? Buddhism, Consumerism, and the Human Environment*, 161–70, Somerville, MA: Wisdom Publications.

"Himalaya Clean-up Drive Held in Leh, Aims to Make Zero-waste Himalayas" (2018), *Reach Ladakh Bulletin*. www.reachladakh.com/news/social-news/himalaya-clean-up-drive-held-in-leh-aims-to-make-zero-waste-himalayas (accessed May 7, 2019).

Huber, Toni (1997), "Green Tibetans: A Brief Social History," *Tibetan Culture in the Diaspora*, 4: 103–19.

Huber, Toni (2008), *Holy Land Reborn: Pilgrimage and the Tibetan Reinvention of Buddhist India*, Chicago, IL: University of Chicago Press.

James, Simon P. and David E. Cooper (2007), "Buddhism and the Environment," *Contemporary Buddhism*, 8 (2): 93–96. doi: 10.1080/14639940701636075.

Jina, Prem Singh (1994), *Tourism in Ladakh Himalaya*, New Delhi: Indus Publishing Company.

Karelia, Gopi (2018), "A Black Hole for Trash Is Leh's Latest Solution to Tackle the Garbage Mountain," *Shachhindia.ndtv.com* (Jammu and Kashmir, News), August 31. https://swachhindia.ndtv.com/waste-management-blackhole-will-help-reduce-waste-in-ladakh-24579/ (accessed May 13, 2019).

Kashmir Reader (2018), "Record Number of Tourists Visit Ladakh in 2017," April 1. https://kashmirreader.com/2018/04/01/record-number-of-tourists-visit-ladakh-in-2017 dir-tourism/ (accessed September 9, 2020).

Obadia, Lionel (2013), "Political Ecology and Buddhism: An Ambivalent Relationship," *International Social Science Journal*, 205 (62): 313–23. doi: 10.1111/j.1468-2451.2013.01811.x.

Pad Yatra: A Green Odyssey (2013), [Film], Dir. Wendy J. N. Lee, Taiwan: Jelly Bean.

Palkit, Nawang (2017), "30% Annual Growth Rate in Tourist Arrival in Ladakh," *Reach Ladakh Bulletin*. http://www.reachladakh.com/news/social-news/30-annual-growth-rate-in-tourist-arrival-in-ladakh.

Patil, Sameer (2018), China Targets India's Ladakh, Gateway House, Indian Council on Global Relations. https://www.gatewayhouse.in/china-targets-indias-ladakh/.

Singh, Upinder (2010), "Exile and Return: The Reinvention of Buddhism and Buddhist Sites in Modern India," *South Asian Studies*, 26 (2): 193–217. doi: 10.1080/02666030.2010.514744.

Stoll, Mark (2012), "Review Essay: The Quest for Green Religion," *Religion and American Culture*, 22 (2): 265–74.

Taylor, Bron Raymond (2010), *Dark Green Religion: Nature Spirituality and the Planetary Future*, Berkeley: University of California Press.

THR Staff (2013), "Pad Yatra: A Green Odyssey: Film Review," *The Hollywood Reporter*, November 27, 2013. https://www.hollywoodreporter.com/review/pad-yatra-a-green-odyssey-660583 (accessed December 18, 2020).

Wangchuk, Rinchen Norbu (2018), "Landfills No More? IAS Officer's Brilliant "Project Tsandgda" is Changing the Face of Leh," *The Better India*, December 25. https://www.thebetterindia.com/167679/ias-hero-leh-ladakh-eco-friendly-waste-avny-lavasa/ (accessed May 13, 2019).

Williams, Duncan Ryūken (2010), "Buddhist Environmentalism in Contemporary Japan," in Richard K. Payne (ed), *How Much is Enough? Buddhism, Consumerism, and the Human Environment*, 17–38, Somerville, MA: Wisdom.

Williams-Oerberg, Elizabeth (2020a), "Buddhism: A Unique Selling Point in Ladakh," in Courtney Bruntz and Brooke Schedneck (eds), *Buddhist Tourism in Asia: Global Networks within Sacred Sites*, Honolulu, Hawai'i: University of Hawai'i Press.

Williams-Oerberg, Elizabeth (2020b), "Buddhist Business and Benevolence in Leh, Ladakh," *Journal of Human Values*, 27 (1): 60–71. doi: 10.1177/0971685820973188.

Williams-Oerberg, Elizabeth (2020c), "When Buddhism Meets Bollywood: The Spectacular Naropa 2016 Festival in Ladakh, India," *Himalaya*, 39 (2): 104–18. https://digitalcommons.macalester.edu/cgi/viewcontent.cgi?article=2538&context=himalaya.

Williams-Oerberg, Elizabeth (forthcoming), "'Little Tibet': Positioning Ladakh as a Homeland for Tibetan Buddhism in India," *Comparative Studies in South Asia, Africa and the Middle East (CSSAAME)*.

Yonnetti, Eben (forthcoming), "When the Snowy Mountains Turn Black: Climate Change, Local Deities, and Buddhism in Ladakh," in Rafal Beszterda, John Bray, and Elizabeth Williams-Oerberg (eds), *New Perspectives on Modern Ladakh*, Toruń, PL: Nicolaus Copernicus University.

Contributors

Saskia Abrahms-Kavunenko is an anthropologist and the author of *Enlightenment and the Gasping City.* She has published on the topics of Buddhism, shamanism, postsocialism, economic anthropology, global warming and pollution, and materiality in Mongolia and India. She is currently a Marie Skłodowska-Curie Fellow within the Center for Contemporary Buddhist Studies at the Department of Cross-Cultural and Regional Studies at the University of Copenhagen. She is the co-founder of Cenote, a travelling multidisciplinary residency program committed to bridging the communicative gap that yawns ever wider between human cultures and the living systems and intelligences which support and co-constitute our existence.

Trine Brox is Associate Professor of Modern Tibetan Studies and Director of the Center for Contemporary Buddhist Studies at the Department of Cross-Cultural and Regional Studies, University of Copenhagen, Denmark. Brox is the PI of the international, collaborative research projects *Buddhism, Business and Believers* and *Waste: Consumption and Buddhism in the Age of Garbage.* Brox has written extensively about contemporaneous issues in Tibet and the Tibetan exile community, including the monograph *Tibetan Democracy: Governance, Leadership and Conflict in Exile* (2016). She has also co-edited the book *Buddhism and Business: Merit, Material Wealth, and Morality in the Global Market Economy* (2020) with Elizabeth Williams-Oerberg.

Jane Caple is an independent scholar with research interests in religion, economy, morality and emotion, and the anthropology of Buddhism. She has held a Marie Skłodowska-Curie Fellowship at the Centre for Contemporary Buddhist Studies, University of Copenhagen (2017–19), and a Leverhulme Early Career Fellowship (2012–15) at the University of Manchester. She is the author of *Morality and Monastic Revival in Post-Mao Tibet* (2019) and is currently working on a book project about Buddhism, wealth, and virtue based on fieldwork in northeast Tibet.

Hannah Gould is a cultural anthropologist studying material culture, death and discarding, and religion. Her research spans new traditions and technologies of death rites, the lifecycle of religious materials, and minimalist movements—in sum, the stuff of death and the death of stuff. Her work has been published in *FOCAAL*, *Anthropological Quarterly*, *The Journal of Material Religion*, and *The Journal of Global Buddhism*. Hannah currently works as a Research Fellow with the DeathTech team at the University of Melbourne and she is President of the Australian Death Studies Society.

Fabio Gygi is a lecturer in anthropology with reference to Japan at SOAS, University of London. He is interested in the intersection of material culture and medical anthropology, with a particular focus on the social, psychological, and material dimensions of disposal. His recent publications include "Things that Believe: Talismans, Amulets, Dolls, and How to Get Rid of Them" (*JJRS* 45, 2018) and "Hôtes et Otages: Entasser des objets chez soi dans le Japon contemporain" (*L'Homme* 231–2, 2019). He is currently working on a book on mortuary rites for dolls in Japan.

Amy Holmes-Tagchungdarpa is an associate professor of religious studies at Occidental College in Los Angeles, CA, the United States. She is the author of *The Social Life of Tibetan Biography: Textuality, Community, and Authority in the Lineage of Tokden Shakya Shri* (2014), and is currently working on a book project about Buddhist material culture in the Himalayas.

Elizabeth Williams-Oerberg is the co-director of the Center for Contemporary Buddhist Studies at the University of Copenhagen. She has worked with Trine Brox on the collaborative research project, "Buddhism and Business" since 2015, and together they have co-edited the volume *Buddhism and Business: Merit, Material Wealth, and Morality in the Global Market Economy*, and a special issue on "Buddhism and Economics" in the *Journal of Global Buddhism*. Since her doctoral research on Buddhist youth and educational migration in India, she has continued her research in Ladakh, India, focusing on Buddhist tourism, economics of Buddhism, Buddhist festivals, ritual, and aesthetics.

Jeff Wilson is a professor of Religious Studies and East Asian Studies at Renison University College (University of Waterloo). He is the author of *Mindful America: The Mutual Transformation of Buddhist Meditation and American Culture* (2014), *Dixie Dharma: Inside a Buddhist Temple in the American South* (2012), and *Mourning the Unborn Dead: A Buddhist Ritual Comes to America* (2009).

Index